Andrey Makarychev

RUSSIA AND THE EU IN A MULTIPOLAR WORLD

Discourses, Identities, Norms

With a foreword by Klaus Segbers

***ibidem*-Verlag**
Stuttgart

Bibliographic information published by the Deutsche Nationalbibliothek
Die Deutsche Nationalbibliothek lists this publication in the Deutsche Nationalbibliografie; detailed bibliographic data are available in the Internet at http://dnb.d-nb.de.

Bibliografische Information der Deutschen Nationalbibliothek
Die Deutsche Nationalbibliothek verzeichnet diese Publikation in der Deutschen Nationalbibliografie; detaillierte bibliografische Daten sind im Internet über http://dnb.d-nb.de abrufbar.

Cover picture: © Thorsten Freyer / pixelio.de

ISSN: 1614-3515

ISBN-13: 978-3-8382-0529-8

Printed in the United States of America

Soviet and Post-Soviet Politics and Society (SPPS)

ISSN 1614-3515

Soviet and Post-Soviet Politics and Society (SPPS)

ISSN 1614-3515

Founded in 2004 and refereed since 2007, SPPS makes available affordable English-, German-, and Russian-language studies on the history of the countries of the former Soviet bloc from the late Tsarist period to today. It publishes between 5 and 20 volumes per year and focuses on issues in transitions to and from democracy such as economic crisis, identity formation, civil society development, and constitutional reform in CEE and the NIS. SPPS also aims to highlight so far understudied themes in East European studies such as right-wing radicalism, religious life, higher education, or human rights protection. The authors and titles of all previously published volumes are listed at the end of this book. For a full description of the series and reviews of its books, see www.ibidem-verlag.de/red/spps.

Editorial correspondence & manuscripts should be sent to: Dr. Andreas Umland, DAAD, German Embassy, vul. Bohdana Khmelnitskoho 25, UA-01901 Kyiv, Ukraine. e-mail: umland@stanfordalumni.org

Business correspondence & review copy requests should be sent to: ***ibidem*** Press, Leuschnerstr. 40, 30457 Hannover, Germany; tel.: +49 511 2622200; fax: +49 511 2622201; spps@ibidem.eu.

Authors, reviewers, referees, and editors for (as well as all other persons sympathetic to) SPPS are invited to join its networks at www.facebook.com/group.php?gid=52638198614 www.linkedin.com/groups?about=&gid=103012 www.xing.com/net/spps-ibidem-verlag/

Recent Volumes

122 Michael Moser
Language Policy and the Discourse on Languages in Ukraine under President Viktor Yanukovych (25 February 2010–28 October 2012)
ISBN 978-3-8382-0497-0 (Paperback edition)
ISBN 978-3-8382-0507-6 (Hardcover edition)

123 Nicole Krome
Russischer Netzwerkkapitalismus
Restrukturierungsprozesse in der Russischen Föderation am Beispiel des Luftfahrtunternehmens "Aviastar"
Mit einem Vorwort von Petra Stykow
ISBN 978-3-8382-0534-2

124 David R. Marples
'Our Glorious Past'
Lukashenka's Belarus and the Great Patriotic War
ISBN 978-3-8382-0574-8 (Paperback edition)
ISBN 978-3-8382-0675-2 (Hardcover edition)

125 Ulf Walther
Russlands "neuer Adel"
Die Macht des Geheimdienstes von Gorbatschow bis Putin
Mit einem Vorwort von Hans-Georg Wieck
ISBN 978-3-8382-0584-7

126 Simon Geissbühler (Hrsg.)
Kiew – Revolution 3.0
Der Euromaidan 2013/14 und die Zukunftsperspektiven der Ukraine
ISBN 978-3-8382-0581-6 (Paperback edition)
ISBN 978-3-8382-0681-3 (Hardcover edition)

127 Andrey Makarychev
Russia and the EU in a Multipolar World
Discourses, Identities, Norms
ISBN 978-3-8382-0529-8

128 Roland Scharff
Kasachstan als postsowjetischer Wohlfahrtsstaat
Die Transformation des sozialen Schutzsystems
Mit einem Vorwort von Joachim Ahrens
ISBN 978-3-8382-0622-6

129 Katja Grupp
Bild Lücke Deutschland
Kaliningrader Studierende sprechen über Deutschland
Mit einem Vorwort von Martin Schulz
ISBN 978-3-8382-0552-6

Contents

Foreword

While this important book is prepared for the printing press, the EU–Russia relations are in their most difficult stage after the collapse of the USSR. This is common sense. Personally, I would say more: Not since the early 1980s, the Russian-European relations were as emotional as difficult, and possibly as hopeless as now.

In this context, a sober and also non-traditional way of assessing this relationship is very much in need. Currently, we are undergoing a quite emotional, biased situation, characterized by failing communication. Or maybe not? Are the differences in assessing the European and global landscape and the role of agrees and institutions maybe very real, and so we may have a successful communication of quite different positions?

Communication is a crucial concept here. According to (not only) non-positivist assumptions, communication is a core approach for properly understanding how state and non-state actors interact—successfully or not. Currently, the dominant impression is that when it comes to European and Russian elites, there is not much left in terms of mutual understanding. I'm not talking here about sharing values and interests, but just—understanding the other side's position.

Currently, there is a broader space of uncertainty regarding the relation between Russia and Europe than maybe ever before after 1961 (construction of the Berlin Wall). Now, again, there is talk about real war. Not openly, not by quite serious policy makers, but nevertheless. This was hardly the case in 1956 (Soviet tanks in Hungary), in 1968 (Warsaw Pact tanks in Prague), 1979 (Soviet invasion into Afghanistan), 1981 (martial law in Poland), and 1982 ff. (medium-range nuclear missile crisis). Neither Ukraine nor Moldova are NATO member states. But Poland is, and the three Baltic states are.

The stereotypes and narratives of the Cold War period were, as it seemed, gone. But maybe we have to think again. The Cold War structure of the international system is indeed gone for good. There is no rest button for globalization, and countless transborder movements of capital, people, information, entertainment, and resources cannot be stopped. But between outdated concepts of the Cold War, helpless search movements in new and complex contexts, mutual misperceptions, and increasing disinterest—the options for exploring and creating some new areas of engagement are very limited.

Andrey Makarychev spent over two years in Berlin, at Freie Universitaet, sponsored by the Alexander von Humboldt Foundation. He used this time to collect many impressions—mostly by talking to people available in Berlin and in other European cities. Andrey is very well suited for this kind of work. He is, in the best possible meaning, a *Grenzgaenger*—a wanderer between his native Russia and West European centers of social sciences, where he is well-established.

On the basis of his careful research and analysis, Dr. Makarychev suggests a careful re-interpretation of EU-Russian ties. His careful analysis suggests that we have at least to keep searching—for a new formula and context between the EU and Russia.

Klaus Segbers
Berlin, March 2014

Abstract

This monograph contains results of my original research at the Institute of East European Studies at the Free University of Berlin as an Alexander von Humboldt Foundation guest professor in 2011–2013. Its primary audience is academic, but rather wide in terms of disciplinary background, career level, and research focus. The position of the book at the crossroads of International Relations theory and empirical study of Russian foreign policy discourses makes it useful for a number of typical university courses worldwide—such as International Relations Theory, Russian Foreign Policy, Global Governance, and the such. I have tried to write the text in plain and comprehensible language to make it accessible for university students at all levels. Given the continuing interest in Russia's foreign policy and its domestic background in Europe and North America, as well as the growing attention to Russia's global role in many other countries and regions, such as China, India, and South America, the book might be expected to be part of a wider debate on models and institutions of multipolarity, and rising powers in a new world order.

The crisis in Ukraine and the EU reaction to Russia's annexation of Crimea confirmed the predictions of a crisis in communication between Brussels and Moscow. Scholarly discourses covering this relationship are also in search of new focal points. Both Russian and European experts in their analysis usually do not go farther than stating a number of more or less obvious symptoms of political stagnation in bilateral relations such as a lack of mutual trust, dissimilar political vocabularies, divergent material interests, etc. As a rule, most of the discourses shaping identities of both actors reproduce the binary logic of these relations either portraying Russia as existentially incompatible with the EU-based normative order, or, vice versa, lambasting contemporary Europe for deviating from its own traditions of democracy, the rule of law, and Christian values. In a more academic vocabulary, the EU is characterized as an exponent of solidarist type of international society (IS), whereas Russia adheres to its more pluralist vision.[1] These two competing

1 Marcin Kaczmarski, "Which Rules for the Global Order? The Global Dimension of the Russian - EU Relationship - The Case of International Crises," *Journal of Contemporary European Research* 7: 2 (2011): 160.

discourses, European and Russian ones, mostly produce "essentialized differences between two spatial markers ('Europe' and 'East'), a practice that is heavily imbued with an identity dimension."[2] The crisis in Ukraine in the aftermath of the revolutionary events of February 2014, followed by Russia's annexation of Crimea, sharply aggravated EU–Russia relations and illuminated the depth of the current splits and ruptures between the two actors.

Today's scholarship of the Russia–EU relations is to a great extent grounded in the recognition of the deep imbalances and miscommunications complicating the dialogue between the two parties. Against this background, the question of why Russia and the EU are such uneasy interlocutors for each other attracts strong academic and political attention. In this book, I stem from a premise that the key problem lies not in Russia's and EU's 'great designs,' but rather in the different conceptualizations of international structures the two actors are embedded in. Both Russia and the EU, in line with this logic, lack coherent policies toward each other; what we see in its stead is a bunch of different and sometimes mutually contradictory approaches grounded in competing, and alternative to each other, understandings of the structures of international relations.

In the traditions of the English school, these structures can be described as different versions of 'IS.' The plurality of models of IS can be understood as a competition of divergent—and alternative to each other—concepts of structural interconnections between key international actors. In the meantime, the variety of international societies as institutional and ideational/mental constructs might serve as an explanatory argument for the corresponding multiplicity of Russian and European foreign policies.

This book is divided into three parts. In Chapter 1, I introduce the research vocabulary and present main theories that organize analysis and conceptualize key approaches to the study of EU–Russia relations. Chapter 2 contains detailed account of different models of IS that are most relevant for comprehending the repertoire of policy strategies of these two actors. Finally, in Chapter 3, I analyze the most controversial policy areas in which Russia and the EU expose markedly dissimilar approaches, building their policies on different conceptual presumptions and, consequently, models of IS.

---

2 Ian Klinke, "Postmodern Geopolitics? The European Union Eyes Russia," *Europe – Asia Studies* 64: 5 (July 2012): 930.

Acknowledgments

I am sincerely thankful to the Alexander von Humboldt Foundation for supporting my two-year research in Germany, and to the Institute of East European Studies, Free University of Berlin (Director—Professor Klaus Segbers) for hosting me during this fellowship. I also express my gratitude to my current employer—University of Tartu (and in particular CEURUS—Center for EU–Russia Studies), which created all possible conditions for finalizing the manuscript in a friendly creative atmosphere.

It is only logical that the book about EU–Russia communicative relations was inspired by both intellectually enriching and emotionally exiting communication with those dearest people whom I consider my best energizers, both personally and professionally. Cities as diverse as Berlin, Lviv, Tallinn, Tartu, Zurich, and Helsinki bestowed on me unforgettable encounters and the strongest inspiratory impulses for transcending borders—in all possible exploratory senses.

March 10, 2014
Tartu

1 The EU and Russia in Times of Uncertainty: Intersubjective Identities and Discourses

1.1 The EU–Russia: Symptoms of Troubles

Current EU–Russian relations are marked by a series of crises accompanied by multiple imbalances, miscommunications, misunderstandings, and mutual accusations. Many of them are of political background. Most European countries are critical of Putin's regime for its digression from the standards of European normative order and growing nationalism. They accuse the Kremlin in mismanaging the country domestically (with emigration and rampant corruption as the most visible evidences of this) and creating artificial impediments for developing professional and civil society-based contacts with European partners. The EU is unhappy with political repressions within Russia, but seems hesitant to make it part of bilateral agenda. In the meantime, to foster Russian democracy, many liberal groups within EU Member States require from their governments a stronger pressure on Putin's regime.

In its turn, Russia pessimistically assesses both domestic developments within the EU and the EU's ability to play a key role in world politics. In the meantime, Moscow does see the EU as its competitor. It is basically for this reason that Russia has refused to partake in the EU-sponsored European Neighborhood Policy (ENP) and from the outset reacted with suspicion to the Eastern Partnership (EaP) program. In a gesture of reciprocation to EU's critique of Russia for the lack of democracy, the Russian Foreign Ministry has started issuing annual reports on the state of human rights in EU Member States. Moscow often claimed that the EU uses conflict resolution agenda for fostering its own influence in Russia's 'near abroad,' and that EU enlargement has weakened Russian influence to its western borders,[3] New EU Member States are portrayed as hindering the effective relationship between Russia and the 'old' EU states.

Economically, Brussels is dissatisfied with the multiple protectionist measures that Russia still keeps applying in spite of its World Trade Organization (WTO) accession. In July 2013, the European Commission has brought its first WTO case against Russia for the so-called 'recycling fees' on

---

3 Oleg Prikhod'ko, "Rossiya v meniayusheisia Evrope," *Obozrevatel'—Observer* 9:10 (2004), http://www.rau.su/observer/N9-10_2004/9-10_04.HTM (as of March 10, 2014).

vehicles. Earlier, the EU Commission initiated a legal trial against Gazprom in an attempt to prove that the Russian gas giant operates in EU Member States in violation of antitrust laws—a serious and consequential charge.

Expectedly, the crisis of Eurozone made Russian discourse on the EU even more critical. A former rector of Russian Diplomatic Academy deemed that nowadays it is time for Russia to say 'good-bye' to Europe until it recovers from the economic troubles.[4] Another Russian author claimed that the EU has fallen victim not only of financial troubles, but also of its either inability or hesitation to articulate more clearly the European identity.[5] Her colleague argued that financial troubles within the EU make it a doubtful partner for Russia and seriously damage the prospects for Russia's European orientation.[6] Europe's weakness may prompt it to more robustly team up with the United States in policies concerning Syria and Iran, and thus to disregard the dangers of a possible destabilization of the larger Middle East for Europe itself.[7] As seen from this vantage point, the only good news for the Kremlin is that a less ambitious and a more inward-oriented Europe may decrease its normative pressure on Moscow, which may open a new chance for reinvigorating Russia–EU relations.[8]

Even among Russian liberals Europe is under a fire of sharp critique. According to one account, at the peak of its strength Europe had based its policies on private property, minimal state, intra-European competition, and a feeling of cultural superiority. In the recent times, as soon as those principles were substituted by social distribution, regulatory powers of the state, pan-European unity, and multiculturalism, Europe's role in the world appears to be declining.[9]

---

4 Alexander Panov, "S.Sh.A.: kurs na sderzhivanie," *Strategia Rossii* 2 (February, 2012): 14, http://sr.fondedin.ru/Publik.pdf (as of March 10, 2014)

5 Olga Butorina, "Evropa bez Evrosoyuza," "Global Affairs" portal (December 15, 2011), http://www.globalaffairs.ru/number/Evropa-bez-Evrosoyuza-15407 (as of March 10, 2014)

6 Sergei Karaganov, "Evropa bol'she ne rastiot," "Global Affairs" portal, December 30, 2011, http://www.globalaffairs.ru/pubcol/Evropa-bolshe-ne-rastet-15437 (as of March 10, 2014).

7 Dmitry Evstafiev, "Glazami konservatora: perezagruzka mertva," *Index Bezopasnosti* 4 (July–October, 2011): 150, http://www.pircenter.org/data/publications/sirus4-11/Review%20Evstafiev.pdf (as of March 10, 2014).

8 Viacheslav Nikonov, "Kak krizis izmenil Evropu." "Politika" Foundation web site, 2011, http://www.polity.ru/articles/08042010.htm (as of March 10, 2014).

9 Yulia Latynina, "Evropa, ty ofigela," *Novaya Gazeta*, August 16, 2011, http://www.novayagazeta.ru/politics/48064.html (as of March 10, 2014).

Moscow often explains the difficulties of communicating with the EU by complicated organizational structure and decision-making procedures in Brussels, but Russia's relations with individual EU countries are no much better. Russian–Polish disputes fueled a harsh discussion on the balance between political and economic instruments in Russia's foreign policy; as an upshot of the Russian–British collision over the Alexander Litvinenko murder case the issues of security were raised in their most conflicting articulations; the Russian–Estonian tug-of-war over a Second World War monument evolved from the debate on collective historical memories to the most sensitive matters pertaining to political identities; Russian–Danish relations were almost frozen due to Moscow's dissatisfaction with Copenhagen's policy of hosting Chechen Diaspora, etc. Even Germany, the key Russian partner in the EU, becomes increasingly critical of—and politically demanding to—the Kremlin. Ultimately, one may argue that none of the frameworks of bilateral relations seems to work smoothly: Economics, along with identity and normative matters, are widely perceived as contaminated by political controversies, while security agenda appears to disjoint the two parties rather than bring them closer to each other.

When trying to explain these troubles, perhaps one has to start with the fact that both Russia and the EU are political subjects in the state of ongoing transformation. Usually it is Russia who is characterized as a transitional country (though for political reasons the Kremlin denies this), but the EU is also significantly changing from the inside. The crisis of Eurozone reshaped political landscape and constellation of political roles within the Union. Demands for more autonomy in regions such as Catalunya; intentions of the indebted Greece to remind Germany of the Nazi war crimes; disagreements between Germany and France on the future of Europe; problems with democracy in Hungary—all these occurrences suggest that the EU may gradually lose its role as an undeniable example of successful integration.

What complicates the picture is that the EU nowadays faces a much more troublesome neighborhood. Countries affected by the Arab spring are perhaps the most visible illustration for this; yet Eastern Europe poses its own challenges to the EU. Many European analysts admit that EU policies toward Belarus and Ukraine are ineffective, which may lead to seriously reconsidering the earlier expectations of the transformative effects of the EU's normative power. Russia is certainly part of this complicated external environment.

From its turn, Russian policy toward the EU seems quite ambivalent. On the one hand, the Kremlin keeps expressing its sympathy to the efforts of keeping the Eurozone afloat, which can be explained not by normative attachment of the Putin's regime to Europe, but rather by more pragmatic—financial and economic—interests of the Russian corporate elite. The Russian government keeps 45 percent of its Reserve Fund and National Wealth Fund assets in Euro, and is definitely disinterested in widening the EU financial crisis. On the other hand, the Kremlin has started to more consistently construct a political borderline between Russia and Europe by discursively articulating Russia's political distance from Europe. This borderline seems to be part of Russia's plans to institutionalize the Eurasian Union and bring its neighbors (especially Ukraine) as close to the sphere of Russian influence as possible. To materialize these projects, Russia under the current regime needs Europe as its unfriendly and weak external Other, which became particularly evident during the crisis in Ukraine in 2003–2014 and the occupation of Russian forces of Crimea in spite of multiple protests from all over Europe.

Thus, the two key actors, the EU and Russia, play ambiguous and highly complicated games in bilateral relations. While Russia tries to take political advantages of the financial crisis in Eurozone by portraying the EU as a moribund entity, the EU seems to be tired of socializing Russia in the European normative order. Against this background, EU–Russia summits turned into ceremonial events of symbolic value, masking deep discords between the two parties and a lack of strategies from both sides.

1.2 Contexts of Normative Disconnections

Arguably, the reasons for stark disagreements between the EU and Russia are grounded in the concept of normativity. It is the normative gap that deeply divides the EU and Russia and complicates a dialogue between them. In the official discourses, the EU and Russia very differently interpret the ideas of freedom, liberty, human rights, and many others. They certainly disagree on the meaning of sovereignty and the importance of trans- and supranational patterns of integration. Ultimately, the normative gap between Europe and Russia boils down to sharp differences between a political community-in-the-making adapting to a postmodern world, and a political community still stuck in reproducing the old patters of modernity with its hierarchical and state-centric thinking. This gap, by and large, stems from Russia's adherence to a set of Westphalian and sovereignty-bound approaches that apparently become less relevant for the EU.

Even when the two parties talk business or discuss seemingly technical issues, normative disconnections still interfere in their dialogue. For example,

Moscow and Brussels have divergent understandings of modernization, dissimilar approaches to energy security, and even differently interpret some of WTO norms and regulations.

The EU–Russia normative disconnections should not, however, be absolutized and ought to be placed in a number of rather nuanced contexts. *First*, along with resisting EU's normative order, Russia tries to re-interpret European values. In so doing, the Kremlin claims that it wants to come back to the 'real'—that is, Christian—roots of European identity. For instance, Moscow does verbally accept democracy as a value, but interprets it mostly as the rule of majority rather than protection of minorities inside the country. This logic, however, turns upside down as it comes to Russia's explications of allegedly 'undemocratic nature' of the regimes in the Baltic states by their maltreatment of Russian-speaking minorities. The result is an ongoing struggle for what academically might be dubbed empty signifiers—concepts of democracy, human rights, equality, justice, individual freedoms, all constitutive of specific types of normative orders and open to various interpretations.

Yet Russia's attempts to portray itself as a promoter of 'international democracy' (in the form of multipolarity, a dialogue of civilizations, etc.) appear to be political moves aimed at pluralization and dispersion of power in the world, which does not necessarily envisage democratic connotations. Indeed, Russia feels pretty comfortable in communicating with many authoritarian regimes. When Russia tries to criticize the EU for its alleged problems with democracy (with traditional references to Russian-speaking communities' rights in the Baltic states), this rhetoric does not resonate in the West.

Second, unlike Russia, the EU rightfully claims to be a normative power, but this is not to say that the EU is *always* a normative actor. The normativity of the EU foreign policy in general (and its policy toward Russia in particular) is manifest in the adherence to a set of democracy-based values in its international agenda (while other, nonnormative/un-normative actors even do not consider to include value-driven issues in their foreign strategies). Therefore, promotion of democracy is certainly part of EU's global philosophy, which, however, does not necessarily imply that in each specific case (in relations with China, Uzbekistan, Russia, etc.) the EU ought to put values before material interests. Apparently, the minimal criteria of a normative power is inclusion of normative/value-oriented matters in foreign policy agenda and advancement of these issues whenever it is feasible and appropriate, while in all other cases adhering to pursuance of more or equally legitimate economic or security interests—which, in their turn, might indirectly facilitate the democracy agenda by opening markets, pluralizing economic and social milieu, and fostering other transformative effects.

Third, the EU and Russia may not share common values, but some common—mostly procedural—norms can form a basis for bilateral relations. These norms are articulated in key documents signed by Moscow and Brussels, including the Partnership and Cooperation Agreement, the Four Common Spaces, the Partnership for Modernization (P4M), etc. Basically they deal with common understandings of security (including terrorism, drug trafficking, environmental protection, etc.), economic reciprocity (based on WTO regulations), and technical standards in many sectors of economy. These norms are basically managerial and nonpolitical, and leave ample space for cooperation even in the absence of common values.

Fourth, on the official level, the value gap persists—basically, due to the Kremlin's obstinacy with sovereignty and attempts to manipulate domestic public opinion by artificially creating the inimical images of the West. Yet on societal level this gap is less certain: The young generation of Russian middle class—urban professionals, students and educators, nongovernmental organization (NGO) activists—has less trouble with either understanding or communicating with their European colleagues and partners. The proliferation of social networks hopefully decreases the importance of value distance as well. This was convincingly demonstrated in 2011 and 2012 by the rise of mass-scale protests in Moscow and other large cities of Russia demanding fair elections, more transparency, and greater respect for human rights and freedoms (assembly, free speech, independent judiciary, and so forth). From a practical viewpoint this means that the more societies interact without governments' supervision, the more chances are for leaving the value gap behind—though still in a rather remote future.

1.3 Clashes of Identities

Against this backdrop, the intricacies and vicissitudes of Russian–European relations can be better grasped through the prism of ideational and, more specifically, identity-related factors. This explains the relevance of constructivist and discursive approaches to studying EU–Russian communicative disconnections.

As Viatcheslav Morozov claims, the development of international studies in Russia since the fall of the Soviet Union has been marked by a dominating obsession with identity, which can be exemplified by the often raised political issues: Is Russia a Western nation or a unique and self-sufficient civilization?[10] Is Russia still a great power, and what needs to be done to retain/restore this status?

Russia's construction of its own identity and subjectivity may be explained with a reference to Alexander Wendt's "projective identification thesis."[11] It might be instrumental in understanding the role of the Other—that is, Europe in reference to Russia—"for displacing unwanted feelings about the Self [...] . Individuals who, because of personal pathologies, cannot control potentially destructive unconscious fantasies, such as feelings of rage, aggression, or self-hatred, will sometimes attribute or 'project' them on to an Other, and then through their behavior pressure that Other to 'identify' with or 'act out' those feelings so that the Self can then control or destroy them by controlling or destroying the Other [...] . A requirement for this process is therefore 'splitting' the Self into 'good' and 'bad' elements, with the latter being projected on to the Other [...] . This can in turn be a basis for the cultural constitution of enmity, since the split Self needs the Other to identify with its ejected elements."[12] The Self is 'casting' the 'Other' in a corresponding counter-role that makes Self's identity meaningful.[13] This might shed some light on Russia's mental—and very artificial—division of Europe into 'weak' and 'strong,' 'false' and 'true,' 'old' and 'new,' with judgmental significance ascribed to each of these dichotomies. According to Wendt's 'projective identification' concept, deep split ('dislocation') within the Russian Self provokes and necessitates corresponding binaries in Russia's imagination about other countries. Almost all accusations Moscow addresses to 'false' European countries—maltreatment of the Second World War veterans, pluralization of historical narratives filled by alternative assessments of the previously glorified past, pro-American sentiments—can be easily found within Russia itself as a testimony for the dislocated nature of Russian identity.

Of course, identity is conceptualized in Russian discourses in many different ways. Some of the interpretations tend to essentialize Russia's belongingness to Europe by explaining it through the prism of geography, culture, or history. As the director of the Institute of European Law at MGIMO (Moscow State Institute of International Relations) deems, "social and political

---

10 Viatcheslav Morozov, "Obsessed with Identity: The IR in post-Soviet Russia," *Journal of International Research and Development* 12:2 (2009): 200.

11 Alexander Wendt, *Social Theory of International Politics* (Cambridge: Cambridge University Press, 1999): 277.

12 Wendt, *Ibid.,* 277.

13 *Ibid.*, 329.

transformation of Russia cannot be considered as a precondition for rapprochement with Europe."[14] Russia's European identity, thus, is simply reduced to the invocations of Russia's 'natural,' 'legitimate,' 'objective' grounds to be considered a full-fledged European nation.[15]

Other authors consider Russia's European identity as a matter of social construction, recognition, and painstaking adaptation of European ideas.[16] The basic intricacy here is that Europe has multiple roles to play and cannot be easily anchored in a single set of meanings. Historically, in modern times Europe was associated with Christianity, balance of power, and monarchic solidarity against republican ideas, but nowadays all these concepts are either relinquished or seriously questioned. The sense of Europe as a 'moving target' was insightfully grasped by Boris Mezhuev:

> "We were thinking of constructing a modern society, as in the West, but it turned out that the West itself is transforming in a direction hardly conceivable for both them and us. We wanted to say farewell to the empire and convert into a nation state, but it turned out that the age of nation states has already gone, and we are on the eve of a new imperial era [...] . We strived for a multi-party system, but we are said that it is moribund in Europe. We wanted public politics, but it occurred that even in the so-called civilized world it is far from sane. We were eager to be modern, but it is exactly in this sense that we have gone hopelessly obsolete."[17]

Besides, almost each of the most controversial policies introduced by Putin's regime—from economic protectionism to increasing intervention of the state in political parties' affairs—usually contains implicit references to various—yet mostly ill-defined— 'European experiences.' Europe indeed is frequently used as an argument for sustaining certain political discourses in Russia, which turns the conception of Europe into a rather broad and elastic signifier. Yet, in spite of this indeterminacy, Europe does play an underlying role for constructing Russia's multiple identities. For liberal thinkers, the EU is "a complex and sophisticated edifice, the main achievement of post-war Europe."[18] Thus, a shift from a 'Europe of nations' to a 'Europe of regions' and

---

14 Mark Entin, "Future Tasks for the Development of the Relations between Russia and the European Union," in Hans-Georg Heinrich and Liudmila Lobova (eds.), *EU-Russia: New Departures and Old Habits* (Vienna: ICEUR Working Papers, No. 3, 2010).

15 *Europe: " 'Real' and 'Unreal*'. Moscow: Report of the Institute of Europe," Russian Academy of Sciences 204 (2007): 7-10.

16 Dmitry Danilov, "Rossiya i Zapad: bol'she ne vragi... a kto?" *Vestnik Evropy* 7: 8 (2002): 17-28.

17 Boris Mezhuev, "Sotvorenie kosmopolisa," *Kosmopolis* 1 (Autumn 2002).

18 Mikhail Borschevsky and Viktor Yaroshenko, "Eta zhivuchaya Evropa," *Vestnik Evropy* 28–29 (2010): 12-18.

networks, and, therefore, from modernity to its radical reconsideration, is viewed as a global trend toward growingly appealing networking type of structures to which Russia has to eventually adapt.[19] For conservative authors, Russia has by all means to help reviving the continental Europe that hypothetically might become its political ally.[20] This implies an explicit disdain to countries of Central Europe that are, in the view of some Russian geopoliticians, overtly pro-American and therefore—according to the Kremlin's logic—Russia-skeptic. The geopolitical recipe sometimes sounds quite paradoxical: Europe ought to display its imperial qualities, and exert hegemony based on its 'cultural majority' for reinventing the forgotten meanings of national identities.[21] This prospect is believed to redress Europe from its current troubles and lay foundation for its stable and sound engagement with Russia,[22] with good prospects for joint management of energy projects instead of confrontation, restoration of Moldova's territorial integrity, incorporation of Turkey in joint Moscow–Brussels political framework, etc.[23] An opposite perspective is described by some Russian authors with a regret: After the failure of its constitutional project, the EU may gradually keep losing its chance to speak with a single voice internationally, and fall victim of intensive migrations unsettling European identity.[24]

1.4 Identities and Discourses

What stems from this is that the concept of identity is strongly and sometimes intentionally politicized, that is, used for political judgments that often spur conflicts of interpretations, involving the issues constitutive for political communities, including democracy, security, legitimacy, collective memories, etc. This is why analysis of identity as the key factor shaping EU–Russian relations requires focusing on its discursive underpinnings. It is through discourse analysis that one may identify and interpret perpetual references to Europe

19 Oleg Nemenskiy, "Kosovskiy precedent i buduschee Evropy" (April 21, 2008), http://www.apn.ru/publications/article19807.htm (as of March 10, 2014).

20 Alexander Dugin, "Evraziyskiy otvet globalizatsii," *Politicheskiy zhurnal* 4:139 (November 15, 2009): 5-9.

21 Mikhail Remizov, "Demokratia plus gegemonia bol'shinstva" (June 24, 2011), http://www.apn.ru/publications/article24379.htm (as of March 10, 2014).

22 Vladimir Karpets, "Imperia neizbezhna," http://www.intelros.org/books/russia_book_karpec1.htm (as of March 10, 2014).

23 Sergey Karaganov (ed.), *K soyuzu Evropy* (St. Petersburg – Valaam – Kizhi – Moscow: The Valday Club Report, 2010).

24 Anatoly Utkin, "Padenie Evropy," *Prognosis* 2: 6 (Summer 2006): 139.

as Russia's constitutive Other for substantiating a set of arguments inherent in Russia's identity-making.[25]

The concept of discourse is of primordial importance for this study since "our own formation as subjects is inextricably woven into the relational webs that constitute the social context in which we live,"[26] and this context is made up of discourses. Placing discourses at the heart of the analysis makes the mapping of social and political spaces more flexible and constantly changing: In some instances, discourses may gravitate to—and reinforce—each other; in other occurrences, they are in a conflict that fuels what could be called 'the battle of the story.' Therefore, a number of different narratives may coexist and intermingle with each other. Within each of them, statements ("order-words"[27]) are given their discursive status and expanse for circulation. Discourses form their semantic fields and may serve certain political purposes. Each discourse produces a certain type of identity embedded in the dominant speech acts. In the meantime, "no discursive formation constitutes a completely closed system, but, on the other hand, it is never totally exterior to other discursive formations."[28]

Discourses of Russia and the EU are not only in the process of constant formation, but both are also *internally dislocated*. By dislocation, one shall understand indeterminacy, instability, uncertainty, and ambiguity of discursive foundations of identity. Both Russia and the EU can be portrayed as deeply divided political subjects incapable of speaking with a single voice internationally. Each of the two parties inevitably refers to its counterpart in the process of constructing its identity, which testifies to nonself-sufficient nature of these identities, and the unavoidable semantic interpenetrations and overlays. For example, Russian international discourse is torn apart between 'sovereignist,' 'exceptionalist,' or 'nationalist' reading of Russia as a country surrounded by fundamentally hostile environment with no reliable friends, on

25 Martin Muller, "Situated Identities: Enacting and Studying Europe at a Russian Elite University," *Millenium: Journal of International Studies* 37: 3 (2008): 3–25.

26 Rob Aitken, "Embedded Liberalism in Counterpoint: Reading Woody Guthrie's Reciprocal Economy," *Millenium: Journal of International Studies* 37: 2 (2009): 30-49.

27 Jon Short, "Outside of Power? Or The Power of the Outside," *Journal of Social and Political Thought* 1: 2 (June 2000), http://www.yorku.ca/jspot/2/jshort.htm (as of March 10, 2014)

28 Mats Braun, "Talking Europe – the Dilemma of Sovereignty and Modernization," *Cooperation and Conflict: Journal of the Nordic International Studies Association* 43: 4 (2008): 400.

the one hand, and 'internationalist discourse' arguing that Russia is harmonious to the international community in managing the most deadly security challenges, on the other. In their turn, a variety of European discourses contain both Russia-skeptic voices and those calling for pragmatic accommodation with Moscow in spite of multiple normative disconnections.

Yet there is also an *external dimension of dislocation* that is manifested by the dependence of Russia's identities "upon an outside which both denies that identity and provides its conditions of possibility at the same time."[29] This dislocates Russia's discourse by representing Russia as a country eager to get attuned to the dominating discourses, and by reinstalling Russia's subjectivity through the re-interpretation of the key components of globally dominating discourses. In this light, Europe may be perceived as a challenge to Russia, but nevertheless Russian identity is constructed through communication with—and reference to—Europe. Even a negative marking of Europe by Russian Euro-pessimists still corroborates the discursive dependence of Russia on Europe as the key signifier for Russia's international narrative.

This leads to another important concept in discourse analysis—that of *re-signification*. It denotes transformative practice of deploying terms in previously unexplored or even 'unauthorized' contexts. Re-signification is mostly used by political agents located at the margins of political structures who wish to change previous meanings by either expanding concepts or by including other meanings into them.[30] This appears applicable to Russia who painstakingly makes efforts to avoid marginalization and raise its world profile by promoting and propagating structural changes in IS to foster greater plurality of power holders and diversification of their resources. In particular, Russia borrowed the concept of multipolarity from the realist vocabulary where it denoted a rather conflictual and unstable type of international system, and re-signified it by ascribing to this concept more positive connotations and making it the key strategic landmark for Russian diplomacy.

Re-signification is closely related to the concept of *language games* that seems to be also appropriate for this study. Following the logic of Wittgenstein, language has neither ontological stability nor unity; consequently, there is no authoritative, determinate collective 'we' that would appeal to a mental

29 Aletta J. Norval, "Theorising Dislocations." Paper presented at "New Stability, Democracy and Nationalism in Contemporary Russia" workshop, Basel, September 26–27, 2008: 3.

30 Birgit Schippers and Judith Butler, "Radical Democracy and Micro-Politics," in Adrian Little and Moya Lloyd (eds.), *The Politics of Radical Democracy* (Edinburgh: Edinburgh University Press, 2009): 80–91.

or metaphysical source of identity or authority, or unveil "literal, uninterpreted truth."[31] The language games approach claims that each concept under a closer scrutiny decomposes into a series of 'pictures' of reality with their "playful and fluid"[32] contexts. Of course, not all language games translate into strong political voices that explain how to change the world, yet at least some of them provide different 'road maps' to the future. This has important repercussions for EU–Russia discursive relations: for example, both parties may formally agree on the importance of the modernization agenda, but treat its meaning differently. As I will show in Chapter 3, for the EU the concept of modernization inevitably presupposes drastic reforms in the Russian system of governance (including eradication of corruption, the establishment of effective public institutions, etc.), while for the Kremlin modernization connotes mainly technical projects of upgrading Russian industrial and financial sectors.

'True' vs. 'False' Europe

The Norwegian scholar Iver Neumann, as well as his Russian colleague Viatcheslav Morozov, distinguished two different versions of Europe—'false' and 'true'—as a key feature of Russia's thinking about Europe. 'False Europe,' in their interpretation, includes countries with strong anti-Russian sentiments and those having lost 'genuine European values.' 'True Europe,' on the contrary, is made up of nations friendly to Russia and adhering to what Russia considers as 'the original spirit of Europe.' 'True Europe' contains, besides what US Secretary of Defense Donald Rumsfeld dubbed 'old Europe' (France and Germany), countries with some degree of cultural affinity to Russia. Politically, the fact that Russia leans toward the French–German 'couple' could attest to its search for a European subjectivity that ultimately is a precondition for Russia's own self-assertion vis-à-vis Europe. Recreation of what could be called 'a great continental family' became a substantial part of Russia's rediscovering of 'old Europe' as its interlocutor.

The 'false–true Europe' dichotomy determines, to some degree, other adjacent conceptualizations. One of them seems to be a contradistinction between 'traditional Europe' and 'post-Europe.' The 'false' features of Europe are associated with the alleged evaporation of national spirit and a growing self-denial of national interests and identities. This Russian discourse, then,

31 Christopher Robinson, *Wittgenstein and Political Theory. The View from Somewhere* (Edinbourgh: Edinburgh University Press, 2009.): 2–13.

32 Robinson, *Ibid.*, 49.

seems to deny what many in Europe are proud of—both the refusal of national egos and the valorization of supranational integration.

The 'false–true' dichotomy may be approached as a discursive frame allowing Russia to assess other European nations according to its own standards, thus stressing Russian subjectivity in European affairs. Russia needs a 'false Europe' in order to reinstall its European credentials and feel at home with what it considers a 'true Europe.' The idea of the alleged 'Russian Europe,' historically exemplified by Novgorod's and Pskov's inclusion into the Hansa medieval trade network and these cities' commitment to a set of democratic procedures, has also to be understood in the light of 'true Europe' concept.

Russia's 'false–true Europe' dichotomy has important historical connotations. Russia's relations with Baltic countries, being fundamentally damaged by different interpretations of the events of the Second World War, are an emblematic case of a history-driven identity clash. The 'battle of words' includes a number of dichotomies: 'voluntary membership' in the Soviet Union or 'annexation,' 'liberation' from the Nazi Germany, or 'occupation' by USSR, etc.

Identity and history debate largely intersects with political discourse that actualized the discursive division of Europe in the aftermath of the Georgia war of August 2008. In the Kremlin's eyes, France and Germany have strengthened their status and reputation of 'good Europeans' (those loyal to Russia), while Poland (who signed the agreement on accommodating the American antimissile system right in the middle of the Russian–Georgian war) and the 'orange' Ukraine (who was accused of selling arms to Georgia and threatening to prevent the Russian Black Sea Fleet from returning to its naval base in Sebastopol in August 2008) are put in a different category of unfriendly states. Again, this way of interpreting Europe contains a great deal of Russia's eagerness to present itself as an unalienable part of 'true Europe' that is threatened by 'false Europeans.' It is not incidentally that Russian Foreign Minister Sergey Lavrov dubbed the treatment by Georgian authorities of Abkhazia and South Ossetia in 2008 'un-European,' which reveals Russian sensitivity to the concept of Europe. In a rather indicative way, Russia did not hide its irritation to the display of the EU flag during Mikhail Saakashvili's public pronouncements—a reaction that was arguably grounded in Moscow's resolve to disavow any European connotations as far as Georgia is concerned.

The othering of Europe frames and conditions the discursive construction of Russia itself, which, in the view of some authors, sometimes thinks of itself as a 'real' Europe, a heritor of century-long European culture. The uncovering of a lack of authenticity in today's Europe leads some Russian scholars to presume that Russia is destined to inherit and incarnate the legacy of the 'genuine,' ancient Greece-based European civilization, while the EU has deviated from these "traditional values."[33] Many Russian political thinkers are convinced in Russia's ability to confess and defend "genuinely Christian and, therefore, genuinely European values, among which the key one is the value of free human being whose freedom is derived from its creation on the basis of the image of the Lord."[34] This type of discourse not only makes today's Europe a poorly self-articulated entity, but also concomitantly questions the strategy of Russia's integration with it.

Yet, of course, the fact that the Kremlin assumes the right to pass judgments on Russia's neighbors from the position of a 'true Europe' does not necessarily imply that Russian foreign policy discourse becomes structured in European terms. Russia does appeal to the norms of Europe, but stops short of applying them to its own policy. As Iver Neumann puts it, "this is a situation where pluralism and some kind of generalized liberalism become increasingly central to European identity, with Russia opting for what looks to Europeans like old-fashioned state building. As a result, Russia is out of synch with the development of European identity."[35] That is why this Russian discourse was never recognized as legitimate beyond Russia itself and thus did not leave institutional traces in Moscow's relations with other countries. Russia's imagined 'special relations' with either of 'real' European powers were never institutionalized; moreover, under a closer scrutiny they may turn into a myth. Russia's policy of ostracizing Estonia for its decision to remove the Bronze Soldier monument from Tallinn's downtown to a military cemetery in 2007 resonated neither in Europe, nor even in Russia's 'near abroad.' Russia's attempts to condition its relations with post-Soviet and postsocialist countries by their adherence to the Soviet/Russian glorious narrative of the Second World War largely failed. Ultimately, Russia had to recognize the politically meaningful role of Poland—otherwise associated with 'false Europe'—in finding a visa facilitation solution for Kaliningrad's residents.

---

33 Viktor Pernatskiy. "Rossiya v mirovom politico-pravovom prostranstve," *Svobodnaya Mysl'* 10: 1605 (2009): 56.

34 Arkadiy Maler, "Pochemu ot Dmitryia Medvedeva ne iskhodit netvarniy svet?" Part 2, *Russkii zhurnal* (April 29, 2008), www.russ.ru (as of March 10, 2014).

35 Iver Neumann, "European Identity and Its Changing Others." Norwegian Institute of International Relations: NUPI Working Paper 710 (Oslo: 2006).

1.5 Intersubjectivity in EU–Russia Relations

With all disconnections in mind, the two subjects in communication, the EU and Russia, are not simply mutually dependent on each other, but—what is even more important—mutually constitute each other's identities. Russia is eager to find its proper place in European political, security, and intellectual milieu but, in doing so, it reinterprets the key terms of the hegemonic discourse and fills them with the content suitable to its needs.

The concept of intersubjectivity can be discussed as defining the nature of Russia's relations with Europe. In Wendt's vocabulary, these relations might be termed micro-structural because they are deployed within deeper structures of IS. It may appear that these relations are 'destined for disconnection' and thrive on separation, "distancing, strangeness, and all the risks of miscomprehension."[36] What these disconnections disclose is the interaction between two identity-based subject positions. In a narrow sense, the concept of intersubjectivity points to the common areas where both parties communicate with each other as partners, and, concomitantly, not only the EU is capable of exerting influence upon Russia, as it used to be throughout 1990s, but Russia may also have some impact too. Intersubjectivity presupposes that each type of influence has its reverse side, a sort of counterinfluence. For example, Russia, being an object of EU-sponsored programs, exerted (perhaps unintentionally) some influence upon the EU in response—through either confirming or disproving the initial premises that framed EU's policies. A Russia who does not meet EU's normative expectations could be an argument in promoting a policy of stronger bordering and enhancing the 'Self–Other' divide.

In a wider sense, intersubjectivity signifies not only a possibility to achieve some practical effects and alter policies of other actors, but also to constitute their identities. It is in this sense that I employ the concept of intersubjectivity in my analysis.[37] In intersubjective relationship, both parties constitute each other in a sense that the formation of Russian identity is impossible without references to European experiences and practices, and vice

36 Jean Baudrillard and Marc Guillaume, *Radical Alterity* (Los Angeles: Semiotext(e), 2008): 31.

37 It is important to note that, in author's judgment, not all relations are intersubjective. For example, countries like Sri Lanka and Uruguay do have certain (diplomatic and economic) relations but they are void of intersubjective background since neither of these two countries defines its identity through the references to its counterpart.

versa. Identities always relate to a "constitutive other,"[38] which was well grasped by Slavoj Zizek:

> when I reconstruct my life in a narrative, I always do it within a certain inter-subjective context, answering the Other's call-injunction, addressing the Other in a certain way [...] . My very status as a subject depends on its links to the substantial Other [...] . [I]n the core of my being, I am irreducibly vulnerable, exposed to the Other[s] [...] . [Yet] confronted with the Other, I never can fully account for myself [...] . I will never get from the Other a full answer to 'who you are' because the Other is a mystery also for him/herself [...] . This mutual recognition of limitation thus opens up a space of sociality that is the solidarity of the vulnerable.[39]

Constructivism treats identity as a social construct grounded in "another-image rather than self-image."[40] Therefore, national identity is to a large extent based on how a state is identified and perceived by other states. Logical consistency does not necessarily need to be a prerequisite for dominating discourses[41] and their combinations, since identities of political subjects are intrinsically split, which explains why states often espouse contradictory and inconsistent premises in their policies. Thus, Russian imagery of international relations is "constructed in relation to the great powers and the West"[42] with whom Russia competes yet simultaneously seeks its recognition and approval.

In light of this approach, the formation of Russian identity in wide historical perspective is impossible without references to European experiences and practices, and vice versa. Identities always relate to their 'constitutive others,' which is well illustrated by the practice of Russia–EU communications. Intersubjectivity makes any subject position dependent on the outside, sensitive to the opinions and approaches of external others, and thus immanently fluid, mobile, and changeable.

---

38 Philipp Casula, "The Loss of the Constitutive Outside: Changing Discourses in East and West after the End of the Cold War." Paper presented on Panel "Metaphors and Power" at the Sixth Pan-European Conference on International Relations, Turin, September 15, 2007.

39 Slavoj Zizek, "Neighbors and Other Monsters: A Plea for Ethical Violence," in *The Neighbor. Three Inquiries in Political Theology* (Chicago and London: The University of Chicago Press, 2005): 139.

40 Anne Clunan, *The Social Construction of Russia's Resurgence. Aspirations, Identity, and Security Interests* (Baltimore: The Johns Hopkins University Press, 2009): 6.

41 Audie Klotz and Cecelia Lynch, *Strategies for Research in Constructivist International Relations* (Armonk, New York and London, England: M.E.Sharpe, 2007).

42 Klotz and Lynch, *Ibid.,* 221.

Seen from an intersubjective perspective, any meaningful political characterization of Russia is possible only through its semantic association—positive or negative—with Europe. The political positioning of Russia as a European country has never been seriously challenged in Russian discourse that asserts Russia as a European country in terms of its history, culture, and civilizational identity. Russian leaders on a number of occasions referred to European experience in order to justify Russia's 'normalcy,' understood as its belongingness to European milieu and alleged compatibility with European political logic. Many in Moscow sustain a thesis of compatibility of Russia-sponsored post-Soviet association and institutional mechanisms of European integrative project—an argument that is meant to substantiate the Kremlin's slogan of 'moving together toward Europe,' addressed to countries with strong pro-European feelings such as Ukraine and Moldova.

Yet intersubjective relations are full of distortions, disconnections, asymmetries, ruptures, and imbalances. The concept of 'the friction of ideas' (or 'ideational friction'), borrowed from Swedish colleagues, makes the case for "deep-seated cultural differences between Europe and Russia."[43] To quote Slavoj Zizek, "language [...] is the first and greatest divider," and this is the reason why we and our neighbors [can] 'live in different worlds' even when we live on the same street."[44] To put it differently, language "provides the boundaries of inter-subjective process,"[45] and "alterity is thus not given but produced."[46] This perspective certainly applies to Russian–EU relations. While frequently using the same normative vocabulary, European and Russian discourse-makers deliberately infuse different meanings in them. Europe, thus, faces not an opposition to its concepts of democracy, identity, and security, but different interpretations of them. Indeed, Russia questions neither of the basic European norms or ideas; instead it seeks to offers alternative visions for most of them.

43 Kjel Engelbrekt and Bertil Nygren, "A Reassertive Russia and an Expanded European Union," in Kjel Engelbrekt and Bertil Nygren (eds.), *Russia and Europe. Building Bridges, Digging Trenches* (Routledge, 2010): 3.

44 Slavoj Zizek, "The Antinomies of Tolerant Reason: A Blood-Dimmed Tide is Loosed," http://www.lacan.com/zizantinomies.htm (as of March 10, 2014).

45 Oliver Kessler, "From Agents and Structures to Minds and Bodies: Of Supervenience, Quantum, and the Linguistic Turn," *Journal of International Relations and Development* 10: 3 (2007): 7-25.

46 Michael Hardt and Antonio Negri, *Empire* (London & Cambridge: Harvard University Press, 2000): 125, 127.

However, intersubjectivity in Russian–EU relationship can be differently interpreted. For example, Fiodor Lukianov explains the predominantly negative portrayal of Putin's Russia in Europe by

> the internal insecurity of the West, and the growing sense that everything is not proceeding quite as it should [...] . Vladimir Putin ... indicates to western partners their mistakes and failures. He criticizes their hypocrisy and double standards, appearing in the role of an idiosyncratic Savonarola whose utterances are especially annoying because they are often true [...] . He plays by the same rules as everyone else but simply doesn't see the need to dress this up in respectable ideological garb. And the fact that – whether by force of luck or by force of a more realistic calculation – he furthermore periodically outperforms his partners, compelling them to take the opinion of that same declining Russia into account, adds a mystical halo.[47]

Yet instead of (mis)presenting the Kremlin as a bearer of a hidden truth for Europe (and implicitly denying a similar role for Europe in its relations with Russia), I share a more nuanced approach to intersubjectivity as an active "power to affect and a passive power to be affected."[48] In other words, even in its role as an object of EU influence, Russia still can—perhaps indirectly—influence debates within the EU and its choice(s) for future actions. For Russia this is especially important, since its ability to influence the EU is limited, which apparently makes the EU–Russia intersubjectivity largely asymmetrical. The EU policy philosophy can be expressed as follows: "If I act toward the other based upon principles I carry with me previously to and outside of my interaction with the other, then it is not really the other I am concerned with. I am imposing my ethical framework upon the other, rather than taking up the other in her own right."[49] As a reaction to the alleged universality of EU's norms, rules, and principles, Russia prioritizes its sovereignty and a great power status that are not expected to be confirmed or approved by anybody, including the EU.[50]

---

47 Fiodor Lukianov, "Putin, Russia, and the West: Beyond Stereotype." Valdai Club web portal (February 15, 2012), http://valdaiclub.com/usa/38620.html (as of March 10, 2014).

48 Yves Citton, "Political Agency and the Ambivalence of the Sensible," in Gabrile Rockhill and Philip Watts (eds.), *Jacques Ranciere: History, Politics, Aesthetics* (Durham and London: Duke University Press, 2009): 122.

49 Todd May, *The Political Thought of Jacques Ranciere. Creating Equality* (Edinburg University Press, 2008): 149.

50 Viacheslav Morozov, "Evropa: orientatsiya vo vremeni i prostranstve," *Rossiya v Global'noi Politike* 3 (May–June 2008), http://www.alleuropa.ru/evropa-orientatsiya-vo-vremeni-i-prostranstve (as of March 10, 2014).

The notion of intersubjectivity is instrumental for understanding the intricacies of Russian–EU relations as interaction of two 'ontologically dislocated,' or unstable, divided, split, and unfixed subjects. European and Russian identities are mutually dependent, but EU's role in molding the Russian identity is stronger than Russia's role for the EU. Russian discourse is mostly Euro-centric, even in its negativity, while the EU discourse is not necessarily Russia-centric. The EU seems to be embedded in "the Eurocentric procedure of imposing its own hegemony by means of the exclusionary discursive strategy of devaluing the Other."[51] This policy can be explained by EU's adherence to the 'thick' (solidarist) version of IS, with clear emphasis on normativity understood as "a way of thinking that emphasizes the central importance of an autonomous legal order for constraining the arbitrary and personal exercise of political power."[52]

Russia plays a different game of rejecting and even challenging its otherness and exteriority that Europe ascribes and imposes to it. A menu of Russia's identity choices may include such roles as a 'different Europe,'[53] a 'non-Western Europe' (along with Turkey), a constitutive part of a wider Europe or of 'Euro-Atlantic civilization.' Russia, therefore, tries not to completely alienate itself from the EU, but rather to discursively divide Europe into different segments and, in the meantime, to make the concept of Europe as broad and imprecise as possible, to be able to fit in anyway. One may see here a double function of Russia's European discourse: forming an image of Europe easy to deal and communicate with, as well as constructing Russia itself through emphasizing the roles it is supposed to play and the qualities it is expected to display internationally.

Since Russia and the EU discursively constitute each other, their subject positions are immanently fluid, mobile, and flexible. In the intersubjective relations the two parties construct the subject positions of each other, which means that these positions are not pregiven. That is why it would be a gross oversimplification to treat intersubjective relations as relations between two (or more) already given political subjects. The two subjects in/of communication, Russia and EU, are not only in the process of ongoing formation, but

---

51 Slavoj Zizek, "Da Capo senza Fine," in Judith Butler, Ernesto Laclau, and Slavoj Zizek (eds.), *Contingency, Hegemony, Universality. Contemporary Dialogue on the Left.* (London & New York: Verso, 2000): 231.

52 Jef Huysmans, "International Politics of Exception." Paper prepared for presentation at SGIR Fifth Pan-European Conference (Hague, The Netherlands, September 9–22, 2004): 7.

53 Nikolay Shmeliov, "Rossiya i Evropa: vmeste ili porozn'?" *Vestnik Evropy* 19–20 (2007).

also what is more important is that both are internally dislocated. Russia can be portrayed as a political subject deeply fragmented by its desire to simultaneously use economic arguments (the case of sanctions against Poland or Lithuania) and normative appeal (the case of lambasting Estonia for the removal of the Great Patriotic War monument in Tallinn in 2007 from the downtown to a military cemetery). It appears that Moscow is eager to speak with many different voices simultaneously—for instance, insisting on the market-based relations with Belarus in the energy sphere, on the one hand, and acknowledging a special role of Belarus in hosting Russian military bases which are considered as an indispensable element of Russian security policy, on the other. In the interpretation of its past, Russia is both a destructor of the Soviet empire (an argument constitutive for Russia's role as a cosponsor of the Cold War termination) and the heritor of the USSR (an argument that explicates Russia's resistance to the Ukrainian and Polish memory politics grounded in remembrances about *Golodomor* and *Katyn*). In terms of Russia's identity under Putin's regime, it seems to be a mixture of a typically *Realpolitik* pragmatism (Dmitry Medvedev argued that Western countries have to accept the 'reality' of secession of the two territories from Georgia and avoid emotional reaction to "virtual situations"[54]), on the one hand, and a liberal assumption that explains foreign policy by domestic developments (in Putin's interpretation, it is the presidential election in the United States that predetermines the position America takes in international conflicts[55]), on the other. Russian policies include both institutional commitments (such as the European Security Treaty proposal) and what might be called 'reluctant unilateralism' (in Medvedev's assessment, Russia and NATO 'may say goodbye to each other,' but it is NATO that has stronger interest in continuing the cooperation). Russian identity mixes up particularist assumptions (admitting that each act of state recognition is individual and singular[56]) and universal explanations (by declaring that what Russia did in South Ossetia and Abkhazia "others have done in Kosovo,"[57] the Kremlin in fact accepted the logic of the 'chain effect').

---

54 Dmitry Medvedev, Interview with Al Jazira TV (Sochi, August 26, 2008), http://www.kremlin.ru/text/appears/2008/08/205783.shtml (as of March 10, 2014).

55 Vladimir Putin, Interview with CNN (August 28, 2008), http://www.government.ru (as of March 10, 2014).

56 Dmitry Medvedev, Interview with "Russia Today" TV Channel (Sochi, August 26, 2008), http://www.kremlin.ru/text/appears/2008/08/205773.shtml (as of March 10, 2014).

57 Dmitry Medvedev, Interview with BBC, (Sochi, August 26, 2008), http://www.kremlin.ru/text/appears/2008/08/205775.shtml (as of March 10, 2014).

1.6 Identity Shifts: Why Russia Is Not the USSR

The menu of Russian foreign policy identities to a large extent depends on a variety of international structures Russia engages with. The differences between today's Russia and the Soviet Union can only confirm this argument.

In the Western discourses, Russia under the Putin regime is often compared (or even equated) with the Soviet Union. This logic is grounded in the resilience of the old Soviet domestic practices and foreign policy ambitions in the area known as Russia's 'near abroad.' However, I share a different approach that is consonant with Ted Hopf's distinction between the Soviet and Russian identity discourses. As seen from (t)his perspective, the Soviet identity was grounded in a number of key signifiers:

- -the idea of 'the new Soviet man,' which makes ethnic or religious identities excessive, harmful, and only tolerable as folkloric rituals;
- the concept of class struggle, hence the class-based foundation of the friends–foes distinction, and the view of the USSR as the vanguard of 'progressive mankind' struggling against the 'world capitalism';
- modernity as the reference point of the Communist strategy, hence greatpowerness as an effect of enforced modernization/industrialization;
- ahistoricity, or a radical break with Russia's historical experience that was regarded as a burden rather than an important identity resource.[58]

Yet after 1991 this set of characteristics was radically altered. Unlike the over-ideologized Soviet Union, Russia has explicitly proclaimed itself 'pragmatic' and depoliticized type of subject, guided by the desire to be recognized in the West as a 'normal' European power. Instead of the unified identity promoted by the Soviet elite, Russia's identity narratives were referring to the multiplicity of Others—external (the United States, or Europe), internal (from oligarchs to self-minded regional elites) and historical (Stalin, Ivan the Terrible, etc., depending on political dispositions). Russia also experienced the renaissance of sub/transnational (ethnic and religious) identities that previously were considered 'obsolete' and 'pre-modern.'

Against this background, Russia may be dubbed a 'post-empire,' which makes it different from the Communist empire of the Soviet Union. However, it is exactly at this point that identity games start: In spite of Russia's longing for the role of a 'normal European power', it is widely perceived in the West as a 'neo-empire' eager to use its energy resources and military force for

58 Ted Hopf, *Social Construction of International Politics. Identities and Foreign Policies, Moscow 1955 and 1999* (Ithaca: Cornell University Press, 2001).

expansionist purposes. This perceptional gap is a constitutive element in the chain of Russian–European discursive disconnections that are perfectly visible in the divergent symbolizations of two key historical momentums of the 20th century by each of the parties. One of them is the Second World War, which is traditionally referred to in Russia as the Great Patriotic War. Russia and Europe not only use different names for it and different dates to celebrate its end (May 9 in Russia and May 8 in the West), but the gaps between the two parties are also much deeper than that. In Russia, the May 9 symbolizes not only Russia's strength as a great power, but also its belongingness to the European geopolitical tradition (the acceptance of Stalin as a full-fledged partner of Western democracies is a good illustration of this power politics argument). Yet, in Europe, the end of the Second World War is a combination of celebration and mourning, since for many East/Central European nations the liberation from the Nazi troops was followed by the occupation of their territories by the Red Army.

Another important historical turning point is the fall of the Soviet Union in 1991. References to 1991 are always part of political discourses, both in Europe and Russia, but the semantic meanings of these references are drastically different, which reveals stark normative cleavages between Russia and Europe. The fall of the USSR is deplored as the 'largest geopolitical catastrophe of the 20th century' by the Kremlin, and celebrated in the West as the key event of the relatively peaceful democratic revolution in the former Soviet bloc. For most Europeans, the dissolution of the USSR was not the major disaster of the 20th century, especially against the backdrop of the experience of the two world wars, and the bloody ethnic cleansings in the Balkans. These comparisons demonstrate how deep the value gap between the official Russia and Europe is.

Yet Russia's identity is far from fixed. The dissolution of the USSR has unveiled a multiplicity of narratives that could make one think of Russia as a country dwelling in different epochs simultaneously.[59] In Russia, indeed, despite the clear shift to authoritarianism associated with Vladimir Putin's reign, there is an ample space for "plurality of contested identities,"[60] and the idea

59 Yurii Pivovarov and Andrei Fursov, "Russkaya Systema i reformy," *Pro et Contra* 4: 4 (Autumn 1999): 178.

60 Vincent Pouliot, "The Essence of Constructivism," *Journal of International Relations and Development* 7: 3 (October 2004): 321.

of "Russia in plural"[61] nicely grasps the diversity of discourses that both constitute and dislocate this country's identity. In a postmodernist manner, some authors think of Russia as a signifier for "what no adequate names can be imagined."[62] On the one hand, even the cursory acquaintance with Russian scholarly literature makes one believe in the possibility of endless scenarios for Russian foreign policy. Yet on the other hand, this seemingly unlimited number of options sometimes is artificially constrained by and locked in elementary dichotomies such as 'integration' vs. 'isolation,' 'liberal reforms' vs. 'conservative retreat,' 'going West' vs. 'going East,' etc. Piles of books trying hard to explain the intricacies of Russia's politics through the prism of concepts circulating exclusively within Russia—such as the proverbial tug-of-war between 'Westernizers' and 'Slavophiles'—add little to the obvious deficiency of concepts capable of bridging the gaps of understanding between Russia and the West. Seemingly, both those believing that 'everything is possible' and those restricting Russia's pathways to a limited number of options are not only far remote from academic accuracy, but also counterproductive for scholarly research. Therefore, the question of how the plurality of Russian foreign policy discourses and the alternatives they entail may be inscribed into international scholarly literature remains in the forefront of academic interest.

The emphasis on a plurality of domestic conceptualizations could be instrumental in demonstrating the fragmentation of Russian political scene. Instead of focusing on the traditional distinction between Slavophiles and Westernizers, I see one of the most important splits differently—between the technocratic and apolitical discourse of the Kremlin, on the one hand, and much more ideological and doctrinal discourses that originate in a wider public space, to include mass media and political parties, on the other.

The official—hegemonic—discourse, to some extent, might be dubbed both postpolitical and apolitical, since it legitimizes itself through the references to something presented as either obvious ('neutral'/technical knowledge formulated in rational terms, that is, with references to a presumably undisputable source of epistemic authority) or essential for national identity and integrity.[63] What is hidden beneath this type of discourse is evidently power ambitions embedded in what seems to appear as presumably rational,

61 Pertti Joenniemi, "Russia's Narrative Resources," *Journal of International Relations and Development* 11: 2 (June 2008): 122.

62 Pivovarov and Fursov, "Russkaya Systema," 180.

63 Slavoj Zizek, *The Ticklish Subject. The Absent Centre of Political Ontology* (Verso: London & New York, 2004): 131.

objective, and commonly shared arguments. The depoliticized discourse turned into an advocacy for reinforcing the state's roles in many policy spheres, both domestic and international. The limitations of individual freedoms under the pretext of security requirements, or the public legitimation of the Georgia war by the alleged humanitarian (human security (HS)-related) reasons appear to be less debatable than the same measures undertaken out of ideological or geopolitical motives.

As far as explicitly ideological discourses are concerned, as I have mentioned above, there is a century-long Russian tradition of using for the purpose of self-description a flat axis usually constructed around two political poles drastically opposing each other. Most frequently they are dubbed 'Slavophiles' and 'Westernizers,' though in other cases the names may differ—'Eurasianists' and 'cosmopolites,' 'liberals' and 'conservatives,' 'traditionalists' and 'modernizers,' 'communists' and 'democrats,' etc. The differences between these dichotomous typologies boil down basically to the names of the poles and the hybrids that might be possibly placed somewhere in-between. Examples might include a number of tripartite schemes such as: (1) "liberal reformists," "national conservatives," and "moderate nationalist centrists"[64]; (2) "liberal Westernizers," "fundamentalist nationalists," and "pragmatic nationalists"[65]; (3) "liberal Westernism," "great power balancing," and "great power pragmatism"[66]; (4) "liberalism," "geopolitical realism," "pragmatic geoeconomic realism," "cultural geostrategic realism,"[67] etc. Yet most of these typologies remain static, and thus oversimplify Russia's ideational landscape, reducing it to a number of 'idea brokers' that seem to be self-organizing and capable of developing independently of each other and the wider international environment.

Besides, what the above mentioned 'flat' conceptualizations of Russia's ideational landscape leave unexplained is the driving forces that stay behind the presumed shifts from one policy platform—and a group that sustained

64 Tatyana Parkhalina, "Impacts of Domestic and Regional Factors on Russia's Foreign and Security Policy," in Kurt Spillmann and Andreas Wenger (eds.), *Russia's Place in Europe. A Security Debate* (Bern: Peter Lang Publishers, 1999): 48.

65 Margot Light, "Foreign Policy Thinking," in N. Malcolm *et al.* (eds.), *Internal Factors in Russian Foreign Policy* (Oxford: Royal Institute of International Affairs and Oxford University Press, 1996).

66 Andrey Tsygankov, *Russia's Foreign Policy: Change and Continuity in National Identity* (Lanham: Rowman and Littlefield, 2006).

67 Christian Thorun, *Explaining Change in Russian Foreign Policy: the Role of Ideas in Post-Soviet Russia's Conduct towards the West* (Basingstoke: Palgrave Macmillan, 2009).

it—to another. For example, what stipulated the transition from Andrey Kozyrev's pro-Western diplomacy at the beginning of 1990s to the Evgeniy Primakov's model of multipolarity? One answer is presumably the force of reflexivity: Following an example of Gorbachev's 'new thinking' given by Alexander Wendt, one may assume that the change might be stimulated by the ability of power holders to analyze the policies they pursue and alter them as soon as they fail to work properly. Yet there is another explanation that points to the changes in Russia's external environment, such as, for example, Russia's involvement in a number of violent conflicts that streamlined its identity (including Transnistria, South Ossetia, and Abkhazia) and thus predetermined the advent of a less 'naïve' and more 'pragmatic' foreign policy. The same goes for the transition from Yeltsin's to Putin's international strategy which may be explicated by a number of factors pertaining to the structure of international relations, including the events in Kosovo, Chechnya, Iraq, the double enlargement of NATO and EU, a series of color revolutions, etc.

Thus, it is insufficient to demonstrate the plurality of domestic discourses and their interrelatedness. What has to be added to this analysis is the external institutional environment these domestic discourses appeal to. From here stems my emphasis on problematizing the 'outer world' which Russia wishes either to integrate into or prevail in.

1.7 International Society: A Meeting Point of the English School and Constructivism

In a more structural sense, the intersubjective nature of Russia's and EU's identities has to be approached through the concept of "the third agency to which we [...] submit ourselves"[68] in the communicative process. This alleged 'third agency' is dubbed by Slavoj Zizek an 'impersonal symbolic Order,' or 'the multitude of empirical others' associated by rules, institutions, and regulations. In other words, cont(r)acting with each other, both parties have to refer and appeal – in one way or another – to a wider set of international norms. Thus, one may argue, we need to move beyond the analysis "of intersubjective practices to look at how these themselves are grounded in deeper structural relations [...] and understand inter-subjective relations [...] as

68 Slavoj Zizek, "Neighbors and Other Monsters," in *Three Inquiries in Politcal Theology* (Chicago: University of Chicago Press, 2010): 139.

rooted in deeper socio-cultural and economic conditions."[69] Within the context of the analysis of the EU–Russia relations, the idea of the 'third agency' can be introduced through the concept of the IS.

The argument I am going to develop below suggests that the menu of Russia's and EU's foreign policy identities to a large extent depends upon a variety of international structures these two actors engage with. In the traditions of the English school, I will call this external environment 'international society.' "A society of states (or international society) exists when a group of states, conscious of certain common interests and common values, form a society in the sense that they conceive themselves to be bound by a common set of rules in their relations with one another, and share in the working of common institutions."[70] The adjective '*international*' here denotes "anything involving interactions across or beyond the boundaries of sovereign states."[71] The noun '*society*' signifies that its members take each other into account in choosing their actions.[72] "English school theorists have focused on global civilizing processes that tame the ability to harm, whether for self-interested reasons or because of the importance of international society,"[73] which explains why the IS "is limited to those state actors, in conjunction with international institutions and nonstate actors, who agree, more or less, on common interests and values."[74]

Methodologically, my approach is grounded in the assertion that "structures have prior causal power over agents. They provide the very conditions within which agents may act, defining and limiting this activity."[75] An important point has to be made at this juncture. For some constructivist authors there is a difference between *structural* approach(es) and *intersubjective* one(s). It may be argued that "seeing a great power an inter-subjectively constituted

69 Jonathan Joseph, "Hegemony and the Structure-Agency Problem in International Relations: A Scientific Realist Contribution," *Review of International Studies* 34 (2008): 128.

70 Hedley Bull, *The Anarchical Society. A Study of Order in World Politics* (New York: Columbia University Press, 2002): 13.

71 Duncan Snidal and Alexander Wendt, "Why there is International Theory Now," *International Theory* 1:1 (2009): 8.

72 Alexander Wendt, *Social Theory of International Politics* (Cambridge: Cambridge University Press, 1999): 249.

73 Andrew Linklater, "Grand Narratives and International Relations," *Global Change, Peace and Security* 21: 1 (February 2009): 10.

74 Richard Beardsworth, "Cosmopolitanism and Realism: Toward a Theoretical Convergence?" *Millenium: Journal of International Relations* 37: 1 (2008): 86.

75 Joseph, "Hegemony," 116.

by the actors of a system is a very different thing from seeing it as structurally constituted by the states system."[76] Alexander Wendt has nicely grasped the difference by saying that "structures of interaction may be called 'micro'-structures because they depict the world from agents' point of view"[77]; in the meantime, there are 'macro'-structures that describe the world from the standpoint of the system. It appears that the macrolevel is 'more structural' and thus stable, while the microlevel is 'more procedural' and thus constantly changing.[78]

The trajectories of the IS concept in Russia are far from easy. In political parlance, it is 'international community' rather than 'international society' which is evoked as a figure of speech whenever references to almost mythical upper-hand authority are needful for authorizing or legitimizing some claims as allegedly 'universally' recognizable. In the meantime, some authors challenge the practicability of applying the concept of society to the sphere of international relations since they appear 'phantoms,' or 'nicknames' for 'real' agents such as NATO, EU, or United States.[79] Others try to (mis)represent Bull's idea of the proliferation of IS as a liberal restatement of an old Marxist obsession with the expansion of "world-wide revolution."[80] Yet even most critical readings of Bull's concept do not preclude Russian international relations (IR) scholars from admitting that the expansion of (world) IS is one of key trends in the current international life. What *is* most frequently challenged is the political machinery that stays behind this trend, including the effects of bordering between the West and "under-West,"[81] or what might be called a strategy of 'crunching,' or 'plowing up' the geopolitical field for the sake of better assimilating the aspirants to joining the Western world.[82]

76 Iver Neumann, "Russia as a Great Power, 1815-2007," *Journal of International Relations and Development* 11: 2 (June 2008): 130.

77 Wendt, *Social Theory*, 123.

78 Petr Drulak, "The Problem of Structural Change in Alexander Wendt's Social Theory of International Politics," *Journal of International Relations and Development* 4 (2001): 370.

79 Vladimir Maximenko, "Proiskhodit li globalizatsiya?" *Pro et Contra* (Autumn 1999): 88.

80 Alexei Bogaturov, "Globalizatsiya kak sindrom pogloschenia v mezhdunarodnoi politike," in Alexei Bogaturov, Nikolai Kosolapov and Mark Khrustaliov (eds.), *Essays on Theory and Political Analysis of International Relations* (Moscow: Academic & Educational Forum on International Relations, 2002): 338.

81 Bogaturov, *Ibid.*, 349.

82 Alexei Bogaturov, " 'Strategia peremalyvania' vo vneshnei politike SShA," in Alexei Bogaturov, Nikolai Kosolapov, and Mark Khrustaliov (eds.), *Essays on Theory and Political Analysis of International Relations* (Moscow: Academic & Educational Forum on International Relations, 2002): 364.

The concept of IS may serve as a meeting point between, at least, two theoretical schools—the English school and social constructivism. "The English school and constructivism are linked by an emphasis on the power of ideas to affect change."[83] In fact, Wendt resorts to the concept of IS as an example of "social systems" or "social kinds,"[84] which give meaning to ideas held on the state level and, I would add, within the state as well. In the English school reasoning, IS seems to be a type of foundational argument, one based upon induction and logic. Foundational arguments cannot be proven true or false, yet they are presented as indispensable conditions of knowledge. "Epistemological and ontological positions, portrayed as bedrock foundations about the structure of the world and our knowledge of it, are beyond refutation."[85] Constructivists appear to share this methodological posture presuming, as Wendt does, that "taking something as given is necessary in any explanatory endeavor by virtue of the simple fact that it is humanly impossible to problematize everything at once."[86]

Hedley Bull makes it quite explicit that IS is an *idea* in the first place, and that it is the distribution of ideas that shapes each specific type of the IS. He repeatedly purports that initially the concept of the IS was conceived by the natural law thinkers, then "converged with historians."[87] In the meantime it would be correct to portray IS a *social construct* as well, which of course does not question the ideational/intellectual background of the concept. The social nature of IS is due to the fact that its norms and principles are widely shared among international actors.

There are at least two important effects stemming from the recognition of the ideational nature of IS. *First*, as Hedley Bull rightly assumes, there is a problem of establishing interlinks between the "ideas of philosophers, international lawyers and historians," "the thoughts of statesmen," and what he calls "the reality of international society."[88] This triad, by and large, corresponds to my research design in this book in two respects. On the one hand, I am interested in how theories (including that one of IS) are related to political

83 Balkan Devlen, Patrick James, and Ozgur Ozdamar, "The English School, International Relations, and Progress," *International Studies Review* 7: 2 (June 2005): 182.

84 Wendt, *Social Theory*, 376.

85 Nuno Monteiro and Keven Ruby, "IR and the False Promise of Philosophical Foundations," *International Theory* 1:1 (2009): 26.

86 Wendt, *Social Theory*, 36.

87 Bull, *The Anarchical Society*, 31.

88 *Ibid.*, 38.

doctrines that motivate policy makers. On the other hand, I pay attention to a more theoretical question of how and whether a certain type of ideas might be fathomed against the so-called reality, whatever one may understand by it.

Second, since the IS roots have to be looked for in the sphere of ideas, it would be quite logical to assume that at a certain time there might be more than one type of IS. "Reality might not be working according to one logic, [and there is] the possibility of the existence of more than one truth simultaneously."[89] Hence, there may be "simultaneously existing social realities where it might not be possible to claim that one is superior to the other,"[90] and the endless plurality of interpretations of reality is embodied in the different descriptions of the IS.

Bilateral relations between Moscow and Brussels are deeply inscribed in structural frameworks of multilateral institutions and practices. This narrows space for individual/agential policies, which is more a problem for Russia than for the EU and its key Member States whose foreign policies by and large are grounded in the logic of collective action and partnership commitments, as opposed to unilateralism favored by Russia. In communicating and interacting with each other, Russia and the EU often stem from different visions and models of IS, and it is these conceptual cleavages that hinder their bilateral relationship and render them ineffective. The most substantial problems arise because Russia and the EU in their policies often adhere to different institutions of IS and, therefore, rely on different mechanisms of international socialization.

The admission of the coexistence of different models of IS challenges two dominating understandings of plurality of international societies as seen from either temporal or geographic perspectives. In other words, the differences between international societies are usually induced from either the temporal shift from one model to another (e.g., from the 'Christian' to 'European' society), or as the grounding of international societies in a predetermined regional context (in this reading, one may speak of 'European,' 'North American,' 'South East Asian,' and other types of IS). Yet I will argue that the idea of plurality of international societies can be also understood as a com-

89 Katalin Sarvary, "Devaluing Diplomacy? A Critique of Alexander Wendt's Conception of Progress and Politics," *Journal of International Relations and Development* 4 (December 2001): 381.

90 Sarvary, *Ibid.*, 381.

petition of different—and alternative to each other—concepts of structural interconnections that are not necessarily bound by the logics of territoriality and temporality.

The multiplicity of international societies might serve as an explanatory argument for the corresponding multiplicity of Russian foreign policies. In many studies, the story of Russian foreign policy since the demise of the USSR is told as a series of models that continuously either destroy or deny their predecessors. Yet what if these models, despite all controversies that divide them, may coexist as different pathways, or vectors that constitute the menu of Russia's foreign policy choices? Thus, the seeming marginalization of the early liberal Westernizers did not mean the effacement of the perspective for Russia's integration into the IS dominated by Western norms; in the same vein, Russia's incorporation of the normative arguments in its foreign policy arsenal does not mean the ultimate refuse from the more traditional geopolitical approaches.

Different types of IS are socially real though invisible constructs. They may serve to denote certain vectors or perspectives of the dynamics of international relations. They are ideal types that are mixed together in practice. In the meantime, different types of IS may be used as independent variables, those applicable for explaining other phenomena, in other words—for emphasizing the causal powers of the structure of the IS in explaining not only state behavior, as Wendt does, but also the mosaics of different discourses within the state. To paraphrase Wendt, these discourses—both theoretical and doctrinal—are "differently structured by the system so as to produce different effects."[91]

Constructivist literature is most helpful in shedding light on the importance of macrostructural matters, as exemplified, in particular, by Pierre Bourdieu's 'structuralist constructivism.' Bourdieu believed that social structures are existent, yet they do not necessarily predetermine agents' actions—they rather develop what might be termed 'collective habitus,' or cultural predispositions to include 'structuring rites' and constraints. Habitus can be compared with 'mental maps,' sets of beliefs and values, or 'unspoken assumptions' on what is thinkable and unthinkable under a given structural environment.[92]

What Wendt added to this conceptualization is that structures not only constrain, but also—what is more important—constructs agents. To adapt

91 Wendt, *Social Theory*,12.

92 Peter Jackson, "Pierre Bourdieu, the 'Cultural Turn' and the Practice of International History," *Review of International Studies* 34 (2008): 164–167.

Wendt's theory for the purpose of my analysis, a number of caveats have to be made. *First*, in this construction process the plurality of external—structural—conditions forcefully diversifies ideational landscapes thus making it possible for multiple theories and doctrines to occupy their intellectual niches. Structural factors, in a way, select ideas, boosting some of them and marginalizing others. These ideas become "logically dependent on the specific external structure" the state is embedded in, and "do not exist apart from external conditions."[93] Structures, Wendt argues then, confront agents "as an objective social fact that constrains and enables action in systematic ways, and as such should generate distinct patterns"[94] of role-taking and role-playing.

Second, what should be added to the Wendtian version of social constructivism is the approach to structures as 'containers' of hegemonic relations. Hegemony can be conceptualized as an "institution of international society."[95] In fact, each of 'social formations' (including each of the types of IS) harbor—if not conceal—what might be dubbed 'hegemonic projects.' Each structure may be approached as hegemonic, and one of the tasks of IR scholars is to uncover these relations of hegemony. As Jonathan Joseph rightly presumes, "hegemony acts as a crucial mediating moment in the relation between structure and agency."[96] Hegemony thus "reaches down to the structural issue of the reproduction of the social formation and the various structural ensembles [...] . Hegemony comes to represent the political moment in the structure-agency relation."[97] What stems from this is the need to understand what kind of hegemony is embedded in each of the types of IS to be discussed further, and how Russia and the EU react to them.

Third, the taxonomy of international societies allows us to see the changing meanings of some of the most important concepts we use in international relations analysis. I will give a few examples of these transformations in meanings. One of the concepts that may be differently interpreted, depending on what type of IS it is placed in, is *marginality*. Under the conditions of unipolarity marginal territories are doomed to be absorbed by the coalition of dominating powers. Thus, marginality is a quality that denotes geopolitical disadvantages and unfortunate submission to the leading centers of power. Yet under certain circumstances marginality may turn into a resource that

93 Wendt, *Social Theory*, 84.

94 Wendt, *Social Theory*,184.

95 Ian Clark, "Bringing Hegemony Back in: The United States and International Order," *International Affairs* 1: 85 (2009): 27.

96 Joseph, "Hegemony," 114.

97 *Ibid.*, 128.

noncentral actors dispose and utilize for shaping their peculiar identities and influencing the seemingly more powerful neighbors. Thus, under a multipolar type of the IS, margins may either find their niches and remain unaffected by the possible rivalry between the competing poles, or plug into the sphere of influence of one of them. Within the framework of what I call the normative integration model marginal regions may formulate their identities in normative terms. Finally, the normative plurality situation will most likely turn some of marginal regions into bones of contention with competing interpretations of their identities. Besides, the practical implementation of the strategy of marginality might bring different effects in different types of IS structures.

Another example may be given by different understandings of a '*New Europe*' concept. Within the unipolar type of IS the 'New Europe' is associated with a strategy of American dominance in Europe. In 2003, the US Secretary of State Donald Rumsfeld has labeled France and Germany an 'Old Europe,' ascribing to them not only reluctance to support United States-led military operations, but also an inclination to protectionism and inability to modify their economies to be competitive. Yet in the norm-based type of IS the New Europe is connoted with an area in which the institutionalized frameworks of subregionalism have emerged, displacing the old East–West divides. In this context, the conception of New Europe is believed to be not any longer about sovereignty, military security, and borders. Thus, the 'New Europe' concept is two-fold. On the one hand, it can be in tune with political realism and the Westphalian worldview, yet on the other, it is open to reinterpret the role of geographically marginal countries as increasingly important international subjects.

In this book, I will explain the menu of Russian international identities by the variety of international societies that coexist and offer alternative policy strategies for Moscow. The unipolar model is rebuffed since Russia rejected to become part of the Western institutions and thus join the dominating coalition of powers. Since mid-1990s Russia turned to an alternative policy strategy of challenging the hegemony of the West through strengthening its own potential for gradually transforming into an autonomous pole of rather regional than global scale; hence Moscow's preference for spheres of influence approach. The role of presumably self-sufficient pole is understood by the Kremlin in predominantly material terms as either 'energy superpower' or military power; what is missing in Russian strategy of adjusting to and taking advantage of the multipolar world is normative aspects of leadership, including soft power resources, which fleshes out the stark differences between

Russia and the EU, especially as seen from the vantage point of their respective neighborhood policies. The same is true with regard to the scenario of normative plurality – to be discussed in Chapter 2 of the book – which Russia overtly sympathizes with, yet unfortunately is capable of only playing a role of a challenger of the Western normative order bereft of its own normative agenda recognized by—and attractive to—other members of IS. Russia seems to understand the width of the normative gap that divides it from the West and fears not a military attack from NATO but rather marginalization within the wider Europe, especially in security domain. This, in particular, explains the launch of a campaign to propose a new set of common rules in the Euro-Atlantic region epitomized by a new European Security Treaty proposal. Yet what drastically diminished the international appeal of such ideas is the unwillingness of the West to legitimize Russia's role as an equal political and security actor, which testifies to the chronic lack of normative and soft power resources in the hands of Russian diplomacy.

1.8 Between the Imperial and the International

The conceptualization of IS can be concluded by a reference to the distinction between *the imperial* and *the international*[98] as two divergent patterns of structuration of world politics. The imperial, along the lines of R.B.J. Walker, is grounded in: (1) 'verticality' (in other words, hierarchies predicated on subordination); (2) exceptionality (i.e., the proliferation of the state of emergency[99] legitimating the imperial subject's acting beyond the existing institutional frameworks); and (3) unilateralism as a form of sovereign decisionism. In contrast, the international connotes 'horizontality' (coordination, as opposed to submission), 'normality' (i.e., playing by the rules), and multilateralism (states' collective—as opposed to individual—diplomatic actions)—a set of legitimate and widely accepted rules that political subjects are supposed to adhere to. 'The international' is characterized, in Walker's view, by four denials: no single imperial form is allowable; no religious wars are tolerated; no 'barbarians' or 'non-moderns' accepted as equals; and neither violence nor coercion can be applied in relations between political subjects.[100]

98 R.B.J. Walker, *After the Globe/Before the World* (Cambridge: Cambridge University Press, 2009).

99 Paul Fletcher, "The Political Theology of the Empire to Come," *Cambridge Review of International Affairs* 17: 1 (April 2004): 58.

100 R.B.J.Walker, "Lines of Insecurity: International, Imperial, Exceptional," *Security Dialogue* 37: 1 (March 2006): 67–71.

These formulae are of course only ideal types of political subjectivity, and in practice it is very rare that a country builds its foreign policy along either of three of Walker's lines. Usually one or two of them are more pronounced, while other(s) might be nonexistent or poorly articulated. This is why 'imperial' and 'international' qualities are matters of degree, and their identification represents a fascinating academic exercise.

Presumably, some of IS models to be discussed in Chapter 2 leave much space for imperial subjectivities. In fact, balance of power, spheres of influence, and great power management (GPM) can be viewed as structural forms of imperial relations, since they imply control, domination, patronage, expansion, absorption, projection of force, etc. In the meantime, procedural approximation, normative plurality, multiregionalism, and multiplicity of civilizations fit, by and large, philosophical premises of the international, as evoked by Walker. Imperial discourses are meant to impose some kind of order in a volatile world,[101] while discourses of the international point to enhancing mechanisms of socialization through institutional commitments and policies of engagement.

Many in Europe would certainly assume that Russia is only hiding its allegedly irremovable imperial nature and concomitant ambitions. The most exemplary cases of Russia's resurgent imperial instincts in recent years were the war in Georgia, attempts to prevent Ukraine from joining NATO and signing the Association Agreement with the EU, and the tug-of-war with Estonia over the removal of the Bronze Soldier monument. Alexander Dugin's utterances of the prospects of Russia's conquest of Europe[102] only add more aggressive notes to this tendency. Although it is undeniable that the concept of empire can be applied as characterization of some aspects of today's Russian foreign policy conduct, it would be an essentializing oversimplification to assume that Russia *is* an empire. In a much less reductionist reading, which I am adhering to, empire represents not an established reality but rather a certain type of discourse, which competes with other discourses in shaping Russia's identity. The surprising resilience of apparently defeated imperial discourse, whatever forms it takes, can be explained by huge elasticity of the term, and its ability to encapsulate a wide gamut of meanings, from nationalist to liberal.

---

101 Gilles Andreani, "Imperial Loose Talk," in Tod Lindberg (ed.), *Beyond Paradise and Power. Europe, America and the Future of a Troubled Alliance* (London: Routledge, 2005): 63–80.

102 Alexander Dugin, "Prisoedinit' Evropu - eto po-russki" (April 11, 2013), http://www.russia.ru/video/diskurs_14028/ (as of March 10, 2014).

Analysis of imbrications and interchanges between the imperial and the international requires a combination of theoretical platforms. One of them is—again—social constructivism with Alexander Wendt's idea of 'role identities' as 'subjective self-understandings,' 'representations of Self and Others,'[103] or social niches that persist as long as someone fills them with certain meanings. In the constructivist reading, role identities are always contextual and relational, that is, they depend upon—and thus can be (re)interpreted through—their various opposites. It is within this logic that the alleged polarity of the imperial—the international dichotomy can be questioned, since Russia's imperial role identity can often be quite compatible with moves—far from successful though—to socialize the country in an international institutional milieu. Walker's scheme seems to be reflecting a European liberal tradition, and needs some readjustments for Russia where the borderlines between the imperial and the international are much fuzzier: Even in its imperial capacity Russia is believed to be able to become not only a full-fledged member of IS, but also its constitutive pillar.

Empires are "self-selected agents to bring geopolitical order where there is disorder,"[104] and are parts of a wide semantic "chain of equivalence" to include "great powers," "super-powers," "world leaders," hegemons, etc.[105] The lines of demarcation and the oppositions that sustain each of these role identities usually prove to be rather fuzzy, producing vast zones of overlap and indistinction. It is critical theories that challenge the very possibility of fixing the meanings attached to imperial and international role identities. This approach seems to boost the argument that the role identity constructed by and through Russia's imperial discourse is highly inconstant and volatile. Paradoxically, it is the dislocated nature of Russian imperial role identity that is a strong additive to its hegemonic proclivity.

What has to be reiterated at this juncture is the intersubjective nature of EU–Russia relationship that is manifested in the dependence of discursively constructed role identities "upon an outside which both denies that identity and provides its conditions of possibility at the same time."[106] Thus, Russia's

103 Wendt, *Social Theory*, 227–229.

104 Noel Parker, "Empires as a Geopolitical Figure," (2009), www.wiscnetwork.com (as of March 10, 2014).

105 Boris Mezhuev, "Nostalgiya kak predchuvstvie," *Russkii zhurnal* (May 2008): 142–151.

106 Aletta J. Norval, "Theorising Dislocations." Paper presented at the workshop "New Stability, Democracy and Nationalism in Contemporary Russia" (Basel, September 26–27, 2008): 3.

self-representations through the concept of empire are closely connected to European and American discourses on their ostensible imperial identities.[107] Indeed, "on the one hand, it is an outside that threatens the inside; on the other hand, it is an outside that is formulated from the inside [...] . Identity is in part constituted by what it opposes."[108] In this light, the imperial identity-building projects of the United States and the EU may be perceived as challenges to Russia, but nevertheless Russian role identities are constructed through some kind of communication with—and reference to—them. Russia's inevitable references to other imperial experiences in the process of distinguishing its own imperial identity from other variants of collective self-identification attest to its non-self-sufficient nature.

Interpenetration of imperial and national identities is also what Russia and some European countries seem to share. "Imperialism as a European enterprise must be viewed as a concerted and purposive contribution to the creation of material wealth and international power for the nation, as well as identity formation of the nation precisely as an imperialist power,"[109] hence the powerful idea of liberal imperialism in Germany in the second half of the 19th century. Similar approaches could be applicable to Russia as well. As some scholars argue, the Romanov empire functioned as a Russian national state, which legitimizes such constructs as "imperial nationalism."[110] For Russian conservatives, empire is a means to the nation's existence,[111] and histories of many other countries know no sharp contrast between empire- and nation-building.[112] The 'liberal empire' idea promulgated since 2004 by a number of Russian liberal economists, such as Anatoly Chubais, echoes the model of British colonial rule[113] and, in more policy-oriented terms, evokes Russian economic expansion into its 'near abroad' and favors mostly financial forms of Moscow's influence in former Soviet republics. The revival of

---

107 Pami Aalto, "Empire Europe Encounters the Post-Soviet North." Background Paper presented at the workshop "Laboratory in the Margins? The EU's and Russia's Policies in Northern Europe," (2004).

108 Saul Newman, "Derrida's Deconstruction of Authority," *Philosophy and Social Criticism 27* (May 2001): 12–18.

109 Matthew Fitzpatrick, *Liberal Imperialism in Germany. Expansionism and Nationalism, 1848–1884* (New York: Berghahn Books, 2008): 4.

110 Evgeniy Yasin, "Fantomnye boli ushedshei imperii," in Igor Kliamkin (ed.), *Posle Imperii* (Moscow: Liberal Mission Foundation, 2007): 5.

111 Denis Dragunskiy, "Izderzhki imperii," *Kosmopolis* 3: 19 (2007/2008): 7.

112 Alexei Miller, *Natsionalizm i imperia* (Moscow: Polit.ru and OGI, 2005): 15.

113 Niall Ferguson, *Colossus. The Rise and Fall of the American Empire* (New York: Penguin Books, 2004): 198.

national identity in contemporary Russia is arguably grounded in its imperial legacy. To rephrase a European historian, it is not so much that Russia created the empire; it is the empire that constructed Russia.[114]

The combination of 'imperial' and 'international' models of political subjectivity gives a broad analytical frame for discussing fluctuations in Russian foreign policy behavior and its vacillation between different conceptual platforms. There are those in Russia who argue that "empires denote a pathway to historical deadlock,"[115] and those who applaud Russia's imperial past as presumably containing much potential for the future. These two articulations construct two different identities for today's Russia, either as a country denouncing its historical experience of imperial hegemony, or as a neo-imperial great power able to, at minimum, secure its spheres of influence (hereby the 'red lines' rhetoric to which Russian leaders repeatedly referred in rejecting Georgia's and Ukraine's prospects for NATO membership), or, at maximum, to balance the dominance of the West.

Arguably, under the presidencies of Boris Yeltsin and Dmitry Medvedev Russia was moving—inconsistently and controversially—from empire to nation state, but this trajectory was complicated and contaminated by multiple comebacks of resurfacing imperial 'syndrome,' or imperial 'inertia.' As a prominent Russian scholar put it, "empire no longer exists, but it still hurts."[116] The Putin regime is widely believed to have reinvigorated the imperial model of Russian policy, based upon the mutually sustaining ideas of exceptionality (in its relations with the major Western institutions Russia demands special status for itself, as verbalized in the lexem of 'strategic partnership') and unilateralism. As the crisis in Ukraine in 2014 made clear, these imperial discourses can thus complicate efforts to institute Russia as a constitutive member of the IS and might rather push it into an outsider's position.

Yet these models are mutually interrelated and constitutive of one another. Thus, the August 2008 war against Georgia was widely considered as fitting the imperial type of conduct. Yet it was the controversial upshots of the war that made Russia return to the philosophy of the international, which in-

114 Alexei Miller, "The Value and the Limits of a Comparative Approach to the History of Contiguous Empires on the European Periphery," in Kimitako Matsuzato (ed.), *Imperiology. From Empirical Knowledge to Discussing the Russian Empire* (Sapporo: Slavic Research Center, Hokkaido University, 2007): 23.

115 Alexander Buzgalin, "Imperskaya model mira i alternativnye ei perspektivy," *International Trends. Journal of International Relations Theory and World Politics* 2: 5 (2004): 114.

116 Yasin, "Fantomnye boli", 5.

cludes 'resetting' Russia–US relations, the recognition of EU's security actorship in the common neighborhood, and finding a compromise with NATO. The reasons behind this conceptual shift could be discussed from at least two perspectives. Some commentators tend to explain Medvedev's sympathies with the discourse of the international by the Kremlin's comprehension of its weakness and the inadequacy of its resources for sustaining its imperial ambitions. One of the striking evidence of the weakness of Russia's imperial agenda is the failure of the Kremlin to hammer out special relations—as one of the most important elements of any imperial identity[117]—with other international actors, including the former Soviet republics and ex-socialist countries. It turned out that Russia's integrative capacities are meagre—the country lacks winning soft power strategies and is severely limited in its own neighborhood policy.

Yet there is an additional, less materialist and more constructivist explanation of Russia's sensitivity to the institutions of international socialization, which questions the practicability of the imperial policies. The key argument of this reasoning is that Russia, having acted within the imperial logic, was ultimately forced to take actions that either it initially considered as inappropriate or too risky (the recognition of Abkhazia and South Ossetia), or left Moscow in international isolation (such as the conflict with Estonia over the Second World War memorials) and, therefore, marginalized it within the IS structures. Consequently, it was the step-by-step comprehension of futility of the imperial logic that pushed Russia to accept the reverse logic of the international, as exemplified by the Kremlin's proposals on the 'new security architecture' in the Euro-Atlantic region.

Yet the idea of re-institutionalization of Euro-Atlantic security is open to different interpretations. It might come in a 'democratic' version implying the inclusive nature of security arrangements that ought to accommodate all actors of this area without exceptions. By the same token, it may also be developed as a version of 'imperial management' (a replica of Bull's GPM concept) predicated on the joint crisis prevention efforts of the United States, the EU, and Russia. Whether the three imperial projects—and the different logics sustaining each of them—might be compatible with each other is an open question.

As for the effects of Russia's dislocated imperial identity, they may be observed from two perspectives. On the one hand, the reformulation of Russia's identity in imperial terms is doomed to remain an inherently unfinished

---

117 Kristin Haugevik, "Dominance Lost? Exploring the Transition from Imperial to Special Relations." Unpublished manuscript (Oslo: NUPI, 2009): 9.

and incomplete discourse, mixed up with alternative representations on Russia's Self. On the other, the intersubjective nature of Russian imperial identity ought to increase the chances for Russia's inclusion into—rather than exclusion from—the IS. The idea of 'joint management between empires'[118] is acquiring some currency in international discourse. According to a Russian reading, the concept of empire—despite multiple voices from Eastern/Central European and Baltic countries—does not necessarily move Russia away from the West. Concomitantly, the imperial role identity turns into Russia's particular leverage not only to achieve world power status, but also to equally play a role of a full-fledged interlocutor in dialogue with Europe.[119] It likewise constitutes an antithesis to barbarianism and chaos, whose return is thus associated with the collapse of the imperial order.

Yet this is not to say that Western countries share this Russian self-perception. They might rightfully claim that, unlike Russia, they did make their *political* choices by relinquishing certain models of development rooted in their histories. Thus, the rejection of colonialism, fascism, and communism was engrained in the European identity, grounded in such key normative signifiers as democracy, civil liberties, human rights, and freedoms. Against this background, Russia's reluctance to unequivocally associate itself with European values provides Western countries with a weighty argument for othering Russia, or representing it as a non-European country.

The political actualization of the concept of empire turns it in a kind of 'moving target,' an attractive metaphor that always remains debatable and ambiguous, and thus requires adjectives—'informal empire,' 'energy empire,' or 'non-colonial empire.'[120] Russia in this sense is a 'quasi-empire': Its imperial discourse is dispersed over the entire gamut of the political spectrum and shared between national patriots, liberal pragmatists, and partisans of regional identity. This finding challenges one of the key points of the critical theory arguing that it is the existence of empty and floating signifiers, as well as dislocations of identities, that makes politics possible.[121] Yet the Russian case opens a different perspective suggesting that split identity may equally produce depoliticizing effects. The case of the Kremlin's legal retrieval of a major Russian Orthodox cathedral in Nice built by the Russian czar before

---

118 Philippe Grosjean and Raymond van Ermen, "The Three Sea Alliance," *Eyes on Europe* (Autumn 2009): 14.

119 Vladimir Kantor, "Rossiiskoe gosudarstvo: imperia ili natsionalizm?" (2008), www.polit.ru/lectures/2008/02/22/russia.html (as of March 10, 2014).

120 George Steinmetz, "Imperializm ili kolonializm?" *Prognosis* 4: 8 (2006): 200.

121 Ernesto Laclau, *Emancipation(s)* (London: Verso, 2007): 40.

the revolution of 1917 gives a good illustration for this argument. By doing this in January 2010, Russia has openly declared itself the heir to the Romanov dynasty. This self-identification appears to be in a contradiction to Russia's role identity as the legal successor of the Soviet Union. This bifurcated—yet, in both cases, imperial—identification, in spite of all its controversies, has at least one rather obvious effect: By avoiding to make political choices between the two imperial models (the czarist and the Soviet ones), the Kremlin tends—quite paradoxically—to depoliticize the imperial discourse by simply reducing its content to the issue of either *material possession* (the case of the Orthodox cathedral in Nice) or territorial control in the areas of its 'near abroad' legitimized by the references to '*natural bonds*' purportedly linking Russians to other Slavic nations. The total glorification of its history can eventually deprive Russia's neo-imperial identity of a strong political appeal. This depoliticization is likely in the long run to undermine the political meanings that imperial identity embraces.

Against this backdrop it becomes apparent that under closer scrutiny the concept of empire, claiming to have ordering effects on the political space it embraces, conceals a number of deep dislocations. First, imperial identity not only fails to identify the boundaries of an entity named Russia—but it also blurs these boundaries. Russia's imperial imagination includes territories where Russian speakers and holders of Russian passports live, which reinforces a sphere-of-influence type of IS. Imperial identity thus treats borders as a relative construct: 'in Russian empire it was never known where Russia's borders are […] . It is still not clear today where the boundary is to be drawn between Russians and Belorussians, Russians and Ukrainians, etc.'[122] This indeterminacy of skepticism about postimperial borders may have become a source of today's conflicts. A good illustration for that are political claims that Sevastopol is 'a Russian city' due to Russia's imperial legacy, or that Russia has a duty to protect militarily its compatriots (holders of Russian passports scattered by the Russian government) all across its borders.

Second, the way Russia actualizes the Soviet imperial legacy in its efforts at identity-building remains very inconsistent. Two different discourses seem to coexist with each other. On the one hand, some authors argue that 'anchoring national identity in the Soviet past is a genealogical feature of

122 Dmitry Furman, "Ot Rossiiskoi imperii do raspada SNG" (September 19, 2008), http://www.polit.ru/lectures/2005/10/05/furman_print.html (as of 10 March, 2010).

Putin's regime,'[123] which explains, in particular, why Ukraine's rejection of the USSR 'was perceived in Russia as being also a rejection of Russia.'[124] Within this reasoning Stalin, for example, might be portrayed as a great Soviet leader to win the Second World War.

Yet, on the other hand, a counter-discourse is also visible. Suffice it to say that the conservative platform developed by the governing 'United Russia' party is openly presented as an opposition to the Soviet-times ideology. The October 1917 revolution is baptized an 'extremist event' orchestrated by revolutionary radicals with foreign sponsorship. In this context, the former Georgian President Mikhail Saakashvili was negatively dubbed an 'heir to Stalin and Beria.' Moreover, according to Putin, 'those who insist that Abkhazia and Southern Ossetia ought to belong to Georgia are Stalinists, since they sustain the decision taken by Stalin.'[125]

What is a matter of debate is to what extent postimperial Russia feels trapped in the Soviet imperial identity. Too much concentration on the Second World War triumphalist narrative does not seem to legitimize anything but the demise of USSR, since none of the Commonwealth of Independent States (CIS) countries supported Russia in her 'historical' dispute with Estonia in 2007 over the removal of the monument to Soviet soldiers from Tallinn's downtown. This isolation of Russia proves that historical parallels fail to construct a common communication space for its 'near abroad' where fears of Moscow's resurrected imperial instincts are evidently stronger than normative/value-driven commitments.

Third, in Russian political discourse, the concept of empire is always a matter of selective interpretations that are battlegrounds for hegemony: Some elements in the imperial past are artificially accentuated and elucidated, while others are intentionally obscured or expelled. As I have mentioned with the reference to Laclau, the meanings attached to empty/floating signifiers might vary according to the context they are placed in, while role identities and identity-driven imaginaries may well be organized around them. This makes empire a relative concept, akin to a metaphor leaving much space for arbitrary usage at one's discretion. It comes with a variety of adjec-

---

123 Viacheslav Morozov, "Evropa: Orientatsiya vo vremeni i prostranstve," *Rossiya v globalnoy politike* (3, May–June 2008).

124 Taras Kuzio, "EU and Ukraine: A Turning Point in 2004?" Paris: Institute for Security Studies, Occasional Papers No. 47 (November 2003): 7.

125 Vladimir Putin, Interview with CNN (Sochi, August 28, 2008), http://www.government.ru (as of March 10, 2014).

tives—empires can be colonial and anticolonial, liberal and orthodox, cosmopolitan[126] or even 'sanitary.'[127] It is precisely this elasticity that opens the concept to political interpretations that can easily change their meanings from negative to positive,[128] or the other way around.

There will always be policy contexts in which a great power's policies may be interpreted as imperial, owing to the multiplicity of the meanings of empire. It is this point that constitutes the theoretical platform of a 'new imperial history' school, in particular, of the *Ab Imperio* journal based in the city of Kazan. Its associates distance themselves from a more traditional approach that perceives empires in predominantly negative terms, in contrast to the inevitable (and, ostensibly from a historical viewpoint, more progressive) 'social order of nation states.' In an 'old' logic, empires were dubbed 'vestiges of the past' and thus opposed to nation states as deficient deviations from the norm[129]. Such an approach not only challenges the teleological inevitability of transition from empires to nations, but also in a wider sense questions the very idea of structural constants. Instead, the *Ab Imperio* group prefers to focus on the so-called 'imperial situations' (or 'imperial formations'), concepts that are instruments to uncover the 'imperial momentum' in the logic of all great powers. This approach seems to be fully consonant with Frederick Cooper's advocacy of 'the potential of empire,' or situations when sovereign nations 'could become empires' or are 'acting like empires.' 'Imperial situations' can be based on free trade ('free trade imperialism') or on democratic governance ('Rome was an empire when it was a republic'[130]).

It is against this background that empire might be called a 'floating' signifier: It easily 'floats' from its 'own' domain to other interpretations of Russia as a nation, a business corporation, and a regionalized state. According to Laclau, a floating signifier is an equivalent 'whose emptiness results from the ambiguity introduced by a plurality of discourses interrupting each other.'[131]

---

126 Artemiy Magun, "Otstranionnoe prostranstvo Imperii," *Levaya politika* 1 (2007): 34.

127 Egor Kholmogorov, "Evropa ot zakata do rassveta," *Russkii zhurnal* (June 18, 2002), www.russ.ru/politics/20020618-holm.html (as of March 10, 2014).

128 Sergey Kortunov (ed.), *Mirovaya politika* (Moscow: Higher School of Economics, 2007): 311.

129 Ilia Gerasimov *et al.*, "Novaya imperskaya istoria i vyzovy imperii," *Ab Imperio* 1 (2010): 20.

130 Jand Burbank and Frededrick Cooper, "The Challenge and Serendipity of Writing World History through the Prism of Empire. Interview with Jane Burbank and Frederick Cooper," *Ab Imperio* 2 (2010): 22–44.

131 Ernesto Laclau, "Structure, History and the Political," in *Contingency, Hegemony, Universality. Contemporary Dialogues on the Left* (London: Verso, 2000): 185.

This is exactly what we see in the intermixture of different versions of Russia's identity. Floating signifiers appear within 'the logic of the displacements' of frontiers and, by and large, do not contradict the idea of empty signifiers. The distance between the two does not appear to be that great: "floating and empty signifiers should be conceived as partial dimensions in any process of hegemonic construction."[132] In our case, this distance appears to be of some significance since it allows for 'debordering' the empire-based 'regime of signification' and for exposing the areas of compatibility between it and other regimes.

132 Ernesto Laclau, *On Populist Reason* (London: Verso, 2005): 133.

2 Multipolarity in Plural: The EU and Russia in Intersubjective Models of International Societies

In this chapter, I will inscribe the idea of intersubjectivity discussed earlier in a variety of institutional settings. I am going to demonstrate that the contours and mechanisms of EU–Russia intersubjective relations are framed by different structural model of IS. It is within these models that the EU and Russia, with all perceptional gaps between them, design their foreign policy imageries and strategies of interacting with each other.

The common denominator proposed for diverse types of IS co-shaped by the EU and Russia is the concept of multipolarity that is accepted both by Russia and the EU as a catchword for redistribution of world power from a United States-led unilateralism to a more pluralist and—at least potentially—balanced world order. Multipolarity as a model is grounded in the ability of sovereign powers to take political decisions of their own.[133] Its reverse side is *unilateralism*, or a logic of sovereign decisions which Russia both adheres to and expects from other countries as well. The Kremlin's multiple suggestions that the Western countries need to be pragmatic and guided by their "genuine interests," as opposed to "imagined ideological clichés,"[134] also fit, by and large, with the multipolar decisionism.

However, the concept of multipolarity needs to be contextualized and faces a number of questions. Perhaps, the most acute of them is the potentially higher volatility and conflictuality of multipolar systems in comparison to unipolar and bipolar ones—an argument based on realist and neorealist pedigree. Arguably, multipolarity may be conducive to further destabilization in the Middle East, strengthening of Iran, military advancement of China and North Korea, etc.[135] Therefore, "the probability of conflict is high in multipolar systems due to shaky alliances and diffuse power-relations. And it is in multipolar systems that we can historically observe the highest frequency of

133 Alexandr Filippov, "Universum ili pluriversum?" *Kosmopolis* 3: 9 (Autumn 2004): 90.

134 Dmitry Medvedev. Interview with BBC (Sochi, August 26, 2008), http://www.kremlin.ru/text/appears/2008/08/205775.shtml (as of March 10, 2014).

135 Vladimir Kulagin, "Globalnaya ili mirovaya bezopasnost," *International Trends. Journal of International Relations Theory and World Politics* 5: 2 (May–August 2007): 50.

power-maximizing behavior."[136] In other words, multipolarity presupposes divides and clashes between a number of 'poles' that might be stronger than—and possibly inimical to—both Russia and the EU.

Yet debates on multipolarity reach far beyond the domain of *Realpolitik*. It is my thesis in this chapter that Russian and European policy- and opinion-makers, having indeed borrowed the concept of multipolarity from the (neo)realist vocabulary, often use it in a broader array of narratives, and therefore attach to it nonrealist meanings, to include issues of identity and nonstate actorship. As I am going to show further, what hides beneath the pretended realist wording is a much more complicated and variegated—though not always consistent—set of policy imageries that shape EU–Russian relations. Against this background, discourses on multipolarity remind patchworks of scattered and loosely tied "metal maps,"[137] based upon—and sustained by—certain visions of the world in the diversity of its actors.

2.1 Multipolarity Re-signified

Since its inception in the realist scholarship, the concept of multipolarity went through a number of substantial transformations. *First*, in the realist reading, it used to be ostensibly state centric. In its more contemporary and reconsidered visions, it may contain important nonstate conceptualizations. One of them is the so-called civilization-based approach that, as I will show below, resonates quite peculiarly in Russia's foreign policy.

Second, in the traditional realist sense power is mostly a material and physical phenomenon and does not always need strong social underpinning. Yet some interpretations of multipolar IS to be presented in this chapter do recognize nonmaterial types of power, since the very concept of the pole, apart from physical resources, implies social content that is well addressed in nonrealist theories, including social constructivism.

Third, for classical realists multipolarity is a rather pessimistic concept heralding conflicts and instability. In the Russian—and, to some extent, European—political parlance, multipolarity, on the contrary, embodies an optimistic worldview, based upon a 'fair' distribution of power among a variety of

136 Peter Toft, "John J.Mearsheimer: An Offensive Realist between Geopolitics and Power," *Journal of International Relations and Development* 8: 4 (December 2005): 401.

137 Oleg Kildiushov, "Vneshnyaya politika," in Vitaly Kurennoi (ed.), *Mysliaschaya Rossiya. Kartografia sovremennykh intellektualnykh napravleniy* (Moscow: Nasledie Evrazii Foundation, 2006): 159.

poles. In *Realpolitik* terms, multipolarity is basically about maintaining *order*, while for nonrealist discourses it is mostly about *management of diversity* in the world that does not any longer constitute an agglomeration of nation states. This makes multipolarity discourses quite compatible with those critical theories that strongly emphasize the issues of 'hybridity' and 'polivocality' in international relations.[138] "The world of singularities" and "the plurality of beginnings as a 'world-forming' experience" (to borrow a few catchwords from Jean–Luc Nancy) repudiate the world of states and focus on human beings and their communities as bearers of diversity and plurality in IS.

Fourth, Russia and the EU seem to be in a discord with one of the key preconditions for a realist mindset—the idea of anarchy. Moscow and Brussels—though in evidently different ways – seek to substitute it with a more or less orderly type of relations. Anarchy is denied by those authors who make sense of multipolarity as a structural condition laying foundation for a greater coordination of major powers' policies, either in the form of a new 'concert,' or within the framework of global governance.

Fifth, for realism social world can be divided into false and true dispositions[139]; therefore, the "correspondence to reality" appears to be a key realist argument.[140] Concomitantly, realists treat multipolarity as almost a 'fact' of the being, if not an axiom that needs neither proofs nor further problematization. This type of reasoning corresponds to the realist "ontological position that claims that objects do exist even if no one is conscious of them or experiences them."[141] The basic problem with this approach is that it leaves unanswered the question of how can we know for sure that a certain concept is 'true' or 'real.'[142] The realist approach can only be feasible if based upon the presupposition of the ontological existence of a presumably all-knowledgeable subject potentially able to distinguish 'real-life processes' from 'virtual' or faked.

138 Gunter Lenz and Antje Dallmann, "Introduction," in Kwame Anthony Appiah *et al.* (eds.), *Justice, Governance, Cosmopolitanism, and the Politics of Difference. Reconfigurations in a Transnational World* (Berlin: Humboldt-Universitat, 2007): 5.

139 Fred Chernoff, "Scientific Realism as a Meta-Theory of International Politics," *International Studies Quarterly* 46: 2 (June 2002): 192.

140 Nuno Monteiro and Keven Ruby, "IR and the false promise of philosophical foundations," *International Theory* 1: 1 (2009): 31.

141 Renee Jeffery, "Australian Realism and International Relations: John Anderson and Hedley Bull on Ethics, Religion and Society," *International Politics* 45 (2008): 55.

142 Wendt, *Social Theory,* 59.

Yet constructivists would argue that multipolarity does not constitute an established reality[143]—perhaps, as unipolarity did not do so either. Following the vocabulary of Alexander Wendt, multipolarity can be better seen as an example of "social systems" or "social kinds"[144] that give meaning to ideas. Therefore, one may presume that there might be more than one model of multipolarity, and these may either correlate or compete with each other—hence the idea of 'multipolarity in plural' which gave the name to this chapter. Hence, plurality of interpretations of reality translates into multiplicity of foreign policy role identities—a situation seemingly consonant with the constructivist understanding of poles as not 'given' subjects but constantly constructed in intersubjective 'games of recognition.'

There is an important methodological point that needs to be addressed at this juncture. One of the research puzzles that the concept of multipolarity brings about lies in its double nature. On the one hand, it would be quite legitimate to view multipolarity as a structural phenomenon in a sense that it is destined to come into being and function almost automatically, as a supposedly natural result of either 'objective' geopolitical dynamics or not less 'objective' internal processes within major world powers that diminish the appeal for a superpower role.[145] Following the English School, multipolarity can be considered as a type of IS[146] embodied in certain institutions.

Yet on the other hand, multipolarity—especially for Russia—is the name for a long-term strategy, that is, something that needs to be promoted and, therefore, requires political investments and agents' policies. Thus, some institutional formats of multipolarity—such as BRICS (a club-like group of "emerging economies" comprised of Brazil, Russia, India, China, and South Africa) are seen as outcomes of conscious effort of a group of states eager to rectify shortcomings of a Western-centric world.

This double-faced nature of the concept of multipolarity partly explains the proliferation of its different interpretations. I will start 'unpacking' this concept on a structural level by proposing a menu of patterns of multipolarity presented in the table below. It is formed on the basis of two kinds of distinctions that appear to be crucial for my analysis, namely between (1) interest-based and normative structures, and (2) state-centric structures and those

143 Boris Martynov, "Mnogopoliarniy ili mnogotsivilizatsyonniy mir?" *International Trends* 7: 3 (September–December 2009).

144 Wendt, *Social Theory*, 376.

145 Leonid Radzikhovskiy, "Koliuchaya mnogopoliarnost," *Rossiiskaya gazeta*, 5001: 177 (September 22, 2009).

146 Bull, *The Anarchical Society*, 1.

reaching beyond the state and, thus, involving a wider gamut of actors. Of course, some authors deem that the concept of multipolarity makes sense only within the context of relations between nation states, while "in a system where the actorship of non-state participants is acknowledged, the notion of multipolarity is devoid of significance,"[147] yet it is my thesis that nonstate actorship can be an important element of multipolar arrangements.

It is within the four resulting blocks that different—yet imbricated—models of multipolarity can be located.

	Interest-based structures	***Normative structures***
State-centered structures	1A: Balance of power 1B: Spheres of influence 1C: GPM 1D: Procedural approximation	2A: Normative plurality 2B: Normative convergence
'State Plus' structures	3: Multiregionalism	4A: Multiplicity of civilizations 4B: Global governance

Four comments to this table need to be furnished. *First*, it is only square 1—with four variations—that corresponds to the realist vision of multipolarity, but it also contains strong English school connotations. *Structurally*, balance of power and GPM are, according to Hedley Bull, institutions of IS. As *political strategies*, they are instrumentalized by Russia to raise its international role without serious domestic transformations, and grounded in Russia's hidden imitation of the major Western powers. As a telling linguistic evidence, references to the 'chess-board' metaphor known for its connotations with Brzezinki's famous book abound in Russian realist discourse, which can be explained as an acceptance of the 'American' rules of the game and an attempt to steer a winning strategy.[148] The three other table cells are domains of modified ('re-signified') versions of multipolarity that either contain more explicit normative accents (democracy- or civilization-grounded) or incorporate actors other than states, or both.

147 Sergei Agafontsev, "Globalniy krizis i regulirovanie mirovykh finansov," *International Trends. Journal of International Relations Theory and World Politics* 7: 1 (January–April 2009): 28.

148 Semed Semedov, "Mesto i rol' Rossii na Bol'shom Kavkaze," *Obozrevatel'-Observer* 6: 209 (2007): 57.

Second, most of the concepts in this table could be simultaneously applicable to both structures and agents' policies, which means that institutional implementations of each of these mental/conceptual structures directly depend on (and presuppose as the condition of their operation) policies of major actors. The only exception is the multiplicity of civilizations that may be viewed as a structure in a Waltzian sense, as an "abstraction" "free of the attributes and the interactions of units."[149] Indeed, plurality of civilizations is regarded by its adherents as immanent (perhaps inevitable) law-like characteristic of socio-political world in its 'natural'—comparable to the physical world—multiplicity, and in this sense does not necessarily require specific actors' strategies.

Third, some of these ideal type models could be quite compatible with each other, while others certainly are in a conflict. The identification of these models and strategies they entail does not necessarily imply the existence of certain policy groups to promote and stay behind each of them. This typology of scenarios is sustained by different articulations of Russia's and EU's role identities in a multipolar world, yet neither of them 'belongs' to any specific political grouping. Neither of scenarios/strategies has its natural 'bearers'; one group within policy-making apparatus may simultaneously adhere to two or more strategies thus demonstrating high volatility of actors' role identities.

Fourth, this line of analysis proffers a contribution to theoretical debates between different schools of foreign policy thought by demonstrating ample room for using classical realist concepts—balance of power, spheres of influence, GPM—for an overwhelmingly constructivist piece of IR research. Indeed, nothing prevents a scholar staying on constructivist grounds to make use and take advantage of the whole series of concepts with seemingly non-realist intellectual pedigree. Arguably, it would be fully consistent with constructivist methodology to claim that some of these models are enduring and resilient, and wield huge resources of influence. Moreover, it is constructivist analysis, with all its subtleties and fine-tuning, that allows to dismantle the simplistic and stereotypical reduction of the EU–Russia disconnections to Russia's alleged adherence to 'old' realist recipes, as opposed to EU's pursuance of a more explicit normative-centered and cosmopolitan type of policy. As I will argue, the EU and Russia are guided by different types of normativity, and the classical Westphalian issues of sovereignty and borders resonate quite strongly and persistently in the EU context.

---

149 Kenneth Waltz, *Theory of International Politics* (Reading, Massachusetts – Menlo Park, California – London – Amsterdam – Don Mills, Ontario – Syndey: Addison-Wesley Publishing Company, 1983): 80.

2.2 Power Balancing: Back to Realpolitik?

The balance-of-power interpretation of multipolarity, though officially repudiated by Russian and European diplomacies as dangerously obsolete, is one of the models that retained certain traction for Russia. As a Russian scholar argues, the multipolar system of international relations can be stable only under the condition of maintaining some kind of balance of power between great powers.[150]

As I have mentioned earlier, one has to distinguish between two dimensions of balance of power. On the one hand, in accordance with Hedley Bull's logic, as one of the institutions of IS, it possesses structural characteristics, and thus focuses rather on institutional results of a process, than on the attainment of goals pursued by particular state actors. To some extent, balance of power seems rather close to the Schmittian concept of pluriverse.[151] On the other hand, balance of power can be connoted with specific policy strategies of major international actors that invest their resources in making this structure functional.

There were those in Russian elites who in the immediate aftermath of the downfall of the Soviet Union anticipated that the post-Cold War order would evolve to a milder (i.e., less conflictual) version of bipolarity,[152] yet as soon as idealism and naïvety of these expectations became obvious, the formation of a more equitable—that is, based on several power holders to contain and balance each other—world system turned into a key priority for the Kremlin's diplomacy. From structural perspective, the balance-of-power vision of IR re-actualizes practices of the Cold War, and recognizes the reality of the West as a United States-led collective political subject whose hegemony ought to be thwarted. The United States and their NATO allies, according to this logic, are destined to continuously reproduce the relations of rivalry with the non-Western world.

Yet the balance-of-power model could be operational only under two chief conditions:

- bloc-based structure of international relations;

---

150 Vladimir Batiuk, "Postbipoliarnaya retrospektiva mirovogo poriadka," *International Trends. Journal of International Relations Theory and World Politics* 8: 2 (August 2010): 87.

151 Alexandr Filippov, "Universum ili pluriversum?" *Kosmopolis* 3: 9 (Autumn 2004): 90.

152 Evgeniy Bazhanov and Natalia Bazhanova, "Kuda idiot chelovechestvo?" *Mir i Politika* 7: 34 (July 2008): 24.

- power has to be understood as mostly material/physical and relatively homogeneous resource that presumably can be more or less equally distributed among a group of key holders[153] for the sake of global stability.

These presumptions, however, can be challenged from a few interrelated perspectives. One counterargument would be that power is not a kind of resource that has a common denominator, and thus cannot be divided or transferred from one actor to another; it always comes in a variety of forms. "What counts as power depends on definitions of the situation,"[154] one may say. This reasoning may be in tune with Michel Foucault's and Gilles Deleuze's theorizing of power as a combination of different spaces that may overlap yet preserve their relative autonomy. Thus, projecting Foucauldian reasoning to the sphere of IS, one may arguably single out domains of *political power* with the five permanent members of the United Nations (UN) Security Council at its core; *military power* with its key holders possessing hard security resources; *managerial power* that manifests itself through the instruments of governmentality, including technical (depoliticized) administration and policing; *disciplinary power* that operates in the forms of regulatory normative mechanisms (including religion); and *biopower* that transnationally takes the forms of 'responsibility to protect' and 'humanitarian interventions.' The fragmentation of power relations into spaces/segments, which is at the core of the Foucauldian approach, seems to be quite consonant with the polycentric worldview, since each of the forms of power presupposes its own key subjects that are in principle unable to balance—in a traditional sense—each other due to different mechanisms, institutions, and resources they are based on.

Therefore, power is by no means a homogeneous resource, and there are many types of it. For instance, poles of economic growth might not coincide with sources of military power, etc. Thus, North Korea, being short of either economic or political might, does possess certain military capabilities; Vatican, having no military resources, is a source of strong spiritual and religious appeal for the world's Catholic community; Switzerland, without any military resources, is definitely one of the key centers of financial power in the world; Nordic countries, lacking meaningful military resources either, compensate their absence with a powerful normative appeal.

153 Kamaludin Gadzhiev, *Vvedenie v geopolitiku* (Moscow: Logos Publishers, 1998): 359.

154 Wendt, *Social Theory*, 331.

Thus, the plurality of power holders may not be a result of the concerted distribution of power among a certain number of states, but rather a consequence of the immanent plurality of power resources as such. Consequently, centers of power are principally dispersed: Economic, financial, political, military, cultural centers may coexist with each other without merging, each one having its own operational and functional spheres. This is what partly was captured by former Foreign Minister Igor Ivanov's reference to a 'real multipolarity' as a coexistence of plurality of international systems, each one grounded in a particular type of resources and influences, both material and ideational.[155]

Another argument, also of a Foucauldian nature, posits that power is something that *produces* agents but *does not belong* to them. Power is not agents' possession but rather a web of relations that forms/makes/constructs political subjects. This implies that different patterns of multipolarity are grounded in the re-activation and instrumentalization of various identity resources that might give different effects. In other words, a Russia of balance-of-power and a Russia committed to global governance are two different international role identities, with different types of international subjectivity inherent in each of them.

The key problem with the applicability of the balance of power concept is that neither experts nor policy-makers have reliable analytical tools for measuring power resources and making sure that balancing does take place. This leads to conceptual difficulties in identifying who is in a stronger and a weaker position in specific situations, and thus in adequately defining one's own place in the world power relations.

The implementation of balance of power as a *policy strategy* is directly conditioned by the maintenance of sovereignty—the key concept for Russian self-determination in the world that is understood by Moscow as a right to control territories rather than as responsibility to the population. Consequently, power balancing can be unilateral and be grounded in the logic of sovereign decisions that Russia favors itself and expects from other most powerful countries as well. Dmitry Medvedev's multiple suggestions that the

155 Igor Ivanov, "Sopernichayuschie modeli i scenarii formirovaniya novogo miroporiadka: sut' i perspektivy realizatsii," *Politiya* 4 (Winter 2004–2005): 11.

Western governments need to be pragmatic and guided by their own "genuine interests"[156] fit, by and large, the decisionist philosophy. As a 'United Russia' party functionary presumed, within the multipolar society "each country is supposed to represent its own interests, instead of delegating them to the EU, NATO and other international organizations."[157] This seemingly anti-institutional and antinormative utterance is a blunt declaration of mistrust to those forms of international subjectivity that entail dispersal and division of sovereignty favored by many political forces within the EU.

As I have noted earlier, the idea of balancing presupposes a certain degree of conflictuality between different poles,[158] which made Dmitri Trenin call the balance-of-power policy "a continuation of the Cold War inertia, which strengthens the arguments of those who would like to see Russia returning to the Soviet policy pathways."[159] Besides, the implementation of this model might ultimately result in Russia's submission to China as its junior partner and, thus, harm Russia's international subjectivity. It is indicative that China has never featured among powers that Russia was intended to balance, which reveals a predominantly anti-Western ground of the balance-of-power concept.

It is from here that another serious trouble for this concept emerges. On the one hand, the balancing strategy indeed presupposes Russia's association with anti-Western identities shaped by postcolonial discourses that emanate from peripheral or semi-peripheral actors. On the other hand, in addressing the most pressing security issues Russia tends to appeal to—and prefers to deal with—the leaders of the West. These two dispositions may not easily sit together, since a Russia sympathetic with anti-Western sentiments will most likely be perceived by the United States and the EU as their external Other rather than recognized as part of Europe.

One may agree that the balance-of-power type of multipolarity "is a direct and unequivocal alternative to globalization,"[160] since it may foster a more regionalized political and security scenery by forging 'regional sub-balances' (in the Mediterranean basin, the Black Sea and the Caspian Sea regions, and so forth). The linkage between balance of power and multiregionalism is not,

---

156 Dmitry Medvedev, Interview with BBC (Sochi, August 26, 2008), http://www.kremlin.ru/text/appears/2008/08/205775.shtml (as of March 10, 2014).

157 *Rossiiskiy konservatizm – ideologia partii 'Edinaya Rossiya'* (Moscow: Center for Social Conservative Policy, 2009): 36.

158 *Strategia-2020* (Moscow: Center for Socio-Conservative Policy, 2008): 23.

159 Dmitriy Trenin, "Nenadiozhnaya strategiya," *Pro et Contra* 6: 1–2 (Winter–Spring 2001): 4.

160 Yuriy Fiodorov, "Kriticheskiy vyzov dlia Rossii," *Pro et Contra* 4:4 (Autumn 1999): 19.

of course, straightforward, yet it may have some parallels with Buzan and Waever's theory of 'regional security complexes' whose existence is preconditioned by local durable patterns of securitization.

The prospects of regionalization of the balance of power type of relationship raise at least two critical points. *Structurally*, the fragmentation of the IS into regional power balancing systems contrasts quite sharply with a hypothetically unified Euro-Atlantic 'security space,' as exemplified by the Kremlin's proposals on 'new security architecture.' As seen from an *agency perspective*, balancing approaches give at least two negative effects. On the one hand, the policy of preserving/maintaining regional sub-balances of power may immobilize Russian diplomacy that is perceived as being aimed not at finding political solutions to regional conflicts but at keeping an uncertain status quo. This is very much so in the South Caucasus where Russia's tactics of balancing between Armenia and Azerbaijan (and, in a wider sense, between the broader coalitions of forces behind each of the two parties) gives no practical results in view of resolving the frozen conflict in Nagorno-Karabakh. On the other hand, as soon as Russia more explicitly positions itself as a hegemon surrounded by satellite states, most of its post-Soviet neighbors "opt for the most natural kind of behavior under the circumstances: they all have become the classical balancers."[161] This explains the resilience of balancing policies not only within the framework of EU–Russia relations, but at regional levels as well—though with very controversial results, as the case of Ukraine makes clear.

2.3 Spheres of Influence

In the frame of this model, the EU and Russia are seen as two power poles struggling for their zones/areas of influence, which implies institutional competition between them in the common neighborhood area. According to this logic, the EU takes rather seriously the challenge posed by the Russia-led projects of reintegrating post-Soviet states, and is willing to act robustly and take maximum advantage of the key Russia's weakness—lack of normative appeal in its neighborhood policies.

Spheres of influence as another realist model of IS seems a structural precondition for Russia's regional domination in Eurasia. Despite the Cold

161 Igor Torbakov, *What Does Russia Want? Investigating the Interrelationship between Moscow's Domestic and Foreign Policy* (Berlin: Deutsche Gesellschaft fur Auswartige Politik, DGAP Analyse, May 2011, No. 1): 11.

War connotations, spheres-of-influence policies are quite resilient, even if decried as allegedly obsolete. Of course, it is mainly Russia who has de facto proclaimed its sphere of vital interests, by and large embracing post-Soviet countries (save three Baltic republics). The very preference of the concept of 'near abroad' over that of common neighborhood is a clear indication of a sphere-of-influence type of thinking in the Kremlin. In blocking Ukraine's and Georgia's membership in NATO—with tacit concord from some EU Member States—Russia has declared that there are 'red lines' that the Kremlin will not allow the West to cross in its attempts to incorporate Russia's neighbors. The victorious military operation against Georgia in August 2008 had led to the fortification of Russia's zones of 'special interest' as a political doctrine. It functions as an overarching imperative and is explicitly EU- and NATO-centric: The realist proponents of spheres of influence choose to keep a low profile in debates on the roles and resources of China, Turkey, or Iran in post-Soviet countries, including those that committed themselves to the Customs Union project.

The spheres-of-influence logic is largely predetermined by the structure of EU–Russia relations where in-between positioning often fails to be advantageous: Thus, it is for economic reasons impossible to be part of a free trade area with Russia and simultaneously with the EU, especially given the stark differences in technical norms between them. This drives the EU (as well as NATO) to engaging in spheres of influence politics by the very denial of such a sphere for Russia. Moreover, in some cases the EU is not far from pursuing policies of spheres of influence of its own. This is, in particular, the case of the EaP and especially EU's policies toward Ukraine, Moldova, and Georgia that are considered the most probable candidates for economically and politically associating with the EU. Since, as we have noted above, Russia and the EU wield dissimilar types of power, the mechanisms of competition for spheres of influence in the common neighborhood are also different. This not only narrows the space for positive interaction between Moscow and Brussels, but also represents a challenge for countries such as Moldova or Ukraine that are objects of two strikingly divergent sets of power instruments.

To some extent, spheres of influence might be viewed as similar to a neo-imperialist approach, based on regional domination or hegemony. In the Chapter 1, I have discussed a problem of great power identities evolving in—or gravitating to—imperial ones. What unites the balance-of-power and spheres-of-influence models of multipolar IS is not only their embeddedness in a realist theorizing, but also their potential openness for accepting imperial subjectivities that can be properly understood as developing within intersubjective frames of relations. Indeed, Russia's self-representations through the concept of empire are closely connected to European and American discourses on their presumably imperial identities.[162] As Viatcheslav Morozov argues, EU's subjectivity encompasses a strong 'imperial moment,' which, however, coincided with the appearance of more accentuated transformation in the direction of "sovereign territorial state" model.[163] Valery Tishkov adds to this that major European countries "for quite a long time retained their imperial qualities but in the meantime were gradually becoming egalitarian nation states."[164]

The imperial inclinations of the United States and the EU may be perceived as a challenge to Russia, but nevertheless Russian role identities are constructed through some kind of reference to the empire-building practices in the West that became inherent parts of Russia's imperial discourse. In many cases, Russia ventured to imitate US international behavior, having incorporated in its political vocabulary the concepts of preemptive strikes, zone of vital interest, and peace enforcement. In constructivist accounts, imitation takes place "when actors adopt the self-understanding of those whom they perceive as successful."[165] As Russian authors put it, the Kremlin "read the American verbal message as a certain semiotic code and then adapted it to its own needs."[166] The Moscow political elite, as frankly admitted by a Russian analyst, all throughout 1990s had "looked at the United States with a mixed feeling of indignation and admiration. Even illegitimate actions in defense of U.S. own interests were perceived [in Moscow] as examples to be followed and reproduced by Russia itself: if Washington does so, why Russia can't?"[167] In particular, many diplomats and military experts in Moscow aver that Russian military bases in South Ossetia and Abkhazia were deployed on

---

162 Pami Aalto, "Empire Europe Encounters the Post-Soviet North." Background Paper to the presentation at the "Laboratory in the Margins? The EU's and Russia's Policies in Northern Europe" workshop, 2004.

163 Viacheslav Morozov, "Evropa: Orientatsiya vo vremeni i prostranstve", *Rossiya v globalnoy politike* 3 (May–June 2008).

164 Valeriy Tishkov, "Chto yest Rossiya i rossiikskiy narod," *Pro et Contra* 3: 37 (May–June 2007): 25.

165 Wendt, *Social Theory*, 325.

166 Igor' Zevelev and Mikhail Troitskiy, *Power and Influence in U.S.-Russian Relations. A Semiotic Analysis* (Moscow: Academic & Educational Forum on International Relations, 2006): 33.

167 Sergei Oznobischev, "Kogo lechit' 'ot Gruzii'?" *International Trends. Journal of International Relations Theory and World Politics* 6: 2 (May–August 2008): 125.

the same grounds as the Americans deployed theirs in Romania and Bulgaria.

One may agree that most of the time Russia has been—though tacitly—fascinated with the United States as a successful country relying upon force without much of reflections about following legal norms and avoiding repercussions. Arguably, Russia's inclination to imitate the American imperial conduct reveals Russia's own proclivity to imperial greatpowerness.[168] In particular, Anatoly Chubais' articulation of the liberal empire thesis appears to echo "the Bush administration's grand strategy that may be imperial, but it aims at creating liberal, rather than autocratic or totalitarian, governance."[169] This is exactly how Russia is perceived by some of its neighbors—as a less successful copy of the United States.[170]

This is also true with regard to Europe. One of the conservative voices in Russia presumes that the formation of EU's subjectivity in an imperial form is a feasible perspective for the future, since the EU potentially has its own ambitions, interests, and ideology that will push it to take certain actions of its own.[171] This trajectory could be beneficial for Russia because of its instrumentality in balancing the US geopolitical preponderance. As a Russian author reports, "should a new, Anglo-Saxon empire take its shape, Russia, instead of resisting, should have start recreating its own empire."[172]

The strategy of imitation was conducive to drawing parallels between the cases of Kosovo, on the one hand, and South Ossetia and Abkhazia, on the other. The Russian military intervention against Georgia and Kremlin's recognition of the independence of two break-away territories were marked by multiple references to the Kosovo precedent. It was the case of Kosovo that Russian authorities used as a legitimating excuse for its actions in defense of the two secessionist republics in the Caucasus. Russia's diplomatic recognition of Abkhazia and South Ossetia in the aftermath of the Georgia war of August 2008 was modeled after the US-inspired recognition of the Kosovo independence half a year earlier. Russian political discourse was ostensibly saturated

168 Alexei Kara-Murza, "Mezhdu imperiei i smutoi" (Moscow: Institute of Philosophy, Russian Academy of Sciences, 1996): 32.

169 Edward Rhodes, "The Imperial Logic of Bush's Liberal Agenda," *Survival* 45: 1 (Spring 2003): 137.

170 Sergei Kizima, "Belorusskiy mentalitet v rossiisko-belorusskikh itnosheniyakh," *Svobodnaya mysl'* 2: 1597 (2009): 58.

171 Egor Kholmogorov, "Evropa ot zakata do rassveta," *Russkii zhurnal* (June 18, 2002), www.russ.ru/politics/20020618-holm.html (as of March 10, 2014)

172 Svetlana Lurie, "Imperskoe vospitanie gosudarstva-gegemona," *Kosmopolis* 4: 6 (Winter 2003–2004): 107.

by alleged similarities between the Balkans and the Northern Caucasus, which seems accordant with both spheres-of-influence and balance-of-power models.

Yet spheres of influence can be operational only under two pivotal conditions. First, smaller countries who find themselves in the orbits of great powers either have to agree to be patronized, or—at least—should not lay claims for associating with an alternative source of authority (i.e., a competing bloc). Second, a great power with ambitions to have its own sphere of influence should develop effective tools of governing the countries falling into this sphere. Both conditions look problematic in the case of Russia and its neighbors. Most of post-Soviet countries would disagree with their inclusion in a Russia-dominated political bloc; moreover, most of them quite explicitly develop multivectoral diplomacies that conceptually challenge the premises of spheres of influence. By the same token, Russia lacks convincing mechanisms of efficient governance in zones of its interest, which questions the efficacy of the spheres-of-influence model in wider Europe.

2.4 Great Power Management: An Oligarchic Type of Multipolarity?

Hedley Bull considered GPM as an institution of IS based on interactions between the strongest actors. It is in this sense that it can be dubbed an oligarchic type of multipolar IS that requires political and security arrangements between "self-appointed guardians of the international system,"[173] as it has been the case, for example, in post-Napoleonic Europe. This model can be achieved through partnerships, associations, or diplomatic bargaining between the leading international players.[174]

Russia nowadays comes up with a number of different interpretations of GPM. One is of geopolitical background: It affirms the utility of various 'axes' and 'triangles' (or other geometric figures) that ought to link Russia to the strongest international actors. In its most radical version—adduced by Alex-

173 Bobo Lo, "Russia: the Eastern Dimension," in Piotr Dutkiewicz and Dmitri Trenin (eds.), *Russia: the Challenges of Transformation* (Social Science Research Center & New York University Press, 2011): 369.

174 Sergey Lavrov, "Russia in the 21st-Century World of Power." "Russia in Global Affairs" web portal (December 27, 2012), http://eng.globalaffairs.ru/number/Russia-in-the-21st-Century-World-of-Power-15809 (as of March 10, 2014).

ander Dugin—the Russian government is urged to make restitution of Kaliningrad and the Kuril Islands in exchange for privileged relations with, respectively, Germany and Japan.

Another—and more widely spread—approach to GPM denotes a pragmatically depoliticized type of bargaining between the world poles. Against this backdrop, historical models of GPM (such as, for instance, the Vienna Congress system) are depicted as a countervariant to the Bismarck-style *Realpolitik*.[175] President Putin himself has referred to historical antecedents of GPM: "the Congress of Vienna of 1815 and the agreements made at Yalta in 1945, taken with Russia's very active participation, secured a lasting peace. And let us remember [the Treaty of] Versailles, concluded without Russia's participation ... Versailles laid the foundation for the Second World War because the Treaty of Versailles was unfair to the German people: it imposed restrictions with which they could not cope, and the course of the next century became clear."[176]

Arguably, the Georgia war, despite the seemingly deep cleavages between Russia and major Western governments it provoked, fostered some elements of GPM. The Russia–NATO relations have reached their peak of securitization in August 2008, yet then have gradually evolved into a more business-as-usual type of bargaining. Under the Obama administration the United States cancelled the deployment of antimissile systems in Poland and Czech Republic, decreased involvement in countries that Russia includes in the sphere of its interest, and discontinued the accession process of Georgia and Ukraine. In particular, Radoslaw Sikorski has said he had an impression that some allies had made commitments to the Russians that the Membership Action Plan (MAP) would not be granted to Georgia and Ukraine.[177] In the meantime, Russia increased its involvement in the operation in Afghanistan and pledged to cooperate against Somalia pirates, which corroborates Alexander Astrov's prediction that GPM tends to evolve into a police-type administering of conflicts[178] with devalorization of normative issues. This

175 Mikhail Mayorov, "Yspytanie avgustom 2008," *Mir i politika* 4: 43 (August 2010): 7–8.

176 Vladimir Putin Meets with Members Valdai Discussion Club. Transcript of the Speech and Beginning of the Meeting. Valdai Club web site (September 20, 2013), http://valdaiclub.com/politics/62880.html (as of March 10, 2014).

177 Angus Roxburgh, *The Strongman. Vladimir Putin and the Struggle for Russia* (London & New York: I.B.Tauris, 2012): 227.

178 Alexander Astrov, "Great Power Management Without Great Powers?" in Alexander Astrov (ed.), *The Great Power (mis)Management. The Russian-Georgian War and*

model implies mechanisms fostering collective (consensual) code/set of rules of conduct that prioritizes technical crisis management (for the sake of order) over ideology (justice); refrains from making loud politically loaded accusations; and criminalizes violence through the application of peace-building procedures. Some of the Russian authors are, for example, sympathetic to the prospects of 'dividing and conjugating' Russian and US policies in post-Soviet area, with special emphasis on joint conflict management and antinarcotic measures.[179]

Partnership between EU and Russia is an indispensable element of different GPM variations. As a result of the Medvedev–Sarkozy talks in August 2008, Russia has de facto recognized the EU as a legitimate security actor in its 'near abroad' area. As INSOR (a Moscow-based Institute for Contemporary Development) argued, the growth of EU's influence worldwide seems to be quite in line with the idea of multipolarity, which constitutes a fertile soil for Russia's partnership with the EU in such spheres as energy policy, transportation projects, and technology transfer.[180]

In its most radical version, GPM may be close to what a Russian scholar called 'a policy of responsible colonialism,' meaning by this a de facto control by the EU, United States, and Russia over regions that represent security challenges for them, including terrorism, migration, human trafficking, etc.[181] This only proves that GPM does not seem to be a workable institution without political agreements between the key 'stakeholders.' Political momentum is necessarily a condition for more or less successful instances of cooperation between great powers, either in the form of external securitization of threats (piracy, drug trafficking, terrorism, etc.), or as a political deal (Russia's support of the United States in the war on terror after September 11 was implicitly conditioned by American support of Russian policies in North Caucasus[182]). Political dimension of EU–Russian partnership consists in preventing Russia from pursuing a strategy of balancing the West through aligning with non-

its Implications for Global Political Order (Farnham and Burlington: Ashgate, 2011): 1–24.

179 Dmitry Riurikov, "Vozmozhnie modal'nosti razmezhevania i sopriazhenia rossiiskikh i amerikanskikh interesov na post-sovetskom prostranstve," *Mir i politika* 9: 48, (September 2010.): 29–34.

180 Igor Yurgens (ed.), *Rossiya – Evropeiskiy Souyz: k novomu kachestvu otnosheniy*. (Moscow: INSOR, 2008): 26.

181 Mikhail Remizov, "Demokratia plus gegemonia bol'shinstva." APN web portal (June 24, 2011), http://www.apn.ru/publications/article24379.htm (as of March 10, 2014).

182 Denga Khalidov, "Moment istiny dlia Rossii," *Obozrevatel'-Observer* 3: 206 (2007): 6–15.

Western governments, including China.[183] When political momentum is weak and major actors choose operating from purely technical positions, conflicts of interest doomed to prevail over cooperative approaches. The ineffectiveness of the Minsk group on Nagorno-Karabakh is perhaps an illustration of great powers' inability to jointly resolve a particular conflict in the absence of political volitions.

One of the biggest problems at this juncture is an explicitly anti-institutional nature of Russian foreign policy manifest in Russia's mistrust to those forms of international integration leading to the dispersal of sovereignty understood rather as the right to control than as responsibility. Dmitry Medvedev all too easily was keen to speak the language of unilateral decisionism: "As far as our military contingent [in South Ossetia] is concerned, I would like to draw your attention to the fact that not a single document, including our joint plan with President Sarkozy, previsions that this contingent would abide by any rules […] . It is up to us to define what troops we need there, where they will be based and what kind of military bases will be deployed over there."[184]

For the Kremlin, political significance of the GPM model is manifest in the prospect of Russia's acceptance as an equal power of its own by the strongest members of IS. In Russian eyes, GPM could serve as a proof for Russia's rising importance for Western countries with whom Moscow is eager to negotiate conditions of cooperation. Thus, Russia is not against the EU or NATO enlargement in principle—it only dislikes expansion of these institutions in the immediate proximity to Russia's borders, which makes clear that Russian interests are ostensibly regional, not global. As far as in 1994, after the inception of the Bosnian crisis, one of the Russian experts nicely expressed Russia's attitude to the West presuming that Moscow could have supported the Western intervention in the Balkans under two conditions: (1) NATO should stop using military force without prior consultations with Moscow, and (2) Russia has to be eventually admitted to NATO. What is hidden between the lines in this utterance is that Moscow is not against applying military force in principle—it wishes to either be consulted in advance, or even participate in interventions on behalf of the IS.[185] It is very telling in this regard that in 2011 Russian diplomats did not rule out co-participation of Russian

183 Jordi Vaquer i Fanes, *Focusing Back Again on European Security. The Medvedev Proposal as an Opportunity* (Barcelona: CIDOB, Seguridad y Politica Mundial, No. 06, September 2010): 20.

184 Dmitry Medvedev, Interview with "*Le Figaro*" newspaper (November 13, 2008), http://www.kremlin.ru/textx/appears/2008/11/209126.shtml (as of March 10, 2014).

185 Tatiana Parkhalina, "Russia i NATO: bezopasnost' cherez sotrudnichestvo," *Obozrevatel'-Observer* 18 (1994).

troops in a land operation in Libya, should the UN Security Council authorize it.

The idea of striking political deals with major Western governments has always been one of the guiding principles of Putin's foreign policy. Only a few months being in office, Putin has openly asked the NATO Secretary General George Robertson whether Russia can be invited to this organization, yet received a very formal response.[186] After September 11, 2001 he offered to Washington Russian logistical help, intelligence assistance, search-and-rescue missions if American pilots were downed in northern Afghanistan, and even the right to military flights over Russian territory for humanitarian purposes. He told the head of the Central Asian states that Russia has no objections to a US role in Central Asia as long as it fights the war on terror, and rejected proposals from Taliban to join anti-American forces.[187]

In the words of Sergey Karaganov, should Russia and the EU make a long-term political deal, the EU eastward enlargement will not be a problem to Moscow.[188] The same logic applies to NATO as well. The Valdai Club report of 2010 calls Russia and the EU to form a Union of Europe – a GPM-type of alliance as the most effective measure to prevent the degradation of both actors and solve most of the security problems, including reunification of Georgia and Moldova, cooperation in the Arctics and Afghanistan, redefinition of NATO global mission as the key security provider, etc.[189]

Yet Russia's attempts to comanage major issues of world politics in the company of Western great powers by and large failed: The United States ultimately rejected Moscow's proposal to make the American military facilities in the Czech Republic and Poland available for Russian inspections; Russian business faced serious troubles with investing in Western projects, etc. The West only pretended that it takes Russia as a great power, thus creating largely imitative institutions such as the NATO–Russia Council.[190] Putin's disappointment with the prospects of a GPM model was profound: "We supported you in the war on terror, we closed down bases, we let you destroy

---

186 Roxburgh, *The Strongman,* 27.

187 *Ibid.*, 39–40.

188 Russlands weltpolitische Verantwortung. Berfedofer Gesprachskreis (Moskau, 141 Bergedorfer Protokoll, Oktober 24–26, 2008): 57.

189 *K Soyuzu Evropy.* Valdai Club Report (St. Petersburg – Kizhi – Valaam – Moscow, 2010), http://vid-1.rian.ru/ig/valdai/Alliance%20rus.pdf (as of March 10, 2014).

190 Roxburgh, *The Strongman*, 86.

the ABM treaty, we didn't even let Iraq get between us, and what did we get in return?"[191], as Alex Roxburgh interprets his logic.

The failure of Russia to get due acceptance as a great power can be only partly explained in material terms by pointing to enormous corruption within Russia's defense sector, and Russia's backwardness in most indicators of domestic strength (life expectancy, drug consumption, etc.).[192] Another explanation embraces normative and identity-related issues—the dominating feeling among the European elites is that "Putin was not quite ready to join the civilized world,"[193] and that "no one would take seriously Russia's security proposals so long as Russia was rolling back democracy at home."[194]

Perceptional gaps that divide Russia and the West indeed constitute a major obstacle for the effective implementation of a joint managerial agenda. Washington usually does not consider Russia as a great power,[195] and this is due not only to economic, but also political reasons too. Thus, the Kremlin's failure "to denounce Stalin's annexation of the Baltic states and Soviet occupation of eastern Europe, (and justification and even glorification of) the Nazi-Soviet Pact and post-war imposition of Soviet-style regimes in eastern Europe […] is both a symptom and cause of Russia's inability to become a successful and modern major power in the 21st century,"[196] Celeste Wallander argues. In result, both parties not only exchange mutual accusations and deny good intentions of the other, but these perpetual denials are also not always sincere: "Perhaps the West accepts that Russia does not see it as a threat; it is instead the West that perceives Moscow as a threat. And perhaps Russia gets that the West accepts it as an equal; instead, it simply feels itself inferior to the West."[197]

Therefore, Russia's status of a full-fledged member of the 'great power club' is rather a theorem than an axiom. At the most critical points of the post-

191 Roxburgh, *Strong Man*,157.

192 Igor Chubais, "Chto takoe status velikoi derzhavy?" Social Network Maxpart (March 1, 2013), http://maxpark.com/user/2692323399/content/1850500 (as of March 10, 2014).

193 Roxburg, *The Strongman*, 100.

194 *Ibid.*, 219.

195 Celeste Wallander, "An Overview of Bush Administration Policy and Priorities on Russia" (Washington, DC: PONARS Policy Memo No. 187, March 2001).

196 Celeste Wallander, "May 9th and Russia: Past, Present, and Future" (Washington, DC: PONARS Policy Memo No. 366, July 2005).

197 Yulia Nikitina, "Lost in Translation. Is There a Way to Overcome the Different Political Languages of Russia and the West?" (Washington, DC: PONARS Eurasia Policy Memo No. 174, September 2011).

Cold War history, such as the war in Kosovo, Russia had to prove its "future role in European security. Russia's outrage at NATO intervention is due to the exclusion of Russia from its proper role in international security affairs and the breathtaking enhancement of NATO's political and military roles [...] . Russian objections are not to the use of force per se, but to the use of force by NATO"[198] without taking Russia into due account.

"The recognition of Russia as a European power is on the top of Russia's agenda. References to the victory over Nazism reaffirm Russia's image of itself not simply as a great power, but as a great European power," Viatcheslav Morozov opines and then continues: "The official story, reproduced in official statements and school textbooks, holds that Russia has always been a European power that has contributed a great deal to the development of European civilization. The defeat of Nazism—an evil originating in the very heart of Europe—was one of the most decisive contributions establishing Russia as a proud member of the European family of sovereign nations."[199] Yet it is exactly this Russia's role identity that is often explicitly or implicitly denied by Europe that assumes that "Russia can undertake activities that can have destabilizing effects on the international system."[200]

Yet the GPM model, in spite of this perceptional unease, still remains one of the most powerful explanatory tools that can be applicable to Russia's claims of an equal status with its key Western partners. US–Russian 'reset,' as well as mutually recognized (at least verbally) strategic nature of the EU–Russia partnership, leave ample room for re-actualization of the GPM debate, which entails a number of practical policy effects. *First*, the success of GPM lies not simply in *any* sort of security cooperation between Russia, on the one hand, and NATO and EU on the other, be it in Afghanistan, Iran, Libya, or North Korea. To be recognized as a great power, Russia is expected to start integrating in the normative and institutional order crafted for decades by the West. In this context, institutions do matter as far as they enunciate "norms which Russia would either visibly adhere to or visibly violate. Even political institutions which are not terribly constraining, such as the Organization for

198 Celeste Wallender, "Russia, Kosovo, and Security Cooperation" (Washington, DC: PONARS Policy Memo No. 58, April 1999).

199 Viatcheslav Morozov, "On a Collision Course: The EU and Russia Revisit Europe's Recent Past" (Washington, DC: PONARS Eurasia Policy Memo No. 20, August 2008).

200 Deborah Yarsike Ball, "How Kosovo Empowers the Russian Military" (Washington, DC: PONARS Policy Memo No. 61, May 1999).

Security and Cooperation in Europe, increased the reputational and linkage costs to Russia of being the 'holdout' and of violating norms."[201]

Second, the police-type security cooperation between Russia and the West "in effect leaves in place old geopolitical thinking and action. The consequences of this are particularly detrimental in the post-Soviet space where Moscow is trying hard to counterbalance the West—apparently without any clear idea of why this is necessary, let alone how this helps achieve the declared goal of modernization [...] . If nothing is done about this predicament, it is bound to produce yet another confrontation at the next sharp turn on the international political scene. Big political issues, such as democracy, human rights, and the future of the international order, must therefore be returned to the agenda."[202]

Therefore, to counter Astrov's logic, GPM can be conceptualized as a normative project rather than as a value-neutral bargain between key world actors. Of course, normative issues may exert divisive impact on communication between great powers. The hegemony "of the West in claiming the power over the meaning of democracy often leaves this notion completely discredited in" countries such as Russia, China, or Brazil which prefer to see democracy as a joint endeavor of the "entire humanity, in which no one [...] should be excluded in advance from taking part."[203] Yet it is hardly expectable that the political domination in the West and understanding of democracy as externalization of Western norms and practices can in the foreseeable future be supplanted by a Moscow-promoted idea of international democracy as plurality of different power holders, irrespective of the nature of their domestic regimes.

The Case of Russia's Policy in the Libya Crisis

This section analyzes Russia's reaction to the Libyan crisis that is an interesting object of study due to two basic reasons. First, Russia's response to the violent unrests in North Africa in general and in Libya in particular unmasked the multiple imbalances and the lack of uniformity in the Kremlin's attitudes to GPM. Second, the deep perceptional gaps between Russian and

---

201 Celeste Wallander, "International Institutions and Russian Security Cooperation" (Washington, DC: PONARS Policy Memo No. 48, November 1998).

202 Viatcheslav Morozov, "Modernizing Sovereign Democracy? Russian Political Thinking and the Future of the 'Reset' " (Washington, DC: PONARS Eurasia Policy Memo No. 130, 2007).

203 Viatcheslav Morozov, "The Forced Choice between Russia and the West" (Washington, DC: PONARS Policy Memo No. 327, November 2004).

European discourses, resulting from the 'Libyan debate,' re-actualized the long-discussed question of Russia's understanding of—and its role(s) in—the IS-in-the-making.

The ups and downs in the Russian foreign policy mechanism were illustrated by such instances as the discharge of Russian ambassador in Tripoli for his alleged disapproval of the presidential policy of condemning Gaddafi, or the Foreign Ministry officials' criticism of the UN 1973 resolution—which Russia consciously did not veto—as 'hasty.' The tug of war between the Russian President and the Prime Minister on the Libyan issue did not remain unnoticed as well. In spite of Putin's parallels between the military operation against Gaddafi and colonial military invasions, Medvedev at G8 summit in Deauville not only shared the Western policies toward Libya, but also publicly confirmed that by brutally oppressing his own people Gaddafi had delegitimized himself. Medvedev has explicitly made clear that the Arab revolutions were caused by authoritarian rule and mismanagement, and not provoked from the outside. He authorized the ban on visiting Russia for Gaddafi and members of his family, and wrapped Russian business operations in this country. As early as in March 2011, Konstantin Kosachov, at that time the head of the international affairs committee of the State Duma, has explicitly supported the prospects of military operation against Gaddafi, thus making both normative (solidarity with the Western conception of sovereignty as responsibility) and political (support to the coalition forces operation in Libya) points. Later Mikhail Margelov, Presidential envoy to Libya, has solidarized with the prospect of bringing Gaddafi to the Hague Tribunal, and claimed that Russia is ready to open its representative mission in Benghazi, based upon the earlier acceptance of the opposition as a legitimate interlocutor.

It appears that the Medvedev administration wanted to use the crisis in Libya for making another bold step to a GPM type of policy through fostering Russia's pro-Euro-Atlantic agenda. Yet the importance of Medvedev's pro-Western turn should not be overestimated for at least three reasons. First, his sympathies to anti-Gaddafi coalition were not more than a technological move aimed at garnering the Western support for the modernization agenda.

Second, for Medvedev the symbolic part of his engagement with the West was more important than its substance: The key to his 'Libyan' narrative was the alleged 'petition' from the Western leaders who asked Russia to mediate between Gaddafi and the opposition, and by doing so confirmed Russia's indispensability as a key security actor at a GPM-type of arrangement. This explains why it was not until the Deauville summit that Medvedev appointed Margelov his special envoy to Libya. The ostensible symbolism of

Margelov's mission as a diplomatic PR move was manifest in his loud declaration of fast 'breakthrough' in negotiations between Gaddafi and his opponents, followed by a later admission that it would be more correct to speak of 'contacts' between the two sides of the conflict than about 'negotiations.'

Third, Medvedev's good intentions should have been viewed not as a well-thought strategy but rather as a by-product of the growing imbalances in the Russian policy-making system. Some of his pronouncements were implicitly rebuffed by much more critical to the West utterances by then Prime Minister Vladimir Putin, as well as Foreign Minister Sergey Lavrov and Vice Prime Minister Sergey Ivanov. The sudden visit in June 2011 to Tripoli by Kirsan Ilyumzhinov, former Governor of Kalmykia and the President of International Chess Federation, only contributed to the impression of disharmony in Russia's Libya policy. As Ilyumzhinov publicly admitted, he was instructed by the Russian authorities to convince Gaddafi to step down, but instead did his best to turn his visit into a gesture of support to the Libyan dictator. Moreover, in comparing Gaddafi with Dzhokhar Dudaev, a leader of Chechen guerillas killed by the Russian missile, he in fact indirectly equated Moscow's offensive against separatists with the NATO-led operation in Libya.

What lies behind these episodes are not only domestic ruptures (the public disagreements between Medvedev and Putin) or attempts by politically marginal figures to intervene in the situation (the case of Ilyumzhinov), but also a set of much deeper disconnections. The Libyan crisis became a matter of tense domestic debate due to its prospective implications for Russia itself. In fact, the Libyan debate was not that much about Libya itself—it was mostly about Russia and its (re)positioning vis-à-vis the West. In this sense, the debate rendered polarizing effects on Russian political scene, widening the gap between those who wish this country to be part of the West, and those who portray the West as a 'dangerous loser.' For the first time in more than a decade the presidential standpoint did not become the dominating policy platform in Russia, and the entire discourse on Libya turned into a battleground between pro-Gaddafi pronouncements and pro-Western gestures. For one group of Russian opinion-makers the wave of North African revolutions and civil wars was inspired from the outside, while for others these developments incarnate the growing sense of civil activism in non-Western world. Consequently, Gaddafi was portrayed either as a tyrant, or an example of principled and ultimate resistance to the United States-led world order.

The Libyan debate was, therefore, important in terms of understanding and assessing Russia's policy of inclusion in the changing structures of IS. The revolutions in Tunisia, Egypt, Libya, as well as mass-scale protests in

Syria and other countries strengthened the worldwide salience of such normative issues as civil rights, accountability, public participation, on the one hand, and fueled discussions on stability of authoritarian regimes all over the world, on the other. In the EU, the 'Arab spring' became an argument for promoting pro-democracy policies toward its neighbors and reversing the previously tolerant attitudes toward tyrants and autocrats. The political and historical parallels that serve the purpose of fixing the meanings of the dominating European discourse are very much normatively loaded, including comparisons of regime changes in North Africa with Eastern European revolutions of 1989 and even with a series of 1848 revolutions, as well as analogies between Benghazi and Srebrenica as two symbols of brutal government-orchestrated repressions.

References to the experience of the breakdown of Communist regimes in 1989 were part of the Russian discourse as well, yet they only unveiled a deep attitudinal gap between Russia and Europe. If in the West the parallels with the previous waves of antiauthoritarian movements were meant to justify the global prospects for democracy, in Russia they took a rather alarmist form, since all most recent revolutionary changes (from the anti-Communist revolts to the 'Maidan revolution' in Ukraine) are widely perceived as challenging and threatening Russia, rather than opening new perspectives for country's integration into IS. There was indeed not a single case when popular protests abroad were interpreted as being in line with the Russian interests as interpreted by the Kremlin.

Russia, generally speaking, in its reaction to the Libyan civil war was stuck between political incapacitation and anti-Western rhetoric. The issue of internationally coordinated actions taken against dictators seems to be quite sensitive for the Kremlin due to the fact that some of its closest allies and partners belong to the problematic category of undemocratic governments. It explains why in Moscow the 'Arab spring' only strengthened the sovereignty-based and antiliberal type of thinking based on a number of quite telling equivalences. One Russian commentator equated ElBaradei with both Mikhail Gorbachev and academician Andrey Sakharov, two symbols of loyalty to the West—at least, in the eyes of those still nostalgic about the times of USSR. The reactualization of the Soviet memories continues this logic: As a positive example, one of Russian experts referred to the Soviet experience of involvement in Africa—from 1956 when USSR took the side of Egypt against the West till 1986 when USSR, according to Ilyumzhinov's interpretation, prevented the West from bombarding Libya. In a different exercise of drawing parallels, it was Dmitry Medvedev who was compared with Gorbachev in his policy of concessions to the West. As an allegedly ultimate outcome of Russia's policies, a former Russian diplomat fantasized about a 'new Crimean war' of the West against Russia—an imagery that appeals to consolidate national power against potential foreign intruders. Within this explicitly anti-Western reasoning, the anticorruption accusations of people such as the popular blogger Alexei Naval'niy are believed to undermine the stability of regime exactly the same way as the anticorruption invectives were part of the arsenal of opposition forces all across North Africa and the Middle East. Other parallels were meant to substantiate the aggressive nature of the US policies (Serbia–Iraq–Afghanistan–Libya), its pursuance of the 'regime change' philosophy (Georgia–Ukraine–Egypt–Libya) which might have negative effects for Russia's south territories (the alleged North Africa–Middle East–North Caucasus linkage) and Moscow's Central Asian neighbors.

Yet this type of nationalist discourse appears inconsistent in portraying its key object that is the West. On the one hand, the West is believed to lack strategic thinking, and its leaders are miserable. Yet on the other hand, it is this debilitated West that has to be resisted. Paradoxically, those in Russia who blame the United States and the EU in sponsoring the Arab revolutions, at the same time depict the military operation in Libya as aimless, ineffective, and thus unveiling the lack of strategy in the West.

The very fact that the Russian debate is strongly influenced by those who believe in a theory of 'American conspiracy,' unveils Russia's provinciality in the IS. Russian public speakers appear to be much less concerned about the most important issue of Russia's influence in the Arab world than about other questions—whether the 'domino effect' may damage Russia itself, and who exactly will ultimately benefit from the regime changes in progress: the EU, the Islamic radicals, or perhaps China. This passive stand was—paradoxically again—sustained by Putin who later assumed that Russia has no special interests in Syria. Foreign Minister Sergei Lavrov joined him by assuming that Russia is not going to play a key role in mediation in Libya and will incite instead activity of the African Union in this country. This type of neutralist thinking uncovers a lack of Russia's global leadership resources. Not surprisingly, Russia did not make any attempt to start a political dialogue with Germany, a major EU and NATO country to abstain from supporting the UN 'no-fly-zone' resolution. In result, Russia took a mostly symbolic role of 'critical bystander' with no real potential of influencing the situation on the ground. In some sense, Russia's criticism of the effects of Western military operation in Libya was formulated in mostly symbolical categories.

A series of revolutions in Arab countries make us assume that the worldview espoused by proponents of 'radical democracy' approach within critical theory—with their emphasis on the growing segmentation of global social milieu and the appearance of political subjects that are not well-established social groups yet are capable of challenging regimes outside the existing institutional mechanisms—are not that far away from reality. Against this background, it is understandable why states' responses to these changes are rather ambiguous and ambivalent, and not always can be institutionally fixed.

2.5 Procedural Approximation

The model of procedural integration/approximation represents a blend of unitary/solidarist and depoliticized visions of IS, and implies that international actors damp their political discords and adhere to a set of presumably universal—and thus depoliticized—rules and regulations. Procedural convergence can be viewed as one of the effects of global neoliberalism bound to the idea of 'the end of politics' and based on such instruments as privatization, structural adjustment policies, coordination of transnational finance, consumerism, and global media markets. Conceptually, this model implies the recognition of 'one single world' based on a set of behavioral standards, which—if needed—might be sustained by police tools (humanitarian interventions, peace-keeping missions, peace enforcement operations, etc.).

Procedural convergence is grounded in Russia's technical cooperation with the West and adaptation to economic and financial rules, as exemplified by Russia's WTO accession, the Four Common Spaces framework for EU–Russia relations, etc. According to this logic, Russian political elites seek an entry into the Western political order rather than replacing it with one of their own. Market principles in energy sphere and penetration of Russian companies into the Western markets are viewed in Moscow as economic effects of procedural universalization Russia is ready to contribute to. This 'technocratic idealism' presupposes the applicability of universal sets of rules and possible projection of business concepts into policy sphere. This model is more a product of a depoliticized—and thus managerial, technocratic—vision of governance, rather than a set of foundational values. It denounces the idea of Russia's irreducible specificity and particularity for the sake of avoiding politically divisive Self–Other distinctions.

The core element of the procedural integration model is the idea of universality, which transforms into Russia's quest for 'normality,' its inclusion in the IS to be governed by a uniform set of rules. The official discourse of the

Kremlin, to a large extent, might be dubbed both postpolitical, since it often legitimizes itself through references to something presented as obvious ('neutral'/technical knowledge formulated in rational terms). Under this logic, the Kremlin's multiple references to the experiences of the West serve as a tool for discursive depoliticization that is one of power resources of Putinism.

Arguably, Putin's regime can only imitate ideology,[204] and remains deeply technocratic. In the sphere of politics, the idea of sovereign democracy was introduced not as what makes Russia ontologically different from the West, but, contrariwise, what includes Russia to the European tradition of modernity. This appeal to the allegedly universal practices translates into a de facto denial of Russia's specificity: Putin presumes that there is nothing peculiar in the Khodorkovsky affair, in the police dispersion of protest actions, in strong presidential powers, and even in the requirement to register externally sponsored NGOs as 'foreign agents.' By the same token, the Kremlin tends to depoliticize the realist approaches by presenting them as allegedly 'normal' state of affairs and by universalizing them. Therefore, the Kremlin's multiple references to the experiences of the West serve as a tool for discursive depoliticization which is one of the most effective power resources of Putinism.

The construction of this type of IS presupposes that the same set of rules—be it the territorial integrity of states or the right for self-determination—has to be applied in all cases that appear analogous to each other. Putin had admitted that even if members of IS once agree to reverse their normative preferences, this has to be a universal move, applicable to each and every specific case: "if someone of the participants of international communication deems that the principles of international law have to be changed, it appears possible, but without imposing anything to any of the conflicting parties."[205] At a different occasion he mentioned: "even if we intend to put the principle of self-determination [...] above the principle of territorial integrity, this approach has to be of universal character and be applicable in other parts of the world, at least in Europe."[206] Putin's stance is thus a conflation of two broad policy frameworks: depoliticized pragmatism, on the one hand, and global idealism, on the other. Putin and Medvedev seem to believe in the

204 Alexander Yanov, "Istoria odnogo otrechenia: pochemu v Rossii ne budet fashizma," *Forum noveishei vostochnoevropeiskoi istorii i kultury* 2 (2010), http://www1.ku-eichstaett.de/ZIMOS/forum/docs/forumruss14/8Yanov.pdf (as of March 10, 2014).

205 Vladimir Putin, Press conference (May 23, 2007), http://www.kremlin.ru/texts/appears/2007/05/130544.shtml (as of March 10, 2014).

206 Vladimir Putin. Interview with journalist of G8 Countries (June 4, 2007), http://www.kremlin.ru/texts/appears/2007/06/132365.shtml (as of March 10, 2014).

global applicability of international norms that are, however, either undetermined or can be mechanically reversed and then reinterpreted. Paradoxically, even by resorting to a normative discourse, the Kremlin appeared to sustain the very decisionist principle it otherwise rejects as allegedly unacceptable and even menacing to Russia.

In the meantime, Kremlin's technocratic indifference and insensitivity to ideological matters is often grounded in a lack of due consistency and authenticity in the hegemonic narrative. Alexander Bastrykin, the head of the Investigative Committee of Russia's Prosecutor General Office and one of the most loyal members of Putin's team, has openly acknowledged considering some time ago a career in one of European Universities and secured a residence permit in the Czech Republic, but then reconsidered these plans for a lucrative job at the top of the reppressive 'vertical of power.' Vladimir Yakunin, the head of the Russian Railways and a sharp challenger of the Western hegemony, has nevertheless welcomed opening Russian transportation infrastructure to NATO cargo. These examples suggest that Russian postpolitical pragmatism may trump ideological or pseudo-ideologized schemes.

All postpolitical discourses are meant to inscribe Russia in a global world and make it part of the dominating trends. In the meantime, there are different visions of depoliticized strategies for Russia.

One strategy emphasizes the importance of legal norms: "Russia presents no set of alternative norms, but insists on respect for the traditional repertoire of international law, above all the adherence to territorial and governmental sovereignty. Russia constitutes itself not as a separate 'order', but seeks to contribute to the creation of a more genuinely universal society."[207]

Another strategy is based on the effacement of ideology from Russian foreign policy[208] and its subsequent economization. As one study concluded, economic arguments are more compelling in explaining the driving forces of Russian foreign policy than those related to security politics[209] where political articulations appear to play more important roles. According to a Russian Foreign Ministry nonpaper, Russia has to strive for "concrete economic paybacks, including privileged conditions for trade, investment and transit, from

207 Richard Sakwa, "Russia's Identity: Between the 'Domestic' and the 'International,'" *Europe-Asia Studies* 63: 6 (August 2011): 957–975.

208 Dmitry Trenin, "Vneshniaya politika Rossiiskoi Federatsii," in Masha Lipman (ed.), *Povestka dnia novogo prezidentstva* (Moscow: Moscow Carnegie Center, 2012): 9.

209 Marcel Vietor, *Russian Foreign Policy between Security and Economics* (Berlin: Lit Verlag, 2009): 12.

rescuing a number of countries (Armenia, Uzbekistan, Iran, Cuba, Syria, Serbia) from international isolation."[210] In particular, considering the confidential relations between Russia and Armenia, it is believed expedient to use the communicative resources available to Yerevan for obtaining important Western technological information. In the same vein, considering the interest by the Republic of Korea in long-term renting of Russian lands in the Far East, it is advisable to facilitate investments from South Korea to Russia. Along with questionable ideas of "creating a free trade area between Russia and Syria" or "inciting the Philippines business to invest in Russia," other suggestions seem to be quite in tune with the model of Russia as a transnational corporation bereft of strong normative driving forces.

In the meantime, there is a third version of Russian depoliticized discourses, which operationalizes cultural arguments. Postindustrial and postnational concepts of development are said to be based on cultural resources[211] that have to be properly managed. Interreligious relations, migration flows, demographic policies, spatial development, border management—all these spheres possess enormously divisive Self–Other potential which can, nevertheless, be assuaged through social engineering and human development projects. For example, even one of the most ideologized concepts in Russian IR discourse—the proverbial 'Russia world'—can be resignified from a geopolitical concept to a geocultural construct grounded in managing human resources rather than in imposing Russia's political domination.[212]

Within the logic of procedurally integrated IS, the most serious threat to Russia is a "settlement that would exclude Moscow from the mechanisms of decision making on the key issues of international politics."[213] What the Kremlin fears is not a NATO military *attack* but any form of *exclusion* from the mechanisms of security decision-making in Europe. The Kremlin believes

---

210 "Programma effektivnogo ispol'zovanoya na sistemnoi osnove vneshnepoliticheskikh faktorov v tseliakh dolgosrochnogo razvitia Rossiiskoi Federatsii," *Russkiy Newsweek*, May 11, 2010.

211 Sergey Gradirovskiy and Boris Mezhuev, "Postnatsionalniy mir tretiey volny." "Russkiy Arkhipelag" web site, http://www.archipelag.ru/geoeconomics/postindustrial-izm/conception/post/ (as of March 10, 2014).

212 Sergey Gradirovskiy and Boris Mezhuev, "Russkiy mir kak obyekt geokulturnogo proektirovania." Center for Humaniaraian Technologies web site (August 21, 2006), http://gtmarket.ru/laboratory/expertize/2006/64 (as of March 10, 2014).

213 Sergey Rogov, "Security Relations between Russia and the Western World," in Kurt Spillmann and Andreas Wenger (eds.), *Russia's Place in Europe. A Security Debate* (Bern: Peter Lang Publishers, 1999): 177.

that all forms of integration *without* Russia are meant *against* Russia.[214] The feeling of being left outside the security governance is the major source of danger for Russia which sees itself as a fully-fledged European power. What stems from this reasoning is that Russia is not intended to launch a wide-scale Cold War-like confrontation for world domination, but rather seeks to bargain for reserving a niche where Russia would feel comfortable and safe enough. Russia's strategies within this model of IS, thus, reveal its fears of marginalization and isolation.

Moscow's proposal on 'new security architecture in Europe,' announced in 2008, by and large fits with the logic of procedural integration. The crux of the European Security Treaty proposal lies in an attempt to join the hegemonic security community of Euro-Atlantic partnership that NATO and EU consider as already established and functioning. As Pertti Joenniemi rightly assumes, inclusion in such a community requires that the applicants become increasingly 'more like us' and, consequently, is premised on a sense of weness and togetherness. In such a community difference and pluralism are externalized, and Russia is one of those outsiders that is perceived as external to the Western security.[215]

Yet even ideology-free approximation of legal norms can imply tensions between the EU and Russia. The EU–Russia Common Spaces Progress Report of 2012 assessing the state of bilateral relations stated that despite Russia's accession to the WTO, Russian sanitary and phytosanitary measures remain nontransparent, discriminatory, disproportionate, and not in line with international standards. In 2012, Russia introduced a number of new restrictions in the veterinary sector, and imposed a ban on nonbreeding pigs and ruminants for all EU Member States. The EU Report states that Russia continues to create problems when it comes to the inspection, and refuses to withdraw undue requirements for a number of commodities (live animals, dairy products, casings, feed of animal origin, composite products, gelatin) contrary to its WTO commitments. Russia threatens to impose restriction on the nursery products from the EU without a scientific justification, and resists EU- supported attempts to further reinforce the sustainability of fisheries in

214 Igor Maximychev, "Russia's Concept of a New European Security Architecture," in Kurt and Wenger (eds.), *Russia's Place*, 197.

215 Pertti Joenniemi, "Difference within Similarity: Transatlantic Relations as a Community of 'Neighbours' ," in Christopher S. Browning and Marko Lehti (eds.), *The Struggle for the West* (London and New York: Routledge, 2010).

the Antarctic environment. It has resisted defining effective capacity management in exploratory fisheries as well as the proposal to establish Marine Protected Areas.[216]

In the meantime, in some cases Russia does acknowledge international rules for toning down conflicts with the EU. For example, Russian Ambassador to the EU Vladimir Chizov admitted that Russia did violate WTO norms by keeping intact additional duties for imported vehicles, and pledged to redress the situation. He also recognized that the EU might have its legitimate economic interests in countries neighboring to Russia, which can be interpreted as a step toward materializing the concept of common neighbourhood.[217]

2.6 Normative Plurality

The next perspective of multipolar IS imbues to it a normative flavor. Normative aspects of multipolarity—in particular, in its balance-of-power version—were noticeable even in realist literature in at least two aspects. *First*, the resort to domestic analogy can draw parallels between the principle of checks and balances as a key institutional tool for democratic government, on the one hand, and the balancing between competing states that has deterring effects, on the other. *Second*, for many realists, the goals of democracy, along with justice and equality, can be "stabilized only by balance of power among states."[218]

Yet the importance of normative issues in Russian foreign policy goes much farther. Arguably, "the age of hyper-pragmatism in Russian politics is giving way to an active search for a new ideology and new values."[219] Starting with the third presidential term of Vladimir Putin, Russia has been moving to

216 *EU–Russia Common Spaces Progress Report 2012* (March 2013), thttp://eeas.europa.eu/russia/docs/commonspaces_prog_report_2012_en.pdf (as of March 10, 2014).

217 Vladimir Chizhov. Interview informatsionnomu agentstvu ITAR-TASS (17 October 2013), http://www.russianmission.eu/ru/intervyu/intervyu-vachizhova-informatsionnomu-agentstvu-itar-tass-17-oktyabrya-2013-goda (as of 10 March 2014).

218 Philip Cerny, *Rethinking World Politics. A Theory of Transnational Pluralism* (Oxford: Oxford University Press, 2010): 64.

219 Fiodor Lukyanov, "Russian Diplomats Move in to the Real World." "Russia in Global Affairs" web portal (March 1, 2013), http://eng.globalaffairs.ru/redcol/Russian-Diplomats-Mov"e-in-to-the-Real-World-15860 (as of March 10, 2014).

the role of "a global harbinger of conservatism, with its principles of non-intervention,"[220] uncompromised sovereignty and territorial integrity.[221] Russia also tries to internationally raise the issues of equality and justice, as opposed to freedom,[222] and portray itself as a beacon for the oppressed and disenfranchized.[223]

The core of the Russian conservative normativist project is not only to articulate Russia's civilizational distinctiveness, but also to disprove the very necessity of legitimizing Russia's international subjectivity by the association with the Western normative order.[224] In particular, the concept of sovereign democracy was meant to serve this purpose – though with little success.[225] It unmasked the key problem with conservative normativism – its discursive production of relations of enmity to and alienation from the West. The whole semantic of Russian conservative normativity is grounded in a negative portrayal of Western norms of freedom and the rule of law as excessively formal and even "primitive in comparison to the Russian philosophy." In this vein, pragmatism is depicted as a Western ideological concept conducive to state degradation and rampant consumerism allegedly alien to the "Russian tradition."[226]

Conservative authors are prone to strictly divide national-oriented and cosmopolitan discourses, the later being described as manipulative and thus

220 Fiodor Lukyanov, "The Year in Global Politics," *The Moscow News* 79 (December 25, 2012 to January 14, 2013): 16.

221 Boris Mezhuev, "Triada Putina i oppozitsiya," *Nezavisimaya gazeta* (February 26, 2013), http://www.ng.ru/scenario/2013-02-26/15_triada.html (as of March 10, 2014).

222 Ruslan Khestanov, "Rossiya i rezhim globalnogo aparteida," *Otechestvennie Zapiski* 3–4 (2002), http://www.strana-oz.ru/2002/3/rossiya-i-rezhim-globalnogo-aparteida (as of March 10, 2014).

223 Nikolay Spasskiy, "Rossiiskiy vek (nekotorye razmyshlenia o meste Rossii v mire)," *Security Index* 4: 95 (2010): 40.

224 Mikhail Remizov, "Sudba rossiiskogo nasledstva", *Strategicheskiy Zhurnal* 1 (2005): 19.

225 Andrey Kazantsev, "Suverennaya demokratia: struktura i sotsialno-politicheskie funktsii kontseptsii," *Forum noveishei vostochnoevropeiskoi istorii i kultury* 1 (2007), http://www1.ku-eichstaett.de/ZIMOS/forum/inhaltruss7.html (as of March 10, 2014).

226 Nikolay Churinov, "Ideologia pragmatizma," *Natsionalnie prioritety Rossii* (January 2009), http://omskmark.moy.su/publ/national_priorities_of_russia/social_humanitarian_problems/2009_churinov_n_m_ideologija_pragmatizma/38-1-0-279 (as of March 10, 2014).

detrimental to Russia.[227] According to Vadim Tsymburskiy, the stronger Russia becomes, the more likely it would be challenged by the West which is believed to justify its interventionist policies by a geocultural distinction between those included in the civilizational core patronized by the West and those excluded from it. Thus, Russia is viewed as both dysfunctional and alienated actor in the West-dominated IS.[228] As another Russian author puts it: "Russia for too long was relocated to the periphery of the Western civilization, which makes impractical today, with the decline of this civilization, to share responsibility for all sins with it."[229]

It is within a plethora of civilization-based discourses that Europe is portrayed as inherently inimical to Russia and applying a variety of instruments to intentionally marginalize it, including the so-called ecumenical projects, ideas of transborder regionalism and federalism, and even the Paris–Berlin–Moscow axis.[230] In Alexander Dugin's words, the Western descriptions of Russia's history and identity are geopolitically biased and meant to either deconstruct or mock the Russian vision of universality.[231] The alternative is Russia's rapprochement with the East that is seen not as an economically driven but a civilizational and identity-based move which itself predetermines economic relations with Russia's Asian partners.[232]

Some of these attitudes are matched by Russian political discourses. Thus, Russian Foreign Ministry spokesman, commenting on the Western reactions to the "Pussy Riot" trial, claimed that "many in the postmodernist West are oblivious to the Christian roots of Europe, deeming that religion constrains democracy. We assume that the disregard to moral norms shared by

---

227 Andrey Paltsev, "Systemoobrazuyuschie tsennosti Evraziiskoi (Rossiiskoi) tsivilizatsii," *Vlast* 4 (2011): 44–45.

228 Vadim Tsymburskiy, "Eto tvoi posledniy geokulturniy vybor, Rossiya?" "Polis" web portal, http://www.politstudies.ru/universum/esse/7zmb.htm#14 (as of 10 March 2014).

229 Dmitry Efremenko, "Pereizobresti Evropu - perevoobrazit' Rossiu," in *Metod*. Moscow Annual Proceedings of Social Sciences. Issue 1: Alternative Models of Natio-Building (Moscow: Russian Academy of Science and INIO, 2010): 75.

230 Vladimir Shtol, "Rossiya: mnogoobrazie tsivilizatsiy i sobstvennaya tsivilizatsionnaya proyektnost," *Obozrevatel'-Observer* 6 (2011): 17–32.

231 Alexander Dugin, "Evoliutsiya natsionalnoi idei Rusi (Rossii) ," *Otechestvennie Zapiski* 3–4 (2002), http://www.strana-oz.ru/2002/3/evolyuciya-nacionalnoy-ideirusi-rossii (as of March 10, 2014).

232 Yaroslava Zabello *et al.*, "Tsivilizatsionniy vybor Rossii," *Otechestvennie Zapiski* 5: 14 (2003), http://www.strana-oz.ru/2003/5/civilizacionnyy-vybor-rossii (as of March 10, 2014).

all world confessions is detrimental."[233] Referring to the gay propaganda legislation, Foreign Minister Sergey Lavrov mentioned that Russia "has its own moral, religious and historical values."[234]

Yet the conservative articulations of these values look weird and sometimes uncomprehensible. Proponents of Orthodox values as a basis for foreign policy philosophy claim that the concept of national interests in Russia is of metaphysical character[235] and lies in the sphere of religious mysticism (such as spiritual communication with the Trinity) and thus requires no practical formulation.[236] Authors from the government-sponsored Russian Institute for Strategic Studies claim that the "Othodox autocracy was a peculiar form of Russian democracy [...] which made the issues of political and individual freedoms of secondary importance."[237] They portray the West as a 'spiritual aggressor,' a prototype of a 'global concentration camp' which prevents Russia from rediscovering itself in imperial restoration.

Of course, each type of normative discourse can be a matter of debate, as the EU case makes clear. Yet there is one key distinction between the EU and Russia in this respect: In the EU, the debate revolves around the consistency of Brussels in practically implementing the value-based policies of supporting democracy and promoting human rights agenda, while in Russia the very content of these values and the Kremlin's determination to embrace them can be challenged both domestically and internationally.

Unlike in the West, Russian normative approaches are overwhelmingly divisive, presenting a fragmented picture of the world political scenery. In conservative normativity the Other is liberalism and democracy, which leads to selective securitization of the West and, concomitantly, artificial desecuritization of the East, including the disregard for Islamic radicalism as a threat to Russia's security.

---

233 Natalia Romashkova, "V etoi situatsii, nesomnenno, est element konflikta tsivilizatsiy," *Kommersant* (August 22, 2012), http://www.kommersant.ru/doc/2006739 (as of March 10, 2014).

234 *Kyiv Post* (February 26, 2013), http://www.kyivpost.com/content/russia-and-former-soviet-union/russias-foreign-minister-defends-anti-gay-bill-320943.html (as of March 10, 2014).

235 Olga Tserpitskaya, "Formirovanie pravoslavnoi tsivilizatsii," *Obozrevatel'- Observer* 5 (2011): 73–78.

236 Olga Tserpitskaya, "Formirovanie v Rossii natsionalnoi idei," *Obozrevatel'-Observer* 7 (2011): 60.

237 Piotr Multatuli and Leonid Reshetnikov, "Rossiya! Vstan y vozvyshaisia!" *Problemy natsionalnoi strategii* 2: 11 (2012), http://www.riss.ru/upload/tfi/138/05_Мультатули,%20Решетников.pdf (as of March 10, 2014).

Academic narratives seem to provide a more fertile ground for articulating conservative messages—for example, in assessing the rise of Russian extreme nationalism as fascism, or in using the Weimer Republic metaphor for characterizing the current Russia's statehood.[238] Official discourse seeks to instrumentalize the conservative ideas for providing ideological basis for its Eurasian Union project and concomitant alienation from the West. In the meantime, the most politicized versions of Eurasianism (such as the 'Orthodox communism' with its global mission) are more universalist than governmental discourses that are rather cautious about going public with Russia's global ambitions.

From a structural perspective, what makes the normative plurality model peculiar is that the pursuance of normative behavior provokes two types of conflicts. *First*, there might be structural conflicts between different constitutive principles of international law—such as, for instance, that ones of territorial integrity and the right for self-determination. The Kosovo situation, as well as Russia's policies toward South Ossetia and Abkhazia, had sharpened collision between these two norms, making governments to choose one over another.

Second, international agents themselves may provoke contests between norms through infusing different meanings in them. One possible example is conflicting interpretations of the energy security concept. For user countries in Europe, energy security is connected with better access to Russia's energy resources through working with 'Gazprom' and other large companies. European countries define energy security as providing acceptable (that is stable and reasonable) prices for oil, gas, and their possible equivalents, derived from reliable and diversified sources. There are two main threats to security from this point of view: high prices for energy and instability of supply. In other words, energy security is a means of creating regulatory regimes that would lower the risks of unexpected price changes, and provide at the same time an appropriate level of openness in the markets. Yet for transit countries, energy security is about controlling the transportation process and receiving rent for it. In the opinion of Lithuanian specialists, for their country "the transit of gas to Kaliningrad is a source of revenue and creates a sense of security. Losing the position of transit state will make Lithuania more vulnerable to

---

238 Mikhail Sokolov, "Izobretaya russkiy fashizm: neskolko kriticheskikh zamechaniy o diskussii 90 godov," *Forum noveishei vostochnoevropeiiskoi istorii i kultury* 2 (2010), http://www1.ku-eichstaett.de/ZIMOS/forum/docs/forumruss14/9SokolovIzob.pdf (as of March 10, 2014).

Russian politics."[239] For Russia as an exporter country the main source of danger is dependence on transit across territories of countries whose political elites are Russia-skeptic. In addition, Russian understanding of energy security encompasses maximizing capitalization of petroleum resources, and using them for promoting Russian economic interests in Europe.

Encounters of Russian and European democracy discourses represent another interesting example of identity-based normative conflicts of interpretation. Two issues are worthwhile to note at this juncture. *First*, many Russian authors speak of a "democratic deficit" in the EU.[240] This argument is apparently borrowed from European discourses and very often merges with political logic of a group of scholars associated with the Institute for Democracy and Cooperation,[241] a misnomer for the Kremlin-sponsored propagandistic institution settled in Paris and New York as presumably the Russian version of Western foundations working in Russia.

Second, some Russian scholars project the concept of democracy to the whole international area. It is within this context that the concept of 'democratic multipolarity' was coined to claim that the idea of democracy, being transferred from the domestic to the international domain, is denotative of a plurality of interests, whatever their nature might be. Democracy here may be understood as a redistribution of power between the leading nations and the developing ones, or those representing the 'middle layer' of international system. Yet this predominantly realist vision of multipolar IS does not resonate in Europe because of the underestimation of institutional and normative mechanisms, which turns the concept of 'democratic multipolarity' into an image of international scene consisting of loosely tied groups of countries whose members share with each other no more than power ambitions.

One may see here some kind of conceptual transfer: The democracy discourse shifted from domestic to the international level of analysis. This shift reduced all semantic contexts of democracy to the legalist (and politically debatable) principle of sovereign equality, as engrained in Russia's interpretation of the idea of multipolarity.

Russia's 'normative offensive' with the issue of 'international democracy' at its core is certainly an explicitly ideological move, since it requires a tacit

239 Tomas Janeliunas and Arunas Molis, "The NEGP Ends Lithuania's Hopes of Becoming a Transit Country," *Baltic Mosaic* 1: 5 (2006): 30.

240 Timofei Bordachov, *Predely evropiezatsii* (Moscow: Higher School of Economics Publishers, 2007): 162–163.

241 http://www.indemco.org/ (as of March 10, 2014)

acknowledgment of allegedly undemocratic nature of the West, and its dethroning from the global normative pedestal. In his 'Munich speech,' President Putin lambasted the American concept of unipolar world as presumed upon "one single center of power," a situation that, arguably, "has nothing to do with democracy." Sergei Lavrov went as far as to promote Russia as "a territory of freedom" in IS due to its resolution to openly raise a set of issues that earlier were either ignored or silenced. All this made a group of Russian authors believe that Russia and the West are in a state of normative contest over the concept of democracy[242]—a situation that politically reactualizes the legacy of the Cold War ideological competition, yet academically can be explicated in more neutral categories of a conflict between pluralist and solidarist versions of IS.

Experimentally exploring the democratic potential of international pluralism as embodied in the concept of multipolarity, Russian leaders project the language traditionally suited for domestic purposes onto the domain of international politics. In doing so, they imply that it is multipolarity that fosters the development of democratic institutions in international arena; in other words, *all* types of multipolarity are believed to be equivalent to international democracy. In this reading, democracy appears to be void of political meanings and reduced to the mere multiplicity of sovereign states, regardless of the internal nature of their political regimes. Not incidentally, Russia recourses to the 'democratic multipolarity' rhetoric basically in communication with countries such as China, Belarus, Iran, Venezuela, India, Cuba, and others, with most of them lacking a convincing record of domestic democratic rule. 'Democratic multipolarity,' understood as a simple redistribution of the 'world power' among several poles of force, makes the issues of liberty, free competition, and other core elements of democracy either irrelevant or equally acceptable along with authoritarianism, totalitarianism, nonmarket economy, etc.[243]

Yet the explanation of international democracy through the concept of multipolarity can be questioned by Russia's employment of democratic rhetoric in quite a different context. Thus, according to the 2008 Foreign Policy Concept of Russia, Russia's policy goal in Europe is not any type of order but a "genuinely open and democratic system of collective security."[244] This statement means that not only pluralism, but solidarism as well can, in the

---

242 Valerian Lebedev and Valeriy Kireev, "Demokratii bez suvereniteta ne suschestvuet," *Svobodnaya mysl'* 9: 1592 (2008): 67–72.

243 Yuri Fiodorov, "Kriticheskiy vyzov dlia Rossii," *Pro et Contra* 4: 4 (Autumn 1999): 21.

244 http://www.mid.ru/ns-osndoc.nsf/0e9272befa34209743256c630042d1aa/d48737161a0bc944c32574870048d8f7?OpenDocument (as of March 10, 2014)

Russian eyes, be democratic, provided that it serves Russian interests of being accepted as a power equal to its Western partners. Therefore, Russia tends to utilize the normative conception of international democracy in ostensibly pragmatic way, as an operational tool to increase its normative power.

The process of re-conceptualizing democracy as key normative concept explains why Russian discourse is often bereft of consistency. On the one hand, Russia is certainly eager to be recognized as a 'normal country' that fits European standards of democracy and sovereignty; yet on the other, it repeatedly relies on the rhetoric of exceptionalism, recalling its alleged specificity and thus hoping to get preferential treatment from Europe. Nevertheless, Russia's intention to be recognized in Europe as an equal partner in norm-setting is not to be understood as an indication of Russia's possession of its 'own' norms that Europe, arguably, either rejects or disregards. Russia seems to be ready to offer an alternative reading of a set of norms constitutive to European identity, but definitely not to substitute them with some kind of Russia-only norms or values.

Russia's normativity is deficient in one more sense – it hardly gives any institutionally integrative effects. Russia's policy of ostracizing Estonia for its ('un-European', in the Kremlin's eyes) decision to remove the Bronze Soldier monument from Tallinn downtown to a military cemetery resonated neither in Europe, nor even in Russia's 'near abroad.' Russia's attempts to condition its relations with post-Soviet (and some postsocialist) countries by their adherence to the Soviet/Russian glorious narrative of the Second World War were ultimately overweighed by more pragmatic economic considerations. Ultimately Russia had to recognize the meaningful role of Poland—otherwise associated with 'false Europe'—in finding visa facilitation solution for the residents of the Kaliningrad *oblast*. These and other examples suggest that the accentuation of Russia's normative positions does not trigger a closer association with either the EU or the common neighborhood countries.

2.7 Normative Convergence

According to this scenario, Russia would gradually accept the basic principle of EU's normative order and integrate into it. In fact, normative convergence is a crucial tool in Russia's attempts to be recognized as an indispensable member of EU-centric IS.[245] Each of the most controversial concepts intro-

245 Dmitrii Trenin, "Integratsiya i identichnost: Rossiya kak noviy Zapad" (Moscow: Evropa Publishers, 2006): 206.

duced in Russia—from measures of economic protectionism to the increasing intervention of the state to the organization of political parties—almost inevitably contains explicit references to a 'European experience.'

Thus, Russia accepted—though reluctantly—the legitimacy of HS discourse because of the awareness that it is precisely through normative lenses that European countries define 'the civilized humankind.' Russia's partaking in the Council of Europe has significantly helped improve its prison system; likewise, launching initial public offerings on European stock exchanges has strengthened Russian corporate governance, social responsibility, and treatment of minority shareholders.[246]

There are a number of documents—both Russian, European, and signed by the two parties—that describe the key premises of the normative convergence scenario:

246 Igor Ivanov, "Need for Europe-Russia Institutional Integration," *Gulf News* (25 November, 2012), http://gulfnews.com/opinions/columnists/need-for-europe-russia-institutional-integration-1.1109828 (as of March 10, 2014).

Four Spaces (4Ss)	***National Indicative Program (NIP) 2002–2003, Russian Federation***[247]	***Wider Europe–Neighborhood (WEN)***[248]	***New Neighborhood Instrument (NNI)***[249]	***European Neighborhood Policy (ENP)***[250]
Economic Space (EcS)	The implementation of the Partnership and Cooperation Agreement (PCA), Common Strategy, and the Northern Dimension (ND)	Extension of the internal market and regulatory structures	Promoting sustainable economic and social development in the border areas	Commitment to shared values
The Space of Freedom, Security, and Justice (FSJ)	Trade and economic relations	Preferential trading relations and market opening	Environment, public health, and fight against organized crime	A more effective political dialogue
External Security Space (ExS)	Political and security issues	Perspectives for lawful migration and movement of persons	Ensuring efficient and secure borders	Economic and social development policy
The Space of Research, Education, and Culture (REC)	Nuclear safety	Cooperation to prevent and combat common security threats	Promoting local, 'people-to-people' type of actions	Trade and internal market
		Conflict prevention and crisis management		Justice and Home Affairs
		Promotion of human rights, and cultural cooperation		Connecting the neighborhood
		Integration of transport, energy, and telecommunication networks		People-to-people programs
		Investment promotion and protection		

First, this table demonstrates different ways that the EU and Russia explored for attaining the goal of normative convergence. For example, within the framework of the NNI, environment and organized crime are pooled together, while in the 4Ss concept they are attributed to different 'spaces.' In "Country

Strategy Paper 2002–2006" security was coupled with 'political issues,' which differs from the approach developed within the 4Ss framework. In WEN, economic and security issues are divided into three separate groups—a fragmentation that was never replicated in other documents.

Second, many elements of the 4Ss overlap. Here are the most noticeable examples:

- the issues of transborder cooperation are mentioned in both EcS and FSJ;
- the information society is part of REC, EcS, and—reportedly—ExS;
- transparency issues are discussed within the frameworks of both EcS and FSJ;
- economic matters (business, entrepreneurship, labor market, etc.) are deployed in both EcS and REC;
- the media are included into both FSJ and REC;
- parts of security-related problems (such as safety of transportation) are attributed to EcS;
- the movement of people is split between REC and FSJ.

Third, security concept is divided between domestic (named merely 'security') and external. This distinction, however, is blurred by the fact that a number of key issues—such as terrorism, minority protection, or discrimination of ethnic groups—are simultaneously mentioned in the two security-related 'spaces' (ExS and FSJ).

The triad 'Freedom–Security–Justice' is also open to different interpretations. One of them is based on the idea of desecuritization: This semantic triangle could be viewed as a means for subordinating security to the values of freedom and justice, instead of deploying it within a political framework as

---

247 *Country Strategy Paper 2002–2006*, NIP 2002–2003, Russian Federation (December 27, 2001).

248 *Wider Europe–Neighborhood: A New Framework for Relations with our Eastern and Southern Neighbours*. Communication from the Commission to the Council and the European Parliament. Commission of the European Communities, COM(2003) 104 final (Brussels, March 11, 2003).

249 *Paving the Way for a New Neighbourhood Instrument*. Communication from the Commission. Commission of the European Communities, COM(2003) 393 final (Brussels, July 1, 2003).

250 *European Neighborhood Policy*. Strategic Paper. Communication from the Commission. Commission of the European Communities, COM(2004) 373 final (Brussels, May 12, 2004).

it was the case earlier.[251] This move could be in tune with Ian Manner's formulae "desecuritization through democracy," "desecuritization through governance," "desecuritization through integration," and "desecuritization through normalization."[252] Yet there could be, in the meantime, a second reading: This 'space' is meant to produce a justice-based security order fostering—in a long run—freedom. In this interpretation, the whole triad may look like a response to those who blame the EU Member States in sacrificing democratic freedoms for the sake of greater security. Finally, a third interpretation places security in-between freedom and justice, or between promoting/fostering the variety of communicative flows and controlling/constraining them. Therefore, security could be regarded as a key notion reconciling the two opposing approaches to a variety of social and economic exchanges and interactions, as a compromising result of intersection between the imperatives of freedom and justice.

2.8 Multiregionalism: A World without Hegemons?

The idea of multiregionalism rests upon plurality of regional orders, or international societies built around regional spheres or clusters. Close to this model is an English school-promoted idea of "regional states-systems or regional international societies," or "many worlds of different regionalism."[253]

In Russia, there are voices that support the idea of multiregionalism as a form of multipolarity,[254] basically coming from liberal segments of Russian academic discourse. Having borrowed most of the Western concepts of region-building, Russian liberal experts adopt many of them for inscribing Russian subnational units into the existing models of transborder regionalization. Most of the writings in this domain focus on the Baltic Sea region (with such widely covered cases as St. Petersburg[255] and Kaliningrad) as a Russian–

---

251 *Common Strategy of the European Union of June 4 1999 on Russia* (1999/414/CFSP), *Official Journal of the European Communities* (June 2, 1999).

252 Ian Manners, *European (Security) Union: From Existential Threat to Ontological Security* (Copenhagen Peace Research Institute, COPRI Working Papers 5/2002): 25–27.

253 Andrew Hurrell, "One World? Many Worlds? The Place of Regions in the Study of International Society," *International Affairs* 83: 1 (2007): 128.

254 Yurii Tzarikaev, "Sovremenniy regionalism i mirovaya politika," *Obozrevatel'-Observer* 3: 242 (2010).

255 See for example: Svetlana Boym, "Leningrad into St. Petersburg: The Dream of Europe on the Margin," in Bo Strath (ed.), *Europe and the Other, and Europe as the Other* (Brussels: Peter Lang, 2010): 311–324.

European communicative interface. Another conceptualization of regionalism relates it to a variety of Russia's linkages with the European North[256] and/or Finno-Ugrian 'world.'[257] Other cross-border regions (the Black Sea and the Caspian Sea regions, the Caucasus and Central Asia) are overwhelmingly covered in Russia from the viewpoint of more realist power balances and competing coalition building.

Multiregionalism, as understood by Barry Buzan and Ole Waever, may be best realizable in the absence of superpowers, which seems to correspond to Russia's vision of IS. It is symptomatic that multipolarity discourse in Russia includes explicit references to the idea of "regionalization of global politics,"[258] which has two meanings within this context. On the one hand, it denotes "a search for regional solutions for conflicts and crises," which implies the avoidance of possible interventions by external powers, among which NATO in general and the United States in particular seem to be the most annoying for the Kremlin. On the other hand, regionalization, in Sergei Lavrov's eyes, could serve as an insurance mechanism to prevent a possible fragmentation of IS as a result of 'deglobalization,' or a reversal of the global momentum. It is through the prism of these two arguments that the conceptual linkage between multipolarity and multiregionality might be traced.

As far as the 'search for regional solutions' is concerned, the Russian stance here appears to be consonant with the idea of regional security complexes (RSCs) introduced by Buzan and Waever. At the center of their theory is a variety of 'security regions' as international subsystems where most of security interactions are internal. "Superpowers by definition largely transcend the logic of geography and adjacency in their security relationships,"[259] they claim. Against this background, RSCs are conceptualized as barriers that prevent superpowers from intervening in security situations at regional level; they are defined as groups of state actors whose processes of securitization and desecuritization are so interlinked that their security practices cannot be analyzed or resolved apart from one another,[260] and do not necessitate projection of external force(s). Therefore, the differences between the

256 Yuriy Shabaev, "Buntuyuschaya etnichnost na Evropeiskom Severe Rossii," *Obschestvennie nauki i sovremennost* 3 (2006): 63-70.

257 Yuriy Shabaev *et al.*, "Finno-ugorskii mir: mif, makroidentichnost, politicheskiy proekt?" *Obschestvennie nauki i sovremennost* 1 (2010): 147–155.

258 Sergei Lavrov, "Mezhdunarodnie otnoshenia v novoi systeme koordinat," *Rossiyskaya gazeta* (October 8, 2009).

259 Barry Buzan and Ole Waever, *Regions and Powers. The Structure of International Security* (Cambridge: Cambridge University Press, 2006): 46.

260 *Ibid.*, 44.

inside and the outside appear to play a key role in the conceptualization of this type of regionalism. This by and large explains why Russia is quite sympathetic with those prospects of regionalism in the EU–Russia common neighborhood that, in the Kremlin's eyes, ought to be decided among local states without external influence.

The second argument introduced by Lavrov also might be dealt with from the theoretical perspective grounded in the English school that treats regionalization as an "approach to world order" presupposing a reorganization of world politics along regional lines. For Hedley Bull, regionalism is a middle ground between states and global organizations. On the one hand, regional organizations are able to fulfill at least some of the functions envisaged for global governance bodies; on the other, they can avoid some of the accusations against global organizations (inclination to establish relations of domination and power projection, etc.). Bull argues that regional organizations may contribute to a more peaceful world order because they defy the concentration of power in the hands of superpowers, encourage small states to strengthen their potential through pooling resources; contribute to lower the dangers of sovereignty-based system by creating institutions beyond states; reduce incentives for wars through webs of interdependence, and tend to insulate regions from dangers of global conflicts.

The concept of multiregionalism in both readings—as a possibility for local crisis management and an insurance against a Hobbesian world—seems to be quite ambiguous. Being one of the possible versions/interpretations of multipolarity, it by the same token questions Russia's exclusive sphere of influence in the common neighborhood. Instead of substantiating a Kremlin-protected 'area of vital interest' that serves as one of the proofs for Russia's status of a major international pole, the multiregionality perspective decomposes the post-Soviet space into several regions that are more effects of EU's enlargement and its neighborhood policy than of Russia's deliberate strategy. Hence, it is through the prism of multiregionalism that the concept(ion) of an allegedly unified post-Soviet space can be deconstructed, and policy gap between Russia and Europe identified. Indeed, the 'mental maps' of Europe's margins are seen quite differently from Moscow and Brussels. The EU deliberately invests its resources and efforts in region-building for both pluralizing Europe's regional scene and making it more adaptable and sensitive to Europeanization. Russia finds itself under a strong influence of this type of policy and wishes to take practical advantage of EU-sponsored regional projects, yet in the meantime often resorts to discursive othering of—

and therefore distancing from—regional groupings which the Kremlin perceives as alien to Russia, and allegedly orchestrated by Western powers. Russia sees no much avail for itself in adapting to the experiences of EU-sponsored regionalist initiatives in the Baltic and Black Sea regions, as well as the Mediterranean.

This raises an important question of whether the idea of region-making as a protection against 'extra-regional forces' can be universally applicable and productive. Even in those cases—such as the Caspian region—where this approach comes into prominence, there are multiple external (including nonstate) actors such as major oil and gas companies playing their major roles and opening up regions to global trends. The RSC-based vision of multiregionalism seems consonant with the so-called 'close regionalism,' which is "aimed at defending region from the negative effects of globalization"[261] and spells an "autarkic policy of reliance upon local forces,"[262] a strategy that is directly challenged by the philosophy of more inclusive and amalgamated projects such as the Kremlin's proposals on common security arrangements in all Euro-Atlantic region.

In the areas of EU–Russia neighborhoods multiregionalism takes different forms, yet unfortunately most of them are either competitive or conflictual rather than cooperative. In the ***Baltic Sea,*** Russia usually prefers to keep a low profile. Moscow had at the outset perceived the Baltic Sea as an EU-sponsored project. Russian caution and skepticism boiled down to the effects of EU enlargement that "may unfortunately add to Russia's relative political isolation."[263] Of course, Moscow was keen to participate in those region-building projects that have material background, but never took political initiative, thus challenging the anticipations of those (mostly Nordic) European experts who expected that the Baltic Sea regionalism, along with initiatives such as the ND, could eventually incite Russia to take a more integration-friendly stand.

The ***Black Sea region*** can be viewed as a combination of nascent collective security mechanisms and balance of power approaches. Both bilateral

261 Mikhail Deliagin, "Puti Rossii v odnopoliarnom mire," in Mikhail Ilyin and Vladislav Inozemtsev (eds.), *Megatrendy mirovogo razvitiya* (Moscow: Ekonomika Publishers, 2001).

262 Vasily Mikheev, "Logika globalizatsii i interesy Rossii," *Pro et Contra* 4: 4 (Autumn 1999): 56.

263 Arkady Moshes, "EU Enlargement in the Baltic Sea Region and Russia: Obvious Problems, Unclear Solutions" (Washington, DC: PONARS Policy Memo No. 171, October 2000).

and multilateral communications seem to be feasible here.[264] Yet, despite a variety of scenarios, under current circumstances a balance of power system is more likely than other options, as exemplified by the US policies of balancing both of the non-Western potential hegemons in this region, Russia and Turkey. The resilience of the balance-of-power approach can be explained by the assumption that "not only are multilateral institutions absent or largely ineffective, critical bilateral relations are also in disarray [...] . [Yet] the convergence of short-term interests between the United States and the Black Sea littoral states for promoting regional stability may compensate for the absence of institutional structures and immediate economic incentives."[265] Russian policy in this region is equally "based on principles of *realpolitik*, and clearly geo-economically and geopolitically motivated."[266]

The Black Sea region vindicates that global/macrostructural concepts—such as balance of power, collective security, multipolarity, etc.—can be projected to the regional level, making regional actors relatively unprotected against this overlay. There are policy implications of this trend. Thus, for example, the Obama administration is believed to set aside 'regional balancing approach' for the sake of 'resetting' its bilateral relations with Moscow at the expense of Washington's engagement with Russia's pro-Western neighbors, including Ukraine.[267] This is a good testimony to the dependence of the regional setting on the constellation of external forces, which, in the meantime, can be considered as a proof for the Black Sea region's incorporation in a global world.

The ***Caspian Sea*** is an example of even less institutionalized and more conflictual regional formation that is also subjected to multiple external overlays. Again, the logic of power balancing seems to play the pivotal role here: "U.S. and Western companies in the region are searching for ways to limit or contain Russian influence."[268] Yet this logic may bring opposite results pushing "Russia and Iran together to obstruct developments in Caspian Sea oil

264 Volodymyr Dubovyk, "The Role of the United States in the Black Sea Region" (Washington, DC: PONARS Policy Memo No. 298, November 2003).

265 George Khelashvili, "Towards a Strategic Respite in the Black Sea Area," (Washington, DC: PONARS Eurasia Policy Memo No. 42, December 2008).

266 Irina Kobrinskaya, "The Black Sea Region in Russia's Current Foreign Policy Paradigm" (Washington, DC: PONARS Eurasia Policy Memo No. 41, December 2008).

267 Volodymyr Dubovyk, "Kyiv and Tbilisi: No Longer Washington's Favorites?" (Washington, DC: PONARS Eurasia Policy Memo No. 93, March 2010).

268 Douglas Blum, "The Russian-Georgian Crisis and Baku-Tbilisi-Ceyhan" (Washington, DC: PONARS Policy Memo No. 252, October 2002).

that favor US companies."[269] That is why the combination of balancing and containment does not seem to be conducive to promote regional integration that necessitates a more pronounced multipolar and inclusive approach to engage both Russia and Iran.[270]

As far as ***Central Asia*** is concerned, there are at least three possible ways to conceptualize this region. The first is to maintain the narrow definition of Central Asia as comprising Kazakhstan, Kyrgyzstan, Tajikistan, Turkmenistan, and Uzbekistan, identifying themselves apart from both the former Soviet Union and the Islamic world.[271] A second possibility is to add to the region the territories of Afghanistan and Xinjiang. A third possibility is to redefine Central Asia as a regional economic trading bloc, thus shifting emphasis to its economic potential and geo-physical realities. In this case, the region has to include the Aral and the Caspian Seas, as well as Iran and Azerbaijan. "Most importantly, there are several natural trade routes between Central Asia, broadly conceived, and China, Europe, Russia, South Asia, and the Middle East. [This vision] approaches the re-conceptualization of Central Asia as a fluid and evolving, rather than a fixed, process and therefore allows a range of future possibilities rather than locking the Central Asian states into a particular path of development."[272]

The key problem with the Central Asian regionalism is that both Russia and the West "tend to look at Central Asia through their global or quasi-global prism [...] . Thus, Moscow willingly accepts the Central Asian states' perception of threats as largely externally driven, because it wants to remain the principal arbiter in the region, and does not have a recipe to resolve the domestic problems [...] . In addition, Moscow has fallen victim to its own [false] explanation of the developments in Chechnya and the North Caucasus in general as being the work of a secretive international network of Islamic extremists. Typically, Russian geopoliticians continue to see the Central Asian states as objects rather than subjects of international relations."[273] Therefore, Central Asia is important for Moscow not as a region of its own, but rather as

269 Douglas Blum, "Russia's Caspian Policy under Primakov" (Washington, DC: PONARS Policy Memo No. 53, November 1998).

270 Fiona Hill, "Russia's International Integration and Caspian Sea Oil" (Washington, DC: PONARS Policy Memo No. 9, October 1997).

271 Pauline Jones Luong, "In Its Own Image: Toward a Re-conceptualization of Central Asia" (Washington DC: PONARS Policy Memo No. 21, October 1997).

272 *Ibid.*

273 Dmitri Trenin, "Central Asia's Stability and Russia's Security" (Washington DC: PONARS Policy Memo No. 168, November 2000).

a "lever to strengthen its position in the Euro-Atlantic framework in which Russia seeks to assert itself as an equal partner."[274]

There is one important policy implication of this variety of views on regionalism. As seen from some of the regional actors' perspective, Russia's policies in regions such as the Black Sea are meant to install their mechanisms sustaining Russia's supremacy, which is indispensable, in Moscow's eyes, for successful implementation of the multipolarity prospects. Yet Russia's 'multipolar world'—enforced through the Georgian war, as the Kremlin deems—may pose a threat to countries such as Ukraine, since, practically speaking, it means the sum of regional 'unipolarities,' based on the dominant power of 'regional leaders' and accepted by other major powers. As seen from Russia's 'near abroad,' a "multipolar world consists of regional 'unipolar worlds' where domination by a regional leader is stronger than a theoretical dominance of a global power in a unipolar world. In extrapolation to Russia's neighbors, the substance of the multipolar world is a de facto limited sovereignty."[275] Seen from this vantage point, the more Russia pushes its vision of multipolarity as a type of global order Moscow is going to basically discuss with either EU and NATO or within the BRICS framework, the more disadvantageous Russian neighbors feel and the stronger their resistance to Russian plans is.

2.9 Poles as Civilizations

In the West civilizational analysis is, by and large, a paradigm rooted in academic expertise and focused on studying plurality of cultural identities, and multiplicity of social experiences and their interconnections. Civilizational analysis contextualizes political institutions by placing them within specific cultural frameworks and explaining multiple dependencies of policy actions from those civilizational contexts.[276]

At some points, Russian reading of civilizational discourse seems quite agreeable with its Western analogs. One example is Dmitry Medvedev's reference to the EU, the United States, and Russia as three branches of the

274 Irina Kobrinskaya, "Is There a Chance for Constructive Cooperation in the CIS?" (Washington, DC: PONARS Eurasia Policy Memo No. 68, September 2009).

275 Olexander Sushko, "Alternative Approaches to Black Sea Regional Security: A Ukrainian Perspective" (Washington DC: PONARS Policy Memo No. 45, December 2008).

276 Johann P. Arnason, "Domains and Perspectives of Civilizational Analysis," *European Journal of Social Theory* 13: 1 (2010): 5–13.

European civilization destined to closely cooperate with each other.[277] Yet from the structural perspective, it takes both the unity of the wider European civilization and compatibility of its different territorial parts (perhaps, as remote as Russia's Far East) almost for granted, as a matter of social reality. This discourse consists neither in developing policies for joining European institutions nor in taking commitments toward Europeanization prospects, but rather in making the West accept Russia's historical belongingness to the presumably common European civilization.[278]

However, as soon as it comes to the strategy level, civilizational discourse turns into a century-long exercise of Russia's identity-making that necessitates a Self–Other delineation with the presumably alien West.[279] Many Russian scholars argue that multipolarity can be successful only being based upon civilizational background[280] and deem that Russia is in possession of its own cultural profile in the world, quite distinct from the West. According to their logic, each of the centers of power in the world can be viewed as a peculiar civilization, including the United States, China, Russia, and India. Thus, the belongingness to civilization becomes one of the key criteria for sovereignty and a justification for Russia's expansion of its spheres of interest. A distinctive from Europe civilizational status is regarded as a possibility for Russia to achieve equality with Europe, while the idea of Russia's belongingness to the common European civilization is believed to be an equivalent to the voluntary acceptance of Russia's backwardness vis-à-vis its more developed Western neighbors. In the meantime, what is metaphorically dubbed 'civilizational immunity' "prevents from implanting to Russia alien to national organism models of democracy."[281]

Seen from this angle, civilizational version of conservative normativity seems to be a cultural argument for the idea of multipolarity. In a politically correct way it can be formulated as a *dialogue of civilizations*, yet in fact it

---

277 Dmitry Medvedev's speech in Berlin (June 5, 2008), http://www.intelros.ru/strategy/gos_rf/prezident_rf/2351-vystuplenie-dmitrija-medvedeva-na.html. (as of March 10, 2014).

278 Vadim Mezhuev, "Iskat' obschiy put' k miru chelovecheskogo edinstva," *Synergia* 7: 16 (2009). http://www.intelros.ru/pdf/synergia_16_09/04.pdf (as of March 10, 2014).

279 Andrei Tsygankov, "Self and Other in International Relations Theory: Learning from Russian Civilizational Debates," *International Studies Review* 10 (2008): 762–775.

280 Boris Martynov, "Mnogopoliarniy ili mnogotsivilizatsionniy mir?" *International Trends. Journal of International Relations Theory and World Politics* 10: 8 (2009): 4.

281 Olga Leonova. Rossiya i mir v XXI veke, *Synergia*, 4 (2010), http://www.intelros.ru/pdf/sinergiya/4_2010/3.pdf (as of March 10, 2014).

more often betrays *"civilizational nationalism."*[282] The idea of Russia as a "state-civilization," first articulated by Russian nationalist thinkers (such as Mikhail Remizov), ultimately became an element of the Kremlin narrative. In spite of its explicitly utopian nature, the idea of civilization is politically welcome due to its expansionist and potentially imperial character.

It is within a plethora of civilization-based discourses that Europe is portrayed as inherently inimical to Russia and applying a variety of instruments to intentionally marginalize it. However, there are substantial structural problems with the perception of this type of civilizational discourses in the EU. First, many European experts claim that appeals to equality and mutuality[283] in international relations often hide demands for impunity. Russia unsuccessfully tries to convince Europe to accept it as it is, without deep domestic transformations. The reluctance of the EU to do so is due to the normative core of the European liberal order that cannot equalize democracy and autocracy, good governance and corruptive economy, etc.

Second, Russia has huge problems with international acceptance of the normative role it intends to play. Russia's traditionalist articulations of such issues as family values, Christianity, or sovereignty[284] get very limited resonance in the world, even beyond the West. The numerous identity cleavages and historical debates within Russia are illustrative of how fuzzy and unstable Russian traditions are; by the same token, Russia's supremacy in Europe in terms of quantity of divorces and abortions makes the Kremlin's moral appeal doomed to failure.[285]

It is worthwhile noting that civilization-based arguments may be politically used for substantiating arguments that are in a conflict with the Russian worldview. For instance, it may become a discursive tool justifying skeptical attitudes to the 'post-Soviet' integration from the part of non-Slavic countries of which Georgia is a good example. The Baltic States refer to Huntington's

282 Alexander Verkhovski and Emil Payn. "Tsivilizatsionniy natsionalizm: rossiiskaya versiya osobogo puti," in Emil Payn (ed.), *Ideologiya osobogo puti v Rossii i Germanii* (Moscow: Kennan Institute and "Tri kvadrata" Publisher, 2010): 171–210.

283 Stanislav Borzykh, "Poniatie globalizatsii: novoe prochtenie," *Vek Globalizatsii* 2 (2011): 18–31.

284 Dmitry Trenin. "Osnovoy ofitsialnogo patriotizma stanovitsa antiamerikanizm," *Kommersant* 3: 5061 (February 19, 2013), http://www.kommersant.ru/doc/2127333 (as of March 10, 2014).

285 Alexander Baunov, "Rossiya – spasatel traditsiy. Novaya natsionalnaya ideya." *Slon* (February 28, 2013), http://slon.ru/world/samozvantsy-914311.xhtml (as of March 10, 2014).

concept of the 'clash of civilizations' as a theoretical justification for alienation from Russia and an anti-Russian discursive tool.

In a more practical sense, references to Ukraine and Belarus are politically self-defeating for proponents of the 'Slavic civilizational unity' since neither Kiev nor Minsk seems to make true the dreams about a Moscow-led integration. The addition of Serbia to the potential members of 'Pax Slavica' makes this imaginary community even more dubious since Belgrade is consistently moving toward the EU and demonstrates more divergence from—than conformity to—the Russian trajectory in Europe. The cases of Poland and Bulgaria illustrate this trend even better. By the same token, the idea of an 'Orthodox unity' is politically discredited by Russia's war with Georgia, as well as tensions with Romania and Moldova in the Transnistrian conflict.

The civilization-based approach can be instrumental in coining the '*European non-West*' concept, with Russia and Turkey playing the key roles in its political implementation. Yet within Russian academic community there are strong voices of those scholars who think that Turkey—in its capacity as a "regional hegemon" and an "order setter"[286]—is more a competitor of Russia than its potential ally.[287]

Therefore, Russian civilizational discourses are split between cooperative pro-European approaches postulating Russia's belongingness to a larger European civilization, on the one hand, and their negation in the form of a more confrontational anti-Western posture, on the other. The latter aims not at rejecting all sorts of universality, but rather at substituting the European version of normative universality with a Russian one, thus recreating—rather than rejecting, as most European civilizational narratives would choose to do[288]—the normative hierarchies.

2.10 Global Governance: Learning to Live in a Postinternational World

The concept of global governance is consonant with the idea of a polycentric world where the state is not in a position to preserve its modern/'Westphalian'

286 Dimitar Bechev (ed.), *What Does Turkey Think?* (London: European Council on Foreign Relations, June 2011): 9.

287 Vasily Ordynskiy, "Turetskoe vliyanie na post-sovetskom prostranstve: vzgliad iz Kazani" (July 11, 2011), http://www.apn.ru/publications/article24468.htm (as of March 10, 2014).

288 Raffaelle Marchetti, "Mapping Alternative Models of Global Politics," *International Studies Review* 11 (2009): 148.

characteristics, and has to undergo deep domestic transformations in reaction to the growing—perhaps enforced—competition with other actors, sometimes more resourceful and normatively appealing than states. A polycentric world embraces such new "configuration of subjectivities"[289] as the prevalence of mobile/ad hoc coalitions based upon multilateral diplomacy and soft power resources, growing asymmetry and turbulence, the multiplicity of political and institutional playgrounds for international subjects, and 'open'—that is, inclusive and nondiscriminatory—model of regionalism[290] grounded in networks of 'centers of growth' and leaving much space for participation of non-state actors.[291] By defying state-centric worldviews, global governance undermines the validity of the 'us against them' type of thinking through questioning and dissolving the essentialized conception of a taken-for-granted 'collective We' as opposed to—or encircled by—inimical identities. It is on these grounds that the idea of global governance is lambasted by those Russian speakers who view it as an effect of deplorable degradation of nation states and the subsequent global imposition of a new version of 'general will' embodied in the United States-led neoliberal model of global governance.[292]

Yet from a structural perspective, the implementation of the global governance model is complicated by the uncertainty of its institutional underpinnings. This is the case of contested interpretations of the G20 and G8 roles—these global institutions may be dubbed "steering committees for the world economy," discussion fora, "talking shops," "old-fashioned concerts of great powers," and so forth.[293] However, it is these global institutions that are seen by many in the world, and in Russia in particular, as elements of the nascent global governance infrastructure. It is through this prism that Russia's engagement with the G8 and G20 has to be analyzed.

As the chair and host country of the ***G8*** in 2006, Russia chose to promote three priority areas. First, it elevated energy to the very top of its agenda, which was a problematic move due to the divisive nature of the issue. Russia's efforts were unable to bridge gaps between producing, transporting, and

289 Vladimir Kapitsyn, "Kosmopolitizm – komponent myagkoi sily i global'nogo upravleniya," *Obozrevatel'-Observer* 10: 237 (2009): 74–75.

290 Kamaludin Gadzhiev, *Vvedenie v geopolitiku* (Moscow: Logos Publishers, 1998): 343.

291 Alexandr Konovalov, "Mir ne dolzhen byt' mnogopoliarnym," *Nezavisimaya gazeta* (September 16, 2008).

292 Elena Ponomariova, "Suverenitet v epokhu globalizatsii" *Svobodnaya mysl'* 11: 1582 (2007): 95–110.

293 Stefan A. Schirm, "Global Politics are Domestic Politics: A Societal Approach to Divergence in the G 20," *Review of International Studies* 39 (2013): 685–706.

consuming countries, which was illustrated by a series of gas conflicts with Ukraine in the years to come, which seriously questioned Russia's trustworthiness among EU Member States.

Second, Russia pledged to focus on education—an area where Russia's global positions appear decidedly less than perfect. The Russian government has become increasingly upset about the low international ratings for Russian universities, migration of professional cadres to foreign universities, and other symptoms of its educational system in crisis. The functioning of transnational educational projects, considered one of Russia's landmarks in this sphere, is hindered by the low effectiveness of Russian educational institutions, and a controversial higher education reform has provoked negative reactions from the professional community of educators and from a part of the ruling elite itself. The rather specific issue of migrant integration through education is certainly a necessary measure, but its social effects were unfortunately overmatched by the growing nationalism and xenophobia across the country.

The third Russian priority as G8 chair was healthcare, one more social area with a huge record of domestic troubles and malpractices, from decreasing life expectancy to the underfinancing of medical institutions in Russia. Besides, the sphere of medicine clearly illustrates Russia's critical dependence on Western technologies and know-how.

In general, the G8 summit of 2006 in St. Petersburg was appraised as more a PR event with insufficient space for civil society voices.[294] In the meantime this problem is not Russia-specific and has a more structural character, since the question of how international NGOs can have their say in the nascent global governance mechanisms is still unanswered.[295]

The ***G20*** is another global organization that Russia chaired in 2013. It was at the focus of Russian diplomatic attention due to the summit in St. Petersburg in September 2013. As President Vladimir Putin assured, Russia's promotion of its key approaches to international politics is directly linked to a series of Russian chairmanships in major international organizations, of which the G20 perhaps plays the key role.

On the one hand, as INSOR, a liberal think tank, wrote, Russia's chairmanship in the G8 and G20 was seen as instrumental for redressing Russia's relations with the West. On the other hand, Russia considers its G20 chairmanship to be in close coordination with the BRICS, which drives Moscow

---

294 Pamela Jordan, "Russia's Managed Democracy and the Civil G8 in 2006," *Journal of Communist Studies and Transitional Politics* 26: 1 (March 2010): 101–125.

295 Andrew Cooper, "Civil Society Relationships with the G20: An Extension of the G8 Template or Distinctive Pattern of Engagement?" *Global Society* 27: 2: 179–200.

toward a policy of balancing and decentering the West, rather than one of cooperation. This is particularly the case with regard to the most politically sensitive issues such as the Syrian and North Korean conflicts.

There were three priority areas in Russia's G20 agenda in 2013. *First*, Moscow has chosen to make an accent on the issues of investment, employment, food security, and human capital development. This seems to be an excessively large basket involving numerous activities in both core economies and financially unstable regions, the overall success and progress of which is hard to measure.

Second, Russia declared among its priorities the building of trust and transparency. Yet as soon as it comes to practice, this area looks lacking in success stories. In the Cyprus debt crisis, Russia and the EU failed—as much as they tried—to find a common approach and thus demonstrate the benefits of collective action crossing institutional divides. Global sports events are mentioned among specific areas where accountability and the eradication of corruption require international efforts, yet it had no impact on the Sochi Olympics project known for its large-scale profligacy and weak financial discipline.

Third, Russia prioritized effectiveness in governance through multilateral trade, antiprotectionist measures, and sustainable development. In particular, the good practices of German corporate business in Russia were discussed at meetings of the B20 (business associations of G20 states) prior to the St. Petersburg summit of 2013. Yet even if Russia does raise some important global issues in organizations such as the G20, its agenda-setting resources and leadership capabilities can be questioned due to the lack of Russia's own success stories in a plethora of fields—from fighting corruption to effective regulation of the labor market. All of this reduces the institutional possibilities for multilateral diplomacy and Russia's soft power appeal.

In fact, Russia's engagement with global institutions reveals a two-tier structure of the Russian foreign policy discourse. One level is explicitly political—with intentional self-alienation from the West and a false ideology of self-sufficiency. Yet there is another discursive stratum where Russia—perhaps reluctantly—has to play a role of the temporal and rotating center of global government, and where self-detachment from the West looks self-defeating. The G20 and the G8 in this sense are institutions that create new discursive spaces, and valorize inclusive—as opposed to exclusive—relations with business communities and civil societies.[296]

In the meantime, Russia is still in a search for a balance between securing a decent place for itself within the framework of Western-led institutions and giving priority to an alternative strategy of forging relations with BRICS states. The idea of multipolarity that nourishes Russian foreign policy philosophy to some extent contradicts the idea of 'thick' global governance institutions. Either Russia—as any other chair—treats the G20 as an institutional embodiment of global governance, or it prioritizes nation state-based coalitions such as BRICS and others, some of them with evident anti-Western bias.

***

In this chapter, I have shown that reformulation of the idea of multipolarity took two forms. First, a variety of nonrealist meanings was infused into this concept, including the issues of culture and identity (normative and civilization approaches). Second, under the influence of nonrealist theories—such as social constructivism and globalism—multipolarity was adjusted to emerging postinternational and postsovereign milieu that encourages the activities of nonstate actors, on the one hand, and the growing appeal of normative regulators, on the other.

My analysis confirmed that the Russian foreign policy discourse consists of a series of 'metal maps' neither of which offers a more or less coherent vision of the idea of multipolarity which, constituting the cornerstone of Russian foreign policy, remains—quite paradoxically—among the least addressed in Russian foreign policy studies. Since conceptions of multipolarity originate in the sphere of ideas, it would be quite logical to assume that at certain time there might be more than one pattern of multipolar arrangements. Each of them gives a different answer to the question as to which pole is composed of—nation states, regions, civilizations, or integrative constructs such as the EU or Customs/Eurasian Union.

In Europe, too, the concept of multipolarity has also reached far beyond its classical realist frames. In the traditions of Hedley Bull, one may assume that the mutipolarity debate contains a great deal of normative potential, since

296 Steven Slaughter, "The Prospects of Deliberative Global Governance in the G 20: Legitimacy, Accountability, and Public Contestation," *Review of International Studies* 39 (2013): 71–90.

it is always about justice vs. order.[297] For Chantal Mouffe, one of the key figures in critical theories, multipolarity is connoted with pluralization of (regional) hegemonies in which agonistic type of conflicts (that one between mutually recognized rivals) would prevail over antagonistic (between enemies).[298] Politically speaking, multipolarity is a challenge to all world actors: In today's German foreign policy debate, for example, multipolarity may signify unilateralism ('going global alone'), which only sharpens the key question of "whether the EU can turn multipolar order into one that works through multilateral cooperation rather than spheres of influence."[299]

As far as Russia is concerned, it does not appear that any of the various versions of multipolarity described above is capable of undermining the Western hegemony. On the contrary, some of the discourse(s) of multipolarity could be quite compatible with the Western hegemonic power. Moscow lacks its own "global project"[300] and, unsurprisingly, the integration with the Trans-Atlantic institutional structures remains the key priority for Russia. Thus, despite protesting against Ukrainian and Georgian engagement with NATO and the EU, Russia itself has restored cooperation with the alliance, particularly in Afghanistan. In spite of conflicts over the EaP program, Moscow continues to refer to strategic partnership with the EU as a priority for Russia's modernization. Thus, despite its sympathies to multipolarity, Russia seems unable to reverse the West-dominated structures of international relations, which explains why it so often adheres to a status quo type of policy that ultimately pushes Russia to the margins of global politics.[301] Harsh polemics with the West and sensitive reaction to external criticism of Russia only mask Moscow's willingness to become part of the core coalition[302] constitutive of the IS-in-the-making. There are voices arguing that BRICS—as an institution which owes its acronym to the world financial elite—can be well inscribed into the future global strategy crafted by the West for engaging China, Brazil, and

297 Nikolai Zlobin, "Mirovoi poriadok kak mirovoi expromt," *Startegii Rossii* 6 (June 2008).

298 Chantal Mouffe, "Demokratiya v mnogopoliarnom mire," *Progosis* 2: 18 (Summer 2009): 16-26.

299 Ivan Krastev and Mark Leonard, *The Spectre of a Multipolar Europe* (London: European Council on Foreign Relations, 2010): 22.

300 Andrey Ryabov, "Globalizatsia dlia Rossii: vyzovy i riski," *Strategii Rossii* 10 (October 2008).

301 Yuri Igritskiy, "Rossiya-XXI: poisk balanse v mirovom disbalanse," *Svobodnaya mysl'* 9–10: 1570 (2006): 45–46.

302 Viktor Martyanov, "Rossiya v transformiruyuscheisia mirosysteme," *Strategii Rossii* 3 (March 2008).

Russia to the World Wide Web of both normative and institutional interdependence.[303] Shanghai Cooperation Organization is not an anti-Western alliance either.[304]

Yet a deeper integration in the normative and institutional order crafted by the West, as my analysis has shown, is complicated by what may be dubbed cognitive dissonances between Russia and the EU. As the balance-of-power version of multipolarity illuminates, Russia's foreign policy philosophy still tilts to a modernist understanding of sovereignty, while the EU seems to a much greater extent adhering to a postmodernist version of governance predicated upon the dispersal of sovereignty as a direct result of trans/cross/supranational integration. Russia prefers to verbalize its messages addressed to the EU as interest-based speech acts with pragmatic overtones, while European countries are inclined to formulate their worldviews in a more normative (identity- and value-based) language that inevitably contains mechanisms of othering Russia, that is, ascribing to her non-European characteristics. It is obvious that the EU is interested not in any type of strategic order, but in that one grounded in a set of liberal values—democracy, the rule of law, and individual freedom. Besides, Russia to a much larger extent than Europe is concerned about hard security problems. The EU focus on soft security agenda leads to further marginalization of Russia that cannot justifiably expect to become a soft security partner of the EU unless it undertakes robust improvements of its democracy record and starts effectively protecting its population against corruption, red tape, environmental decay, etc. While Russia's policies of multipolarity have strong connotations with sovereignty, self-assertiveness, and self-sufficiency, the competing EU logic embraces a different chain of meanings, to include integration, dispersal of sovereignty, norm-based identity, soft/HS, democratization through Europeanization as the key policy signifiers. Consequently, the two parties—Russia and the EU—still have different understandings of the nature of diversity and pluralism as constitutive features of IS they are embedded in. Besides, Russia tries to pursue the policies of multipolarity and multilateralism without having reliable friends and allies,[305] which was proven in August 2008 by the fact that Russia did not consult with Collective Security Treaty Organization members prior to launching the military operation against Georgia.

---

303 Vladimir Pavlenko, "Gruppa BRICS v global'no-upravlencheskoi strategii anglosaxonskogo Zapada," *Obozrevatel'-Observer* 11: 238 (2009): 29–30.

304 Anatoliy Shutov, "Shanhaiskaya Organizatsiya sotrudnichestva: problem ne ubavliaetsa," *Mir i Politika* 4: 31 (April 2009): 10–12.

305 Ilya Leviash, "Est' li u Rossii soyuzniki?" *Svobodnaya mysl* 3: 610 (2010): 45–58.

All this makes Russian efforts to push forward the multipolarity agenda—in the variety of its formats—ineffective. The problems Russia faces lie in an obvious lack of institutional support to what might be dubbed 'inter-polarity,' or a structure of interdependent relationship between the major world powers. Neither bilateral relations with European capitals nor interest-based alliances in which Russia participates—the Collective Security Treaty Organization (CSTO), the Shanghai Cooperation Organization (SCO), and BRICS—can institutionally match (or win emulation with) norm- and value-based organizations, NATO and the EU included. As the demise of the Gaddafi regime in Libya in August 2011 demonstrated, NATO and the EU—despite serious intrinsic splits – are still the dominating political forces capable of steering and streamlining the reshaping of crisis-ridden and strategically important regions.

The debates on multipolarity in its multiple forms can be inscribed into a dichotomy of '*politics of being*' and '*politics of becoming*.' The "politics of being refer to existing configurations of power," while the "politics of becoming" denotes "constant process of renewal" and shifts in identities and institutions.[306] In this sense, the multipolarity discussions are very much related to the 'politics of becoming,' since most of policy strategies they entail require not only accommodation to the changing global structures, but also to Russia's active actorship. Yet, undoubtedly, "there are no free foreign policy pathways,"[307] and each of possible Russia's strategies in a multipolar world has its political price to be paid. Domestically, it is indispensable that Russia undertakes deep internal reforms to decrease the current institutional distance with the West. Internationally, Russia should concede that the policy of fueling 'frozen conflicts' in its neighborhood not only is economically unsustainable, but also damages the prospects of strategic partnership with the West. In other words, before charting different schemas of multipolarity, Russia needs a frank assessment of its own profile in the IS and a serious discussion on what kind of pole it is willing and capable to become.

---

306 Roland Bleiker, "Visualizing Post-national Democracy," in David Campbell and Morton Schoolman (eds.), *The New Pluralism. William Connoly and the Contemporary Global Condition* (Durham and London: Duke University Press, 2009): 136–138.

307 Viktor Kremeniuk, "Rossiya v global'nom soobschestve," *Obozrevatel'-Observer* 11: 178 (2004): 34.

3 Competing International Societies: Four Cases of EU–Russia Interactions

In this chapter, I will continue exploring the cognitive and explanatory resources embedded in the variety of IS models by more specifically addressing a number of policy areas that illuminate the already mentioned gaps between the EU and Russia. As in the previous chapter, I explain these gaps not only as results of incompatibility of individual choices of Moscow and Brussels, but also rather as effects of grounding their policies in different structural models of IS. Each of the four cases that I have selected for this analysis in its own way illustrates the structural conditions of EU–Russia disconnections and put them in a wider set of conceptual perspectives.

3.1 European Neighborhood Policy and Eastern Partnership: EU's and Russia's Approaches

In this subchapter, I will argue that the European Neighborhood Policy (ENP) in general and the Eastern Partnership (EaP) in particular reveal a deep perceptional gap between Russia and the EU. Brussels' approaches, being intrinsically contradictory, are split between *normative unification* and *multiregionalist* models, on the one hand, and spheres of influence, on the other. Yet Moscow either denies or ignores normative components in EU policies, and takes it as an undue expansion into Russia's presumed *sphere of interests*.

Yet in spite of this gap, the EU and Russia, two dissimilar political subjects, do interact with each other in a contested area dubbed 'near abroad' by Kremlin and—alternatively—'common neighborhood' in major European countries. What certainly deserves a closer attention is that both different patterns of communication between the EU and Russia in this vast area consisted of a dozen countries with post-Soviet legacy, and the process of regionalization within this area.

In the academic literature, a number of models of regionality are widely discussed: regional complex/system, regional society, regional community, etc. [308] All of them are conceptually grounded in the idea of interna-

308 Attila Agh, "Regionalisation as a Driving Force of EU Widening: Recovering from the EU 'Carrot Crisis' in the 'East' ," *Europe-Asia Studies* 62: 8 (October 2010): 12–44.

tional/cross-border socialization as developed by both English school and social constructivism. As seeing from this vantage point, two communicative processes take place simultaneously: the EU–Russia interaction, and a more complex regional socialization that involves a much wider array of actors. Both processes are deeply intersubjective. Being key shapers of regional dynamics in their common neighborhood, Russia and the EU are themselves objects of influence from the part of their neighbors. Neighborhood is a concept against which EU's and Russia's identities are constantly (re)articulated. Russia defines itself as an actor able to cope with economic and security challenges originated in adjacent countries, while the EU claims to be capable of effectively using transformative mechanisms spurring normative changes in its neighbors.[309]

In this subchapter, I argue that it is insufficient to uncover the transformative mechanisms that the EU applies toward its multiple neighbors. What is of primordial importance for my analysis is to show that EU's political subjectivity is to a large extent dependent upon its neighborhood that is in a position to at least partly streamline the contours of EU's identity. In this interpretation, the EU is equally a region-maker and a product of regionalization dynamics unfolding in close proximity to its borders.[310] The same is true for Russia, though it is noteworthy that Russia's integrative Eurasian Union project is short of explicit normative dimension, which leaves the issue of norms acceptance of rejection beyond the otherwise intersubjective framework of Russia's relations with its neighbors.

In addressing the multiple experiences of identity-formation on a regional level in the EU–Russia shared neighborhood, I stem from a constructivist presumption that "regions are what states and other actors make of them [...] . Regionness, like identity, is not given once and for all: it is built up and changes."[311] Accordingly, regional identities—key elements of successful region-making projects—are constructed by both political discourses and cultural practices to be scrutinized in more detail in my analysis.

309 Pertti Joenniemi, "Turning into a Sovereign Actor? Probing the EU Through the Lens of Neighborhood," *Geopolitics* 17 (2012): 27–38.

310 Christopher Browning and George Christou, "The Constitutive Power of Outsiders: The European Neighborhood Policy and the Eastern Dimension," *Political Geography* 29 (2010): 109–118.

311 Louise Fawcett, "Regionalism from a Historical Perspective," in Mary Farrell, Bjorn Hettne, and Luk van Langenhove (eds.), *Global Politics of Regionalism. Theory and Practice* (London and Ann Arbor: Pluto Press, 2005): 26.

Policy Framework for Analysis

The interest in regionalism in a wider Europe is due to a few factors. *First*, there is a growing regional momentum within the EU where the financial crisis reactualized a number of regional for(u)ms of cooperation such as the Visegrad Four (V4), the 3+1 (Germany plus three Baltic states) format, etc. This new regional dynamics is to have inevitable repercussions for EU's policies in the East, since many regional projects are designed as "bridges between the internal and external regionalization of the EU."[312] Each of (intra-)European forms of regionalism necessarily has repercussions for EU's relations with its neighbors: the Nordic Europe has strongly influenced the practices of regionalism in the Baltic Sea region, the Central Europe (as exemplified by V4) is instrumental in engaging the countries of EaP, etc.

Many of the current modalities of European regionalism are quite compatible with the much debated idea of the 'Core Europe' as encompassing Germany, the Central Europe, the Baltic Sea region, and the Nordic Europe. Intrinsically, this alliance can envelop countries with effective and responsible models of social and economic development, as well as a record of successful outward policy transfer practices.[313] The Core Europe, being a product of overlapping region-making projects, will be most likely dominated by Russia-skeptic countries lobbying for a more active engagement with Russia's neighbors independently of relations with Moscow.

Second, the area known as either 'near abroad' in Russia or common neighborhood in the EU goes through a steady process of regional differentiation. This is to a large extent due to the fact that this neighborhood spans a series of meeting points between European and non-European practices of territoriality and regionalism. From a practical perspective, regionalization within the area of common EU–Russia neighborhood questions the appropriateness of applying to it unified political instruments—be it the Brussels-sponsored EaP or Moscow-patronized Eurasian Union. Regional fragmentation opens more space for different identities and institutional affiliations, with borderlines between regions-in-the-making (the Black Sea region and South Caucasus, South Caucasus and the Caspian Sea region, etc.) being immanently fuzzy and blurred.

---

312 Attila Agh, "Regionalisation as a Driving Force of EU Widening: Recovering from the EU 'Carrot Crisis' in the 'East' ," *Europe-Asia Studies* 62: 8 (October 2010): 12–41.

313 Andras Simonyi, "Central Europe's Pivot to the North Is a Good Idea" (May 14, 2013), http://www.huffingtonpost.com/andras-simonyi/central-europes-pivot-north_b_3274253.html?utm_hp_ref=fb&src=sp&comm_ref=false (as of March 10, 2014).

The Neighborhood Regions: An Inside–Outside Perspective

Russia and the EU as two key shapers of regions constituting the area of their common neighborhood adhere to drastically different attitudes to the mechanisms and institutions of region-building. Russia prefers the concept of 'near abroad' to 'common neighborhood' and overwhelmingly perceives this area in terms of zero-sum-game and spheres-of-influence politics.

For the EU the central question of its policy toward Eastern neighbors is how to create a zone of peace and stability at the Union's borders without offering the prospect of full membership as an incentive.[314] By and large, this dilemma is tackled by two discourses—civilizational and geopolitical ones. Civilizational discourse is about the transfer of values in a process of 'education' and norms diffusion with the purpose of transforming the neighbors. In geopolitical discourse, neighbors are viewed as transit countries that constitute a buffer zone ('our backyard') against the unfriendly 'Big Other.' Russia is accepted as a geopolitical player,[315] which only exacerbates the need for control over resources, security protection, and spheres of influence. Against this background, EU's Eastern frontiers are effects of "geopolitical decisions" stemming from a "battle for Europe"[316] and its borderlines.

Arguably, the key factor that determines EU's and Russia's policy tools is their status of either insiders or outsiders in region-making projects developing in the area of their common neighborhood. In my further analysis, I will single out four possible models of EU–Russia interactions based on this criterion: (1) Russia is an outsider, while the EU is an insider; (2) vice versa, Russia is an insiders, while the EU is an outsider; (3) both the EU and Russia are insiders; and (4) both the EU and Russia are outsiders. Each of these four models is considered below from the viewpoints of a combination of identities, institutions, and patterns of external overlay.

Model 1—in which Russia is an outsider, and the EU is an insider—encompasses two regions: Nordic Europe and Central Europe. Of course, they differ from each other in many respects, with one of the most striking

---

314 Alessandra Nervi Christensen, *The Making of the European Neighborhood Policy*. (Baden-Baden: Nomos, 2011): 64.

315 Christoffer Kolvraa and Jan Ifversen, "The European Neighborhood Policy: Geopolitics or Value Export?" in Federica Bindi and Irina Angelescu (eds.), *The Frontiers of Europe: A Transatlantic Problem?* (Rome and Washington: Scuola Superiore della Pubblica Amministrazione and Brookings Institution Press, 2011): 50–61.

316 Federica Bindi and Irina Angelescu, "Introduction: Defining the Frontiers of Europe from a Transatlantic Perspective," in Federica Bindi and Irina Angelescu (eds.), *The Frontiers of Europe: A Transatlantic Problem?* (Rome and Washington: Scuola Superiore della Pubblica Amministrazione and Brookings Institution Press, 2011): 2.

dissimilarities being a desecuritized nature of the Nordic regionalism, as opposed to the ongoing securitization of energy policy and military matters for Central Europe.

However, both intra-European regions are firmly embedded in the European/Euro-Atlantic institutional structures and produce their own languages of self-description. Their normative coherence is sustained by a variety of cultural underpinnings. In both regions, institutional density fosters effective mechanisms of regional socialization that give spill-over effects: The Nordic Europe is keen to project its experiences to the Baltic Sea region, while the Central Europe is eager to share its success stories with Eastern European neighbors.

For both regions Russia is obviously an external force, though the inside/outside relationships are not identical: Central European identity, along with the very distinction between Central and Eastern Europe, is grounded in a political setoff against Russia, though radicalization of Russia's alterity is by and large avoided for practical reasons. In the meantime, the concept of Nordicity leaves some routes for Russia to share certain elements of the Northerness. In some cases, Russia tries to pragmatically take advantages of regionalist initiatives undertaken by its neighbors (as it was the case of the Finland-sponsored ND program), while in others it chooses to ignore region-building capacities of its Western neighbors (which is mostly the case of Central Europe[317]).

In unpacking Model 1, I will further focus on the region of Central Europe due to its stronger relevance for the common EU–Russia neighborhood. Institutionally, this is a very dense region that encompasses the V4, the Central European Initiative, and the Danube regional strategy. These three institutional frameworks reveal three different facets of Central European regionalism: The Poland-led V4 is focused on tackling energy and military security issues among its Member States and is eager to develop flexible communicative formats with adjacent countries; the Central European Initiative extends the concept of Central Europe to the Balkans, and the Hungary-driven Danube-based regionalism is basically about jointly managing a plethora of soft security and transportation projects.[318] Among the three it is the V4 that has the most immediate bearing for the EU's relations with Russia in their common neighborhood area.

317 Wojciech Zachaczkowski, "Ignorirovat Tsentralnuyu Evropu nepravilno." Rosbalt Information Agency web site (April 9, 2013), http://www.rosbalt.ru/main/2013/04/09/1115575.html (as of 10 March, 2014).

318 http://www.danube-region.eu (as of March 10, 2014)

The V4 identity discourses focus on two mutually correlative nodal points—the historical trauma of imperial submission and well-articulated democratic attitudes. This is why EU's core narratives—Europeanization and normative expansion—find a fertile ground here. The V4 strongly positions itself within a transatlantic security community and calls for boosting EU security functions, including conflict management resources: By 2016 the V4 pledged to form a Visegrad battle group as a regional contribution to European hard security. Cyber security and energy security—including mechanisms for mutual support in case of energy disruptions[319]—are also matters of pivotal importance, including in the framework of V4's cooperation with Eastern partners.[320]

The outward role of the V4 appears to derive from the group's European commitments. The four Central European countries are eager to engage their East European neighbors in developing the 'V4 – Eastern Partnership' program. By the same token, the V4 members support the Southern Energy Corridor facilitating the access of countries of Central-, East-, and South-East Europe to gas and oil supplies from the Caspian Sea region and the Middle East, thus reducing their dependencies from Russia.[321] They also advocate measures for liberalization of energy market and competitive energy prices, support the continuing Europeanization of EaP countries, and are critical to the human rights situation in Russia.[322]

Obviously, Russia's attitudes to the region of Central Europe are drastically different. For Moscow most of Central European nations are culturally close but politically unfriendly. Indeed, the V4 countries share the history of challenging the Soviet Union whose fall in 1991 was characterized by Vladimir Putin as the greatest geopolitical catastrophe of the 20th century. Poland's role as the strongest lobbyist for Ukraine in Brussels seems geopolitically inacceptable and irritating for Russia.

---

319 Declaration of V4 Energy Ministers (Bratislava, January 25, 2011) http://www.visegradgroup.eu/2011/declaration-of-v4-energy (as of March 10, 2014).

320 For a More Effective and Stronger Common Security and Defence Policy. Declaration of the Visegrad Group Foreign Ministers (April 19, 2013), http://www.visegradgroup.eu/declaration-of-the-130419 (as of March 10, 2014).

321 Press Statement of Prime Minister Gordon Bajnai delivered after the Extended Energy Security Summit of the V4 Countries (February 24, 2010), http://www.visegradgroup.eu/2010/press-statement-of-prime (as of March 10, 2014).

322 Meeting of Foreign Ministers of the Visegrad, Nordic and Baltic countries (Gdansk, February 20, 2013), http://www.visegradgroup.eu/documents/official-statements/meeting-of-foreign (as of March 10, 2014).

Thus, the countries of Central Europe are still in the process of carving out their proper role identities within the EU and simultaneously developing their outreach strategies. They are sources of multiple institutional initiatives aimed at engaging a wider circle of countries into the Europeanization process, yet in the meantime they themselves are objects of criticism from major EU actors for insufficient compliance with European normative standards (in particular, this is the case of Hungary, yet the governments of Poland and Slovakia have also earlier had similar problems). Despite those cleavages the attempts to draw political lines between 'old' and 'new' Europe—initially articulated by Washington and then reinterpreted by Moscow as a distinction between 'good' and 'bad' Europeans—by and large failed, leaving scarce leverage for Russia to build its European strategy on dividing its neighbors into different identity-framed categories. The inception and maturing of the Berlin–Warsaw axis is a political move that not only legitimizes Poland's role as a partner for Germany in Europe, but also facilitates closer coordination of their policies toward Russia and the common neighborhood countries.[323]

Model 2—in which the EU is an outsider, while Russia is an insider—embraces two regional cases: non-EU Eastern Europe and the Caspian Sea region. This model starkly differs from the first one discussed above. It is characterized by weak—if ever existent—institutionalization: neither of the two regions is cemented by more or less binding institutional commitments. They also lack common identity discourses, as well as external spill-over effects—neither Eastern Europe nor the Caspian Sea region think of themselves as model regions eager to project their norms to other regions. In both cases, Russia claims to have an upper hand in shaping regional milieux, and takes—sometimes aggressively—protective stand against EU's attempts to have its say there.

Eastern Europe is a very volatile region, where interests and identities of key actors are far from fixed. The region is mostly shaped by a competition between Moscow and Brussels, but it cannot be easily divided into 'Russian' and 'European' segments—in fact, being 'pro-Russian' or 'pro-European' is a matter of interpretation. The elites in Ukraine, Moldova, and—to a certain extent—Belarus often choose to portray themselves as being different from Russia, in the meantime being aware of their dependence on Russian energy resources and military power. Russia, from its part, does its best to present itself as a country belonging to this region that it alternatively might call 'a

323 The Visegrad Group and Germany Foreign Ministers Statement on the Eastern Partnership (Bratislava, March 3, 2011), http://www.visegradgroup.eu/2011/the-visegrad-group-and (as of March 10, 2014).

different / non-Western Europe.' However, the very structure of EU's—as well as Ukrainian and Moldovan—discourses grounded in the inescapable choice between joining Russian and European models of integration ascribe to Russia external characteristics by placing it in the same category of outsiders as the EU.

In fact, it is Eastern Europe's positioning between the EU and Russia and the structural impossibility to make either identity-based or institutional choice between Moscow and Brussels that constitutes region's specific role identity, which is particularly the case of Ukraine. This situation enhances two interrelated foreign policy models: a multivectored diplomacy of balancing between the two hegemonic poles, and a zero-sum game bargaining (presuming that the more EU turns out of Ukraine, Moldova, and Belarus, the more they are to cooperate with Russia). As an ideal model for foreign policy, most of the regional actors seem to prefer multilateralism with collective consultations and decision-making by multiple parties.[324] Yet this is hardly a completely feasible option within the system of spheres of influence that leaves little room for Russia's Eastern European neighbors' political strategies of their own. Power-based system of international relations reduces the role of Ukraine, Moldova, and Belarus to junior partners of great powers, and forces them to the spheres of influence shaped by the EU that will always prevail as a source of normative power, and Russia with its domination in hard security and energy domain.

In the *Caspian Sea region*, Russia's legitimate belonging to the regional milieu cannot be contested, but Russia faces a strong competition from external powers, including the EU. Moscow and Brussels take incompatible positions toward the whole set of energy issues: The EU supports the Southern Gas Corridor with Nabucco and the Trans-Caspian Pipeline System as its key elements,[325] while Russia develops the South Stream project. Besides, the EU has its say in the regional dynamics via EaP (where Azerbaijan is a member) and European energy companies working in the region.

It is the absence of common approaches to the key energy issues—the delimitation of the Caspian seabed and the competition in gas transportation

---

324 Bobo Lo, "Russia: The Eastern Dimension," in Piotr Dutkiewicz and Dmitri Trenin (eds.), *Russia: the Challenges of Transformation* (New York: Social Science Research Council & New York University Press, 2011): 369.

325 http://europa.eu/rapid/press-release_IP-11-1023_en.htm?locale=en (as of March 10, 2014)

projects—that created preconditions for securitizing regional milieu.[326] In particular, Russia increasingly considers Astrakhan' as its military outpost in the Caspian Sea.[327]

The Caspian Sea region, as well as Eastern Europe, clearly demonstrates that even being a regional insider Russia has to compete for the influence with the explicitly extra-regional powers.[328] This drastically differs from the regions—such as Central Europe and the Norden—that are plugged in the EU project and where no external power has chances for a comparable impact. Apparently, it is the lack of normative resources and soft power traction, as well as institutional weakness that make Russian positions in the two regions of this model vulnerable and unstable, and Russian policies more reactive than pro-active.

Model 3—where both Russia and the EU are regional insiders—encompasses the Baltic Sea and the Black Sea regions. It is mainly in these two regions that the EU offered "Russia an access to regional-level international societies with a thicker set of institutions than are available in its relations with the United States and Asia."[329] With all controversies, the Nord Stream project can serve one of the few examples of economic compatibility between Russia and major gas-consuming countries in Western Europe. In the same vein, with all its limitations, the Russian–Polish agreement on visa-free border-crossing regime for the residents of Kaliningrad *oblast* and two neighboring Polish *voivodships* is a good argument for a more comprehensive visa facilitation bargaining between Russia and the EU.[330]

Yet paradoxically, an equal status of region-shapers, however, is hardly conducive to a fruitful dialogue, since Russia is fully aware that from 1990s Estonia, Latvia, Lithuania perceived the Baltic Sea regionalism as a step toward EU and NATO membership, along with Romania, Bulgaria, Ukraine,

---

326 Ioannis Michaletos, "Caspian Sea's Part in the Great Game" (November 8, 2012), http://www.worldpress.org/Europe/3944.cfm#down (as of March 10, 2014).

327 Hiroaki Hayashi, Julia Kusznir, and Arbakhan Magomedov, "Modern Russian Energy Policies in the Caspian Basin in Context of Military Strategy." Valdai Club web site (February 21, 2013), http://valdaiclub.com/near_abroad/55280.html (as of March 10, 2014).

328 Mazen Labban, "The Struggle for the Heartland: Hybrid Geopolitics in the Transcaspian," *Geopolitics* 14: 1 (2009): 1–7.

329 Pami Aalto, "Russia's Quest for International Society and the Prospects for Regional-Level International Societies," *International Relations* 21: 4 (2010): 459.

330 Jakub Korejba, "The Kaliningrad Triangle: a New Directorate for Central Europe" (November 17, 2012), http://www.neweasterneurope.eu/node/526 (as of March 10, 2014).

and Georgia for whom the Black Sea region-making was in one way or another inscribed in their Europeanization drive. Consequently, many of the regional actors were redefining "their identities in opposition to the 'Other' symbolized by Russia - the imperial, barbaric neighbor."[331] From its part, Russia proved unable to counter this negative othering by promoting its own long-term regional projects in either Baltic Sea or Black Sea regions, and has chosen to compensate the shortage of normative strategy with distancing from the EU and refusing to join the EU-centered normative order. Russia's—mostly rhetorical—claims for equality in the absence of long-term alternative strategies of region-building were conducive to the reproduction on the regional level of communicative disconnections between Moscow and Brussels.

In spite of optimistic expectations for a thicker EU–Russia convergence on regional levels,[332] the two parties are steadily drifting apart from each other. Identity-wise, Russia's association with the European idea—with all undeniable intersubjectivity of Russia–EU relations—turn out not that strong. Even the market—as an international institution potentially conducive to a more solidarist type of interaction—played a divisive role in both regions of the third model due to different conceptions of energy transportation routes. Solidarity within the Black Sea region is undermined by a competition between the Russia-sponsored South Stream project and its EU-supported alternative Nabucco. The Baltic Sea region is a home to two other competing approaches to energy business: The Russian–German Nord Stream project that may potentially enlarge to the Netherlands and the United Kingdom, on the one hand, and a nascent strategy-in-the-making of a group of Baltic and Central European states eager to rid themselves of excessive energy dependence from Russia by means of diversifying their supplies and investing in alternative sources of energy production (renewables, shale gas, nuclear energy, etc.), on the other. In the Roadmap of the EU–Russia Energy Cooperation till 2050 both parties have agreed on two most important points—energy interdependency (Kaliningrad on Lithuania, the three Baltic states on Russia and Belarus) and diversification of energy supplies, yet these two notions are differently understood by the parties involved. As the head of the Russian Permanent Mission in the EU Vladimir Chizhov argued, instead of interdependence some Baltic and Central European countries are longing for

---

331 Felix Cuita, "Region? Why Region? Security, Hermeneutics, and the Making of the Black Sea Region," *Geopolitics* 13:1 (2008): 133.

332 Aalto, "Russia's Quest," 471, 474.

energy independence from Russia, which is hardly achievable technologically. As for diversification, this is exactly what Russia believes to contribute to by developing South Stream and planning for constructing new legs of the Nord Stream.[333]

Moscow often portrays the Baltic Sea Region as one of interfaces where Russia is confronted by serious problems in dealing with the EU. The Kremlin in fact accuses the EU in applying allegedly protectionist measures against Russian investments, impeding Gazprom's business and derailing for political reasons joint projects such as the launching of a unified energy system to embrace Russia, Belarus, Latvia, Lithuania, and Estonia. The growing tensions between Russia and the EU (and its Member States) in the Baltic Sea region are particularly consequential due to the widely discussed perspectives of the concept of 'Core Europe' to potentially encompass Germany, Northern Europe, Central Europe, and the Baltic Sea region. Should a new constellation of economic and political forces take a more concrete shape in the long run, the future contours of EU–Russian relations will to a very large extent be dependent on a number of developments either spurred by countries belonging to these regions or unfolding in their premises. The most important political problem for Russia is whether the potential of the existing mechanisms of Russia's engagement with its Baltic partners (the Nord Stream project, the German–Poland–Russia triangular diplomacy, etc.) would be sufficient to counter a well-pronounced series of opposite moves (such as the legal process against Gazprom spurred by Lithuania and Czech Republic, the energy security policy coordination mechanisms between the V4 and the Baltic countries, etc.).

By and large, the future of the Baltic Sea region is defined by the collision between at least two different versions of energy regionalism. One is the model of the Russian–German energy condominium rhetorically supported by Brussels and some Scandinavian countries. Another model is shaped by alternative visions of energy security mainly emanated from the three Eastern Baltic states in conjunction with their V4 partners. Their strategy includes a heavy accent on practically implementing the idea of energy diversification that presupposes forming coalitions to balance the Russian influence and preventing Gazprom from acquiring new assets in the region. For Baltic and

333 Vladimir Chizhov, Intervention at the Conference "Third Investment Energy Summit" organized by "The Economist" (Brussels, May 29, 2013), http://russianmission.eu/en/interviews/intervention-ambassador-vladimir-chizhov-conference-third-investment-energy-summit-organi (as of March 10, 2014).

the V4 states the Nord Stream project is problematic since it maintains non-competitive prices and technically creates preconditions for disrupting Russia's energy supplies to the Baltic states while continuing deliveries to Western European consumers.[334] Baltic countries are also wary of EU's policies of introducing stricter environmental protection regulations that can eventually lead to the rising energy prices due to new investments in expensive technologies and potentially to the growing dependence from Russia. This explains the interest of Baltic states in the exploration of shale gas reserves, building of liquefied natural gas terminals, investing in renewables, and the search for alternative transportation routes.

In spite of the tensions between different visions of regionalism in the Baltic Sea, in this region Russia and the EU possess a better record of cooperation than in the Black Sea. As the military exercises of 2013 demonstrated,[335] for Moscow the Black Sea is mostly a region emanating threats to Russian security than an interface for cooperation. Again, it is the lack of a normative appeal that seriously undermines Russia's policies in both regions.

Model 4—under which both the EU and Russia are formally outsiders—embraces South Caucasus and Central Asia. In these cases, there are potentialities for both cooperation (the EU mediating between Moscow and Tbilisi after the Georgia war in 2008) and competition (basically in soft power domain) between Moscow and Brussels. Multiple external overlays (by China, Turkey, United States) are indispensable elements of regional policy constellations, which can be explained by almost nonexistent institutional basis for regional cohesiveness and the deliberate preferences of regional actors for multivectored diplomacies.

It appears that Central Asia and South Caucasus represent a strong challenge for the EU international role identity since the widely used otherwise normative discourse does not bring here the desired communicative outcomes (perhaps, with the exception of Georgia). This is why the EU had to refocus/recalibrate its normative agenda from promoting human rights and civil freedoms to supporting good governance and sustainable development.[336]

334 Triinu Tarus and Matthew Crandall, "Is Russia a Threat to Estonian Energy Security?" *Baltic Journal of Political Science* 1 (December 2012): 77–90.

335 Fred Weier, "In the Wee Hours, Putin Ordered Impromptu Russian War Games," *Christian Science Monitor* (March 28, 2013).

336 The EU and Central Asia: The New Partnership in Action (Brussels, June 2009), http://eeas.europa.eu/central_asia/docs/2010_strategy_eu_centralasia_en.pdf (as of March 10, 2014).

Yet Russia as well had to partly adjust its policies to the Central Asian regimes. This is especially the case of the Russian-speaking population that in most of other post-Soviet regions is elevated to the highest rank in Russian priorities. Yet, in Central Asia, Moscow has never seriously raised this flammable issue, which might be interpreted as part of Russia's policy of accommodating Central Asian dictatorships and avoiding conflicts with them.[337]

As we see, countries of the regions under consideration are reluctant to accept either European or Russian normative supremacy, yet are they capable of producing their own norms instead? Examples of Central Asia and South Caucasus depreciate one of the key claims of postcolonial theorizing, namely that one presuming the ability of non-Western regions not only to reject Western norms, but also to "replace or modify them with ones which are consistent with their interests and identities."[338] The situation on the ground looks less certain: In fact, both Central Asia and South Caucasus are examples of under-regionalized areas that suffer exactly from the lack of norms to institutionally bind the countries. This normative deficit is exacerbated by either inability or unwillingness to adopt European norms and, consequently, to integrate with a Europe-centric normative order.

The experiences of the two regions also question the relevance of the principle of 'regional solutions for regional problems' that is portrayed as key to non-Western regional actors' search for their autonomies in regional settings.[339] None of Central Asian and South Caucasian countries seriously stands for keeping outsiders aside as a principle of their policies; moreover, some of them (especially Kazakhstan, Kyrgyzstan, Azerbaijan, Georgia, and Armenia) welcome the actorship of external powers and do their best for taking practical advantages of competition between them (a practice known as multivectored diplomacy).

Implications for the Eastern Partnership

From the EU part, the EaP is a combination of *normative unification* and—to a much lesser extent—(soft) *power balancing*, yet for Russia it is a mix of *spheres of influence* politics and regional *balance of power*. The key problem

337 Alexei Malashenko, "Tsentralnaya Azia: na chto rasschityvaet Rossiya?" (Moscow Carnegie Center, December 6, 2012), http://carnegie.ru/2012/12/06/центральная-азия-на-что-рассчитывает-россия/ewu5 (as of March 10, 2014).

338 Amitav Acharya, "Norm Subsidiarity and Regional Orders: Sovereignty, Regionalism, and Rule-Making in the Third World," *International Studies Quarterly* 55 (2011): 99.

339 *Ibid.*, 102.

with Russia's explicit or implicit discontent with the EaP is that the policy of preventing Russia's neighbors from participating in EU-sponsored projects questions the sincerity of Russia's declaratory 'European choice.'

In March 2003, the European Commission presented its Communication on "Wider Europe Neighborhood: A new framework for relations with our Eastern and Southern Neighbors," outlining the basic principles of the ENP. Its purpose was to build friendly relations with the EU's new neighbors in the postenlargement era. In October 2003, the European Council welcomed this initiative and urged the Commission and the Council to take it forward. Since then, the Commission has also held exploratory talks with partners in Eastern Europe and the Southern Mediterranean, which already had Partnership and Cooperation Agreements or Association Agreements in force.

In the 1990s, Moscow was mostly positive about EU's regional initiatives and encouraged Russian border regions to participate in various trans- and cross-border collaborative projects—mostly within the ND framework. Russia was also eligible for participation in the ENP project, yet declined the proposal to join, arguing that the ENP failed to provide Moscow with a special status in its relations with Brussels. Russia felt that, because of its previous intense cooperation with the EU and its geoeconomic and geopolitical role in Europe, it deserved more than a position of merely one of many neighbors of the Union.

In 2002–2003, when Poland tried to launch the Eastern Dimension initiative, aimed primarily at engaging Belarus, Ukraine, and Moldova and, only in the second place, the Russian region of Kaliningrad, Moscow became more suspicious of Brussels' regionalist projects on its doorstep. Some Russian strategists tended to believe that such initiatives had a secret goal of undermining Russia's positions in its traditional sphere of influence. For this reason, Moscow received them rather coldly. It was also unhappy with the universalist approach of the ENP: The point was that Russia did not want to be treated in the same way as Belarus or Morocco, and rather claimed a special status and special relationship with Brussels. Likewise, Moscow was also discontented with the ENP concept in that, in contrast with other regional cooperation projects, it leaves almost no room for Russia in setting the bilateral cooperative agenda. The concept, as viewed from Moscow, seemed to be based on the assumption that the EU's neighbors should simply accept its rules and upgrade their legislation in accordance with the European standards, rather than the EU developing specific models for each country.

The EaP represents another source of disagreements between Russia and the EU. Promoted by Poland and Sweden, this program can be understood against the background of such factors as the 'Eastern fatigue' in Europe, and the scaling down of the US commitment to the Eastern Europe and the Caucasus as an effect of the Moscow–Washington 'reset.' Yet Russian diplomacy considers EaP as a political project ultimately aimed at undermining Russian positions in Eastern Europe.

The EU indeed views Russia as a revisionist power trying to regain its former control over the post-Soviet space. Brussels interpreted the Russian–Georgian military conflict of 2008 and the 'gas wars' with Ukraine as evidence of Russian imperialist intentions. Yet in the meantime, the EU capabilities to effect serious changes in the six EaP countries and transform them into prosperous states sharing European values are quite limited. The EU might find it difficult to achieve the desired result, since the present generation of post-Soviet politicians is prepared only to pay lip service to democracy and liberalism rather than to actually put these values into practice.

Against this backdrop, Russia wants to play its own game in the post-Soviet region by forging a "community of unaccepted" to the Western institutions.[340] On the one hand, Moscow claims that the EU's plans to enlist EaP countries' support in constructing Nabucco or White Stream without Russia's participation are doomed to failure. On the other hand, Russian diplomats remain either negative or skeptical about the EaP which they see as an encroachment upon its 'near abroad' sphere of influence. Russian discourse is contaminated by a number of either highly judgmental or falsifiable hypotheses—such as the belief in a "common mentality the majority of post-Soviet people,"[341] etc. It is not always that Russia's policies are in tune with its neighbors' policies: Moscow seems to be interested in depoliticized forms of regionalism, but its neighbors (such as Ukraine) look for much more normative and value-based models of regional integration as a wider Europe. The key problem with Russia's policy of preventing its neighbors from more closely associating with the EU is that it questions the sincerity of the 'European choice' proclaimed by Russia itself.

Russia, who claimed its status 'above' the ordinary EU neighbors, is evidently eager to develop its own integrationist project. Only a few days after having announced his decision to run for presidency in the March 2012 elec-

340 Leonid Bliakher, "Vozmozhen li post-imperskii proekt: ot vzaimnykh pretenziy k obschemu buduschemu," *Politia* 48: 1 (2008): 6–16.

341 Alexander Galkin, "Rossiya kak subyekt mirovoi politiki," *Politia* 44: 1 (2007): 17.

tion, the then Prime Minister Vladimir Putin published an article in the '*Izvestia*' newspaper to enunciate his foreign policy priorities for the next years in office. In that Putin called the Customs Union a nucleus for post-Soviet reintegration, and made clear that the Kremlin will heavily invest in this project that is doomed to present an institutional challenge to the EaP. Yet the Russian initiatives on the Customs Union and Eurasian Union are more a resource for increasing the status of Russian leadership internally and externally than a well-thought economic strategy. Such pompous moves are immanent to the nature of the Kremlin regime that needs great missions and success stories, even those existing only on paper.

Yet the reality on the ground looks much more difficult. The key problem at this juncture is that Russia's adherence to a *Realpolitik* type of thinking is conducive to underestimation of nonmaterial ('soft') instruments of power. This incapacitates Russian diplomacy as soon as it comes to situations shaped by issues of values and norms.

Russia clearly lacks resources (both material and ideational) to play the role of the dominating subject in the post-Soviet region. The ruling elite in the Kremlin is too technocratic and pragmatic for lavishly disbursing money to the neighboring countries (as many of them certainly expect) without immediate payback. Besides, the negative memories of the Soviet Union who sponsored its allies until the complete disintegration of the system are still alive. What is more, in spite of Putin's rhetoric, integrating the post-Soviet area does not look like the real essence of Russian economic policies that, due to the heavy dependence on energy export, in practice seek to foster cooperative projects with the EU and China, and not with neighboring countries such as Ukraine. Most experts have quite bluntly assessed the ceremonial opening of the Nord Stream pipeline by Dmitry Medvedev and Angela Merkel in November 2011 as an event conducive to further weakening of Ukraine—which Moscow deems one of potential members of the Customs Union—in international energy markets.

The key *structural* problem with the content of EaP is an ambiguous balance between its political and technical sides. In a study of the Slovak Foreign Policy Association, the EaP was criticized for 'unclear political leadership' and 'missing political guidelines.' This is indeed a crucial issue, since the EaP from its very inception has been a political project aimed at supporting fragile democracies in Eastern Europe after the Russian–Georgian war in August 2008. This explicates the rhetoric of the Warsaw summit of EaP that claimed that "the Eastern Partnership is based on a community of values and principles of liberty, democracy, respect for human rights and fundamental freedoms, and the rule of law. All countries participating in the Eastern Partnership are committed to these values through the relevant international instruments."[342] There are two main problems with this evidently politicized approach. First, it looks like a wishful thinking: The concept of 'deep democracy' appears to be too premature and too hasty in times when even elementary democratic norms do not seem to be the evident guidelines for many ruling elites in EaP capitals. Second, the initial political design of the EaP is not substantiated by the political commitment from the part of Brussels in the core issue of the membership perspectives.

It is this lack of long-term political commitment that Brussels is eager to compensate with visa liberalization and the Deep and Comprehensive Free Trade Area. In this sense, the EaP may be dubbed a modernization project, [343] focusing on tackling the issues of mismanagement, corruption, shadow economy, lack of due transparency and accountability, clan economy, etc. Within this logic, democracy cannot be a precondition for membership in the EaP, since neither of its countries corresponds to EU's democracy standards. Against the backdrop of the prevailing managerial logics within EaP, it becomes understandable why the EU is so hesitant to intervene in a series of violence-prone overpoliticized situations in those EaP countries facing the challenges of clashing identities, contested borders, complex interplay of inclusion and exclusion, etc.

In almost all six countries covered by the EaP this program faces implicit or explicit criticism, basically for the lack of incentives and prospects for membership. There are at least three issues that fuel skeptical attitudes in the EaP countries. The first is of perceptional nature: While the EaP governments (except Belarus) view this initiative as a sort of a common interface with the EU, for Brussels it is only an institutional platform for EU's own policies toward the six neighbors. The second issue stems from the first one: Since the EaP is an EU tool designed for its own needs and convenience, it inevitably becomes part of a broader system of EU's external policies. On the one hand, both Brussels and Berlin have to implicitly commensurate the tempo and the depth of EaP with EU's relations with Russia that include the negotiations on

---

342 EaP after the summit in Warsaw (June 10, 2011), http://www.easternpartnership.org/community/debate/eap-after-summit (as of March 10, 2014).

343 Alexander Duleba and Vladimír Bilčík, *Taking Stock of the Eastern Partnership. Preliminary Findings and Discussion Points* (Research Centre of the Slovak Foreign Policy Association, supported by the Friedrich Ebert Stiftung and the International Visegrad Fund, October 2011).

visa-free regime, the Meseberg initiative,[344] etc. On the other hand, Brussels has to accommodate preferences of other EU Member States, who are not willing to pursue a 'Russia-first' policy. To be viewed in the framework of EU–Russia relations seems inacceptable for countries located between these two powers and perceiving themselves as important elements of the pan-European order. Under these circumstances, maneuvering between different poles becomes the core strategy of most EaP countries, of which Ukraine is perhaps the most notorious – and least successful – example.

Third, the bilateral relations between the EU and each of the six 'Eastern partners' evidently prevail over the common EaP agenda. The reasons for this are much deeper than simple failures in EU policies: The differentiation and fragmentation within the post-Soviet space are so profound that neither of major world actors (including EU, NATO, or Russia) is in a position to contrive a common framework to incorporate most of them. What is more or less clear is the growing disparity within the group of six counties: Belarus is institutionally bracketed out from the project, the regimes in Ukraine (under Yanukovich) and Armenia (under Sarksyan) alienated themselves from Europe, Moldova tries to overcome its lengthy political deadlock provoked by deep divisions within the ruling elite, Georgia strives to maintain its higher profile as a pioneer in the good governance reforms, and Azerbaijan is more interested in fostering relations with Turkey than with the EU. This explains why the EU prefers to tackle the most urgent issues on a country-specific basis, rather than approaching its partners as a group.

It would be fair to describe the EaP as an experimental EU project that, as the experience of other similar initiatives previously launched by the EU (ND and the Barcelona Process) demonstrates, will in the future most likely undergo serious institutional transmutation. Coming back to the analytical models of EU–Russia relations, the GPM practices are unlikely to be implemented. On the contrary, Russia is strongly challenged by a group of EaP-interested countries who do their best to turn the EaP into a platform for competition between the six countries for reaching European normative standards. In this sense, the EaP is seen as a framework for emulating European

344 The June 2010 Meseberg Memorandum, signed by Chancellor Angela Merkel with President Dmitry Medvedev at Merkel's initiative, envisages creating a EU–Russia Political and Security Committee. This could potentially give Russia a voice in the EU's decision-making processes. To facilitate this, Berlin is asking Moscow to demonstrate its bona fides as partner to the EU by facilitating a resolution of the Transnistria conflict.

practices and implementing the ambitions of those countries interested in associating themselves with Europe.

The implementation of these plans sends a clear message to Russia. The competitive model of EaP evolved into an open conflict between the EU and Russia. The previous experience shows that the Kremlin gets tougher on those countries—such as Moldova and Ukraine—that achieve the best results in their bids for association with the EU. Russia has claimed that should Moldova 'choose to lose its sovereignty' (i.e., join the EU), Moscow would reconsider its (though mostly rhetorical) support for Moldova's reintegration. Russia overtly keeps refusing to discuss the issue of troop withdrawal from Transnistria as unacceptable, and argues that it is not a precondition for effective negotiations. Thus, Moscow is reluctant to see the Meseberg initiative as a test case for Russia's security relations with the EU, and unfortunately one should not expect too much flexibility from Russia in the years to come.

Against this backdrop, Moscow interprets normative sympathies to Europe in many post-Soviet states as effects of hegemonic imposition of Western instruments of domination. The Kremlin's estrangement from Europe is in a sharp contrast with much more variegated and multifaceted discourses developed by those Russian neighbors who feel attached—in one way or another—to Western institutions, either due to security reasons (Azerbaijan, Georgia), commercial interests (Kazakhstan), or because of their pro-European identity dynamics (Ukraine, Moldova).

In spite of Russia's strategy of institutionalizing a sphere of influence of its own, most of the neighboring countries keep dealing with Russia as an important economic (and partly security) partner, but are reluctant to take commitments stretching beyond mutually beneficial business projects. In many respects, Russia's policies toward former Soviet states are conditioned by Russia's relations with other major players, including EU Member States.

Conclusions

In concluding this section, I would like to briefly compare Russia's and the EU's policies as region-makers, bearing in mind their different role identities and instruments.

As an insider to regions of common neighborhood, Russia faces serious competition with the EU (as well as other major actors) and tries to avoid it by downplaying the dissimilarities between the Eurasian Union project and the European integration. In some cases (such as in Eastern Europe) Russia advocates inclusive versions of regional integration presupposing some debordering connotations (the rhetoric of a closer cooperation and even convergence between the 'Western' and 'Eastern' flanks of integrative processes in a wider Europe), while in other situations Moscow sticks to clearly articulated bordered approaches (e.g., in the Caspian Sea). Yet, by and large, Russia has voluntarily closed for itself the possibilities for both co-making/co-sponsoring region-building projects with the EU, and pragmatically using regional institutions as a means for diversifying its channels of communication with Europe. This added strong notes of conflictuality in Russia's communication with the EU in various regional formats.

As an outsider, Russia pursues a policy of alluring its South Caucasian and Central Asian neighbors in the Moscow-sponsored integrative project of the Eurasian Union mainly through soft power mechanisms. Simultaneously, Russia tries to challenge its status as an outsider by strengthening its military presence in South Caucasus (in Abkhazia, South Ossetia, and Armenia) and Central Asia (Tajikistan). In the meantime, Russia's impact on the Nordic and Central Europe is miniscule, which attests to Russia's scarce resources for influencing developments to the west of its borders.

As an insider, the EU hosts a number of regional projects that maintain institutional diversity within the Union, on the one hand, and are instrumental in developing rather variegated policy approaches to EU's neighbors, on the other. In fact, it is countries forming the regions of Nordic Europe and Central Europe that are the most instrumental in shaping EU's *modus operandi* in the adjacent regions, with the Baltic Sea and the Black Sea regions remaining the key laboratories of EU–Russia communications with all their complications and inconsistencies.

As an outsider, the EU combines 'soft' securitization of its Eastern neighbors with attempts to normatively transform them. The key problems are the lack of EU's security resources in frozen conflicts,[345] as well as limited utility of the normative power policy. EU's norms projection implies the distinction between European Self and a variety of regional Others with different degrees of adaptability to EU norms. In some cases, the EU has to reconsider the universality of its normative appeal and recognize the limits of its applicability even within the EaP.

The different patterns of regionalism analyzed in this section can hopefully elucidate the variety of role identities between the EU, Russia, and their

---

345 Marco Siddi and Barbara Gaweda, "Bystander in Its Neighborhood? EU's Involvement in Protracted Conflicts in the Post-Soviet Space" (Institut fur Europaeische Politik: IEP Policy Papers on Eastern Europe and Central Asia, No. 1, 2012): 23.

common neighbors. As analytical models, they may be used for better comprehending the dynamics of the inside–outside relationship based on a combination of discursive and institutional practices.

3.2 Modernization Partnership and EU–Russia Normative Cleavages

For Russia, P4M[346] is mostly about *technical and procedural approximation*, while for the EU it has to be viewed as the key element of *normative convergence*. Evidently, the EU strategic vision of P4M presupposes a certain degree of asymmetry and challenges one of the mantras of Russian foreign policy—the concept of equality in relations with the West.

Modernization is a concept that has originated in a scholarly discourse and is seriously contested academically. Its key conceptual underpinnings—a causal link between economic and political development and a postulate of a universal model of modernity (to be distinguished from mere contemporaneity)—are strongly attacked by its numerous opponents.[347] Yet in spite of its debatable academic profile, the idea of modernization is paradoxically relatively popular in policy circles of many countries. This is what constitutes the key research questions in this section: What are the political trajectories of this concept as seen from Russia and the EU? And what are the divergent contexts in which modernization is articulated by the two parties?

Methodological Rejoinder

Intensive criticism of Russia's modernization agenda for its lack of practical results only sustains the validity of approaching modernization as a peculiar type of discursive practice. Methodologically, I stem from the presumption that discourse is not simply "a collection of words that represent non-linguistic things of reality,"[348] but is the crucial shaper of meaning-making. Each type of discourse, in spite of inherent instability, contains its 'nodal points' of epistemic salience, through which key speakers acquire and consolidate

346 The P4M was initiated by the EU–Russia Rostov-on-Don summit (June 1, 2010). A Work Plan was adopted in December 2010 and is being regularly updated.

347 Richard Sakwa, "Modernisation, Neo-modernisation, and Comparative Democratisation in Russia," *East European Politics* 28: 1 (2012): 43–57.

348 Peter Ives, "Language. Agency and Hegemony: A Gramscian Response to Post-Marxism," in Andreas Bileler and Adam Morton (eds.), *Images of Gramsci. Connections and Contentions in Political Theory and International Relations* (London and New York: Routledge, 2006): 66.

power.[349] In a Foucauldian way one may argue that "there can be no possible exercise of power without certain [...] discourses of truth [...] . We are subjected to the production of truth through power [...] . Power never ceases its interrogation, its inquisition, its registration of truth: it institutionalizes, professionalizes and rewards its pursuit."[350] Modernization is certainly one of these nodal points meant to underpin Russia's transformation and thus to contribute to the constitution of the hegemonic discourse of the Kremlin. What sometimes remains unnoticed is that the idea of modernization partnership with Russia is one of the key shapers of EU's foreign policy and international identity.

Along the lines of critical discourse analysis, I approach modernization as an "empty universal,"[351] or an "organizing metaphor" for a "discursive polity."[352] In Richard Sakwa's words, modernization is "a form in which universal goals can be couched in particularist form."[353] Modernization can be viewed as an 'empty'—that is, not attached to any specific meaning—signifier in a number of ways. First, it may have both academic and political interpretations, and be used in each of these discursive registers. Modernization is an academic term migrated to political discourse, and it is this migration that constitutes interest for this analysis. Second, due to its breadth the concept constantly requires specifications in the form of multiple adjectives, depending on whether it is political, social, or economic modernization that matters most. Third, modernization inevitably overlaps with other adjacent concepts such as development, progress, Westernization, Europeanization, and civilization, which often adds an ideological flavor to it.

The logical linkage between modernization as a policy and modernity as a scholarly concept seems to be of utmost importance for this analysis. Seen from this angle, modernization implies: (1) the construction of a modern nation state guided by rational calculations of benefits and advantages that

---

349 Terrell Carver and Samuel Chambers (eds.), *Michael J. Shapiro. Discourse, Culture, Violence,* (London and New York: Routledge, 2012): 2–4.

350 Michel Foucault "Disciplinary Power and Subjection," in Steven Lukes (ed.), *Power* (Oxford: Basil Blackwell, 1986): 230.

351 Jacob Torfing, "Discourse Theory: Achievements, Arguments, and Challenges," in David Howarth and Jacob Torfing (eds.), *Discourse Theory in European Politics. Identity, Policy and Governance* (Houndsmills, Basingstoke: Palgrave and Macmillan, 2005): 16.

352 Yanis Stavrakakis, "Passions of Identification: Discourse, Enjoyment, and European Identity," in Howarth and Torfing (eds.), *Discourse Theory*, 96.

353 Richard Sakwa, "The Soviet Collapse: Contradictions and Neo-modernisation," *Journal of Eurasian Studies* 4 (2013): 75.

modern institutions can bring; and (2) its inclusion in the dominating model of IS that is ostensibly grounded in a Eurocentric set of norms and institutions.[354] The policy of modernization in this sense may restrain the power of individual states by imposing certain limitations on their domestic and international conduct. It is through this angle that I unveil the external repercussions of Russia's modernization agenda as intimately linked to the perspectives of this country's international socialization, a process in which the EU appears to be the key driver.

A Tug of Interpretations

While Russia is mostly interested in European investment and high-tech transfers under this program, the EU tried to develop a more normative vision of modernization (including its legal and socio-political aspects). The EU insisted on the importance of ensuring an effective, independent functioning of the judiciary and stepping up the fight against corruption, encouraged Russia to further develop an appeal system for criminal and civil court cases, and insists that an active involvement of civil society institutions in the reformist process should be a part of the modernization 'package.'

Yet Russia wants to avoid situations in which the EU could take a role of an indisputable example, a standard to be adapted. Russian diplomats propose to remove the issues of democratization and human rights as a precondition for modernization partnership, and in its stead focus on Russia's acceptance of technical norms and rules that successfully work in the EU and can be projected on Russia (energy efficiency, customs regulations, educational exchanges, environmental protection, etc.).

However, Russia's obsession with equality in conditions of structural inequality in bilateral relationship only sustains a rift between political rhetoric and the practice of EU–Russia interaction. According to the P4M progress report,[355] the most dynamic development of the program take place in those areas where Russia pledged to adopt European rules and regulations, thus acknowledging their higher standards. Russia promised to ratify the Espoo

354 Barry Buzan and Richard Little, "World History and the Development of Non-Western International Relations Theory," in A. Acharya and B. Buzan (eds.), *Non-Western International Relations Theory. Perspectives On and beyond Asia* (London and New York: Routledge, 2010): 206.

355 *Progress Report Agreed by the Coordinators of the EU–Russia Partnership for Modernisation for Information to the EU–Russia Summit of December 21, 2012*, http://eeas.europa.eu/russia/docs/2012_p4m_progress_report_signed_en.pdf (as of March 10, 2014).

and (similar) Aarhus conventions on assessment of environmental impact in transboundary context. The EU awarded grants for projects to nonstate actors on education and awareness raising for energy auditors, managers, and engineers, and set a EU–Russia laboratory on energy efficiency in Cannes. A project on energy efficiency in north-western Russia is being implemented within the Northern Dimension Environmental Partnership.

Despite the general progress in the P4M implementation, this program has also evoked some tensions between Brussels and Moscow. For example, in the energy sphere the main bone of contention is Moscow's unwillingness to ratify the European Energy Charter (EEC) that Russia signed under the President Boris Yeltsin but later interpreted as discriminatory. The main obstacle to Russia's ratification of the EEC is Moscow's unwillingness to separate production, reprocessing, and transportation of gas from each other. In practice, the Charter's requirements mean reorganization of monopolist companies such as Gazprom, Rosneft, Transneft, etc., and better access by foreign companies to the Russian lucrative energy sector. To counter the EEC the Kremlin suggested an energy charter of its own in 2009, but Brussels did not endorse the Russian initiative, and this part of the EU–Russia energy dialogue is almost frozen.

Modernization in Russian Discourse: Between Depoliticization and Politicization

The Putin regime, being a domestically depoliticized—that is, based on managerial and administrative approaches—type of power, from the very beginning was looking for a politically neutral language of communication with the EU, grounded in the idea of Russia's indisputable ('natural') belonging to the European tradition of modernity. The very reference to Europe thus serves as a powerful tool for discursive depoliticization and 'normalization' of Russia. It is against this background that the significance and the applicability of the idea of modernization have to be contextualized. The proliferation of different versions of modernization unveils a strong technocratic idealism as the constitutive feature of the Putin regime, including a belief in the applicability of the universal logic of administrative wisdom, legal provisions, and managerial efficiency, and the projection of business concepts into the policy-making and social domains.

The dominant Russian interpretation of modernization might be dubbed both postpolitical and apolitical. Yet what it hides is power ambitions embedded in presumably rational, objective, and commonly shared arguments. Ultimately, the depoliticized discourse of modernization turns into advocacy for a reinforced role of the state in many policy spheres, both domestic and international. Besides, the mix of postpolitical and authoritarian versions of modernization that prevails in Putin's Russia creates discursive disconnections in relations with Europe, where socio-political connotations of this concept resonate much stronger. It is not rare that in Europe the debate on modernization is intentionally put in a broad context of Russia's controversial relations with the West, including the most divisive issues of security, geopolitical clashes in a common neighborhood, dissimilar identity narratives, etc.[356]

For Russia, P4M is mostly about technical and procedural convergence, while for the EU it is a key element of the expanding European normative order, which also means approximation of norms within Russia to EU and Council of Europe standards. While Russia is mostly interested in European investment and high-tech transfers under this program, the EU tried to develop a more normative vision of modernization, including its socio-political and legal aspects that are indispensable for European businesses interested in expanding their operations into the Russian market. The EU insisted on the importance of ensuring an independently functioning judiciary and stepping up the fight against corruption. The EU encouraged Russia to develop further an effective appeal system for criminal and civil court cases, and believes that an active involvement of civil society institutions in the reformist process should be an indispensable part of the modernization 'package.' The EU also uses Russia's high interest in visa liberalization for conditioning a facilitated visa regime—or its lifting—by other measures that the Russian government has to undertake to correspond to EU standards, including the independent judiciary, effective police, safer system of document protection, integration of migrants, and many others.[357]

Evidently, the EU strategic vision of P4M presupposes a certain degree of asymmetry and challenges the concept of equality in relations with the West. Russia wants to avoid situations in which the EU takes the role of an example, a standard to be adopted by its neighbors, including countries of the EaP. Politically this removes the issues of democratization and human rights from the modernization partnership agenda, yet on technical levels Russia cannot avoid accepting regulatory norms and rules that successfully

356 Dieter Dettke, "Europe and Russia; from Neighborhood without a Shared Vision to a Modernization Partnership," *European Security* 20: 1 (2010): 127–142.

357 Report from the Commission to the European Parliament and the Council (2013). First Progress Report on the implementation by Russia of the Common Steps toward visa free short-term travel of Russian and EU citizens under the EU–Russia Visa Dialogue (Brussels, 18 December 2013, COM(2013) 923 final).

work in the EU and can be projected onto Russia – in energy efficiency, customs regulations, educational exchanges, environmental protection, etc. In most cases what is in a politically correct way dubbed the 'approximation of EU and Russia's systems' boils down to the alignment of Russia's technical regulations with that of the EU, often funded by the latter.[358]

Debates on modernization are conducive to a couple of conceptual challenges for the Kremlin, both evoking—though in different ways—political reverberations. One problem stems from the wide interpretative possibilities intrinsic to the idea of modernization, while another deals with its inscription into the debate on the universality of the European conception of modernity.

First, the broad variety of interpretations of modernization by different schools of thought makes the concept imprecise and even fuzzy. References to modernization in countries such as China or Iran[359] not only widen the concept, but also deprive it of its key contraposition with traditionalism and ultimately turn into a synonym for any type of development, regardless of its normative content. Since the conception of modernization seems to be far from self-sufficient and self-explanatory, it requires adjectives that infuse in it political connotations. In Russian discourse modernization can be 'liberal' (as opposed to 'conservative,' otherwise dubbed 'archaic')[360], 'deep' (as opposed to 'uneven,' 'apical,' 'peripheral,' or 'spasmodic'), 'comprehensive' (as opposed to 'fragmentary'), 'real' (as opposed to 'putative'), etc.

The conceptual breadth and uncertainty of the modernization concept triggers inevitable politicization, that is, its contestation and adoption for different political projects. Arguably, when elevating the modernization discourse to the very top of Russia's domestic and international agenda, the Kremlin underestimated the politically divisive effects of the concept, as exemplified, for example, by the robust denial of the model of authoritarian modernization by authoritative experts.[361] These discursive interventions con-

358 EU–Russia Partnership for Modernization: Two New Projects to Boost Trade and Economic Relations (May 23, 2013), http://www.enpi-info.eu/eastportal/news/latest/33184/EU-Russia-Partnership-for-Modernization:-two-new-projects-to-boost-trade-and-economic-relations (as of March 10, 2014)

359 Irina Kudriashova, "Iran kak sluchai islamskoi modernizatsii," *Politicheskaya Nauka* 2 (2012): 121–151.

360 Eduard Chekmariov, "Teorii modernizatsii i sovremennaya Rossiya," *Obozrevatel'-Observer* 9 (2009): 18.

361 Bobo Lo and Lylia Shevtsova, *A 21st Century Myth – Authoritarian Modernization in Russia and China* (Carnegie Moscow Center Report, 2012), http://www.carnegie.ru/publications/?fa=49116 (as of March 10, 2014).

strain the Kremlin's capacity for pragmatically utilizing the teleology of modernization for the sake of legitimizing the managerial and administrative practices of the ruling elite.[362] The very emptiness of the concept, therefore, constitutes a logical trap for the Kremlin that seems to be unable to control the proliferation of political meanings attached to modernization. A good example of politically divisive connotations of the concept of modernization is the controversy over Ukraine's discontinuation of the negotiations with the EU on the Association Agreement on the eve of the Vilnius summit of EaP in November 2013: For many European experts the nature of the problem boiled down to Ukraine's reluctance to modernize its economy.[363] Concomitantly, Russia who torpedoed the whole association process, in this interpretation stands as an antimodernization force, unfit to the European normative order. Modernization is thus not simply a technical notion but rather a terrain for political collisions in which the EU and Russia are on the opposite sides of barricades. Of course, this politicization was not among Medvedev's initial intentions, but it became more obvious after his presidency, which to a large extent explains Putin's reluctance to publicly articulate this concept during his third term in presidential office.

The Kremlin's response to the politicization of the idea of modernization boiled down to the attempts of anchoring it in a Russia-specific context and thus stabilizing its semantic dispersion. It is in this context that we may interpret the multiple attempts to inscribe modernization in religious or civilizational narratives[364] that, in spite of their supposed authenticity, on many accounts match the arguments of the Western 'critical neo-modernization' approach. Ultimately, in many cases, debates on modernization are substituted by—or transform into—debates on civilizations, which testifies to the weakness of modernization discourse and its leaning to other concepts. Politically, the Kremlin—especially with Putin resuming his presidency in 2012—is eager to take advantage of the fluidity of modernization discourse in order to detach its meanings from European roots, and to deny linkages between

362 Olga Malinova, "Eschio odin ryvok? Obrazy kollektivnogo proshlogo, nastoyaschego i buduschego v sovremennykh diskussiyakh o modernizatsii," *Politicheskaya Nauka* 2 (2012): 76.

363 Stefan Meister, "What if … the EU had offered membership perspective to Ukraine?" (Berlin: European Council on Foreign Relations, 2013), http://ecfr.eu/content/entry/commentary_what_if_the_eu_had_offered_membership_perspective_to_ukraine230 (as of March 10, 2014).

364 Vladimir Pavlenko, "Pravoslavie i modernizatsiya," *Obozrevatel'-Observer* 3 (2010): 17–35.

modernization and (liberal) Europeanization. Partnerships for modernization between Russia and several Asian countries (China, Korea, and Japan) serve to prove Moscow's intentions to place modernization in non-Western contexts, though practical effects of these agreements are hardly visible.

As Philipp Casula demonstrated, the concept of modernization may well be in line with some nodal points of Putin's narrative (such as depoliticization), yet in the meantime may contradict others (such as populism). This only confirms its characterization as an empty signifier politically adaptable to the needs of the ruling elite that, however, cannot fully control its meanings.[365]

Second, the very fact that academic theorizing produced two competing versions of modernization—one as a global projection of Western normative order, and another as coming in multiple forms conditioned by vernacular cultural identities—constitutes a significant political problem as well. In spite of the rhetoric on multipolarity and multiplicity of civilizations, the Kremlin by default pragmatically (though not necessarily publicly) accepted the Western—and, more specifically, European—foundations of the modernization paradigm. The most illustrative proof for this acceptance is the fact that it is the EU that is Russia's main international partner for modernization. Should the Kremlin genuinely believe in the idea of 'multiple modernities' and see strong impulses for modernization beyond Europe, it would certainly turn modernization into the key concept within the BRICS, or use it as a constitutive principle of the Eurasian integration project.

Yet the implicit acceptance of the Western origin of the concept of modernization will hardly bring palpable political dividends to the Putin regime, since it contradicts its core ideological assumptions of 'rising from the knees' rhetoric and maturing into a self-sufficient international pole. It is the EU that offers programs of modernization to its neighbors,[366] including Russia, and not vice versa. Of course, from the formal viewpoint, it was the Russian Ministry of Economy that co-drafted the actual partnerships with the EU and its Member States, yet the implementation of specific policy tracks leaves little room for rhetoric of Russian uniqueness.[367] The work plan for the implementation of P4M contains multiple indications of Russia's de facto recognition of

---

365 Phillipp Casula, "Sovereign Democracy, Populism and Depolitcization in Russia," *Problems of Post-Communism* 60: 3 (2013): 3–15.

366 Dieter Mahncke and Sieglinde Gstohl, "New Neighbors – New Challenges?" in Dieter Mahncke and Sieglinde Gstohl (eds.), *Europe's Near Abroad: Promises and Prospects of the EU's Neighborhood Policy* (Brussels: College of Europe's Studies 4, 2008): 9.

367 Emil Payn, "Istoricheskiy beg po krugu," *Obschestvennie nauki i sovremennost'* 4 (2008): 5–18.

EU's supremacy in many spheres—Russian municipal officers were studying the experiences of urban restructuring in European cities, Russian students and scholars extensively take advantage of the EU-sponsored programs of Erasmus Mundus, Tempus, Jean Monnet, Youth in Action, etc. The EU–Russia Common Spaces Progress Report of 2012 clearly indicates that the work plan of the P4M emphasizes the importance of associating Russia closer to European standard organizations (CEN/CENELEC). The document mentions that the EU has offered the Russian side its availability to organize training activities on antidumping. The EU has launched a new program on climate change for 2013–2016 involving Russia and aimed, in particular, on improving Russia's access to information on the EU climate change policies. Russia agreed to accept EU airline designation and hence to align all bilateral air transport agreements with EU legislation. The EU supports Russian NGOs joining child protection network.[368] There are many other facts that prove this trend as well – Russian phytosanitary norms and legislation regulating automotive sector are gradually being harmonized with EU standards; the EU funded a project aimed at upgrading the appeal system in Russia's judiciary; Russia benefited from TAIEX-funded activities on police cooperation and witness protection programs, as well as from ENPI-funded programs of journalist training, etc.[369] Having adapted the language of modernization, Russia, therefore, implicitly pledged to acknowledge the legitimacy of the European normative order and its own intention to find a proper place in it, which is not guaranteed by the virtue of either geography or history.

By the same token, the acceptance of Western primacy runs against Russia's search for *equality* with the West, since the launch of the modernization partnership implicitly confirms Russia's role as a junior partner of the EU. In late modernity, one may argue, "the non-West remains a silent spectator"[370] of the predominance of the West. Russia's status as a modernizing country could thus be comparable to those Third World countries that were the initial objects of modernizing by the United States-led West in the 1950s

368 EU–Russia Common Spaces. Progress Report (2012), http://eeas.europa.eu/russia/docs/commonspaces_prog_report_2012_en.pdf (as of March 10, 2014).

369 *Ibid.*

370 M.K. Pasha and M.K. Islam, " 'Soft' Orientalism and Hegemony: A Gramscian Rereading," in A. Bieler and A.D. Morton (eds.), *Images of Gramsci. Connections and Contentions in Political Theory and International Relations* (London and New York: Routledge, 2006): 155.

and 1960s.[371] Russia's obsession with equality in conditions of structural inequality only sustains the rift between the political rhetoric and the practice of EU–Russia relations. It is indicative that in those spheres where Russia insistently claims its sovereign rights to define its political priorities beyond coordination of its policies with the EU, the evidences of success in the modernization work plan are almost nonexistent. This is the case of the EU proposal to make EU–Russia Civil Society Forum a key element of the modernization agenda, which the Kremlin certainly dislikes due to its domestically restrictive policy toward NGOs often referred to as 'foreign agents.' Yet in much less politically pronounced areas—such as in the expected elimination of trade barriers—Russia shows no sufficient signs of cooperation, which can be explained by the Kremlin's fear of losing competition with EU products in Russian domestic markets. Lack of progress in another area—developing common approaches to food security—is due to Russia's policy of using quality of food products as a political tool against targeted countries, including EU Member States. Thus, having introduced a ban on Lithuanian dairy products in October 2013, Russia claimed that since this issue concerns the safety of consumption, it stays beyond WTO regulations—a logic that the EU is hardly to accept.[372] In spite of the fact that under the aegis of the P4M Russia acceded to a number of international legal acts aimed at protecting children (the 1980 Convention on the Civil Aspects of International Child Abduction and the 1996 Convention on Jurisdiction, Applicable Law, Recognition, Enforcement and Cooperation in Respect of Parental Responsibility and Measures for the Protection of Children), Russia's restrictive policy on foreign adoption is still an issue that betrays either political motivations, or deep ideological gaps between Russia and Europe—in particular, in such sensitive policy fields as LBGT rights.

Implications for Russia–EU (Mis)Communications

The debate on the essence of the concept of modernization unveiled deep political gaps between the two partners. *First*, as the joint letter of Foreign

---

371 D. Efremenko, "V poiskakh modernizatsionnykh orientirov v epokhu mezhdutsarstviya moderna," *Politicheskaya Nauka* 2 (2012): 13–14.

372 Vladimir Chizhov, Interview informatsionnomu agentstvu ITAR-TASS, (October 17, 2013), http://www.russianmission.eu/ru/intervyu/intervyu-vachizhova-informatsionnomu-agentstvu-itar-tass-17-oktyabrya-2013-goda (as of March 10, 2014).

Ministers of Germany and Poland, Guido Westerwelle and Radoslaw Sykorski to Lady Ashton[373] made clear, the modernization agenda in relations with Russia is more about EU's assistance to—than about partnership with—Russia. The EU claims to remain "Europe's main embodiment of modernisation,"[374] especially in such areas as good governance, transparency, accountability, sustainable development, civil–military relations, etc. The chances of Russia accepting this approach are miniscule. Moreover, Russia's fierce resistance to Ukraine's policy of adapting to EU norms through signing the Association Agreement is a good vindication of Russia's reluctance to modernize its legal and economic systems to be as competitive on the Ukrainian market as European producers. In this light, the questions of whether Russia can modernize[375] and how it can spur demodernization all across former Soviet Union[376] receive increasing resonance.

Second, for European governments modernization is predominantly a political process aimed at establishing an effective modern nation state, which definitely encompasses policies of eradicating corruption and mismanagement. "Modernization requires institutional change – indeed the development of a range of independent institutions and of the rule of law, and the curtailing of the power and privileges of the bureaucracy and of a gigantic, inefficient, subsidized, and anticompetitive state corporation."[377] This agenda in most European countries is largely completed, which leads to highly divisive political effects of the modernization concept: EU–Russian relations within the P4M framework are inevitably destined for asymmetry and inequality, and contain strong bordering ('Us' vs. 'Them') components. After Putin's resumption of presidential powers in 2012 it became a commonplace for EU experts to assume that the ruling regime in Russia shows no signs of interest

---

373 Joint Letter of Foreign Ministers Radoslaw Sikorski of Poland and Guido Westerwelle of Germany on EU–Russia Relations (2011), http://www.mfa.gov.pl/en/news/joint_letter (as of March 10, 2014).

374 Petr Kratochvil and Elsa Tulmets, *Constructivism and Rationalism in EU External Relations. The Case of the European Neighborhood Policy* (Baden-Baden: Nomos, 2010).

375 Alena Ledeneva, "Can Russia Modernise? Sistema, Power Networks and Informal Governance" (Moscow: Valdai Club, 2013), http://valdaiclub.com/books_english/61782.html (as of March 10, 2014).

376 Mikhail Minakov, "Demodernizatsiya na prostranstve byvshego SSSR," *Vedomosti* (November 14, 2013).

377 R. Lyne, "The Imaginary Curtain," in P. Dutkiewicz and D. Trenin (eds.), *Russia: the Challenges of Transformation,* (New York: Social Science Research Council & New York University Press, 2011): 281.

in comprehensive modernization. The European message sent to Russia implies that in the postindustrial age modernization cannot be based on authoritarian mechanisms of mass mobilization and administrative centralism, and requires different concepts [378] premised on good governance practices grounded in horizontal interaction, policy networks, public–private partnership, etc.[379]

Third, what complicates the EU–Russia conceptual disconnections is that the EU does not identify itself unequivocally any longer with the idea of modernity. In the opinion of many European experts, the concepts of sovereign great powers, spheres of influence, and balance of power, to which Russia largely adheres, are 'too modern', 'too Westphalian,' and therefore seemingly inadequate for—and even incompatible with—today's idea of Europe.[380] A Russia adhered to a pretty modernist concept of power balancing and zero-sum-games will certainly be stigmatized by Europe for subscribing to obsolete worldviews. In particular, there are voices in Europe claiming that the Putin's regime maltreatment of the LGBT community is exactly what makes Russia "unmodern."[381]

This raises a question of whether modernization is a sufficient tool for fulfilling Russia's double task of domestic reforms and international socialization. To Europeanize itself, Russia has to adapt to some of the practices of postmodernity and postsovereignty (networking/post-Westphalian diplomacy, supranationality, cross-border flows and exchanges, multiple and unfixed identities, etc.). Unfortunately, while reproducing obsolete social and political practices, reminiscent of feudal times (such as, e.g., in the relations between the federal center and regions, or between the Kremlin and corporate business), Russia moves away from both Europe and the very idea of modernization.

Modernization, officially articulated as one of the foundations for partnership between Russia and the EU since 2010, from the outset was a form of legitimizing Russia's place in Europe, on the one hand, and promoting the economic interests of major EU industrial and financial actors, on the other.

---

378 Dmitry Trenin, "Of Power and Greatness," in Dutkiewicz and Trenin (eds.), *Russia,* 419.

379 Andrew Hurrell, *On Global Order. Power, Values, and the Constitution of International Society* (Oxford: Oxford University Press, 2009): 95.

380 Derek Averre, "Competing Rationalities: Russia, the EU and the 'Shared Neighbourhood' ," *Europe-Asia Studies* 61: 10 (2009): 1691, 1693.

381 Sergey Khazov, "Russia's Anti-Gay Own Goal," *Open Democracy, 2013,* http://opendemocracy.net/od-russia/sergey-khazov/russias-anti-gay-own-goal (as of March 10, 2014).

On both accounts, the position of the EU seems to be of crucial importance for the prospects of the modernizations partnership between the EU and Russia. Seen from a discursive perspective, the idea of modernization promoted by the ruling elite in Moscow comes mostly in a technical form and thus lacks due social and political appeal. As this analysis suggests, modernization does not seem to be capable of sustaining the dominating narrative of Russian grandeur, since what it underlies is recurrent failures of previous attempts to modernize the country along the lines of the most successful nations, as well as deep disconnections with the Europeanization framework. Russia's backwardness appears particularly visible against the background of those states that are successfully adapting to a postsovereign, post-Westphalian, postnation world that is rebuked by Putin's regime.

The debate on modernization had as its effect the strengthening of Europe's discursive and normative predominance over Russia, which triggered a counterreaction from Moscow. The structure of modernization discourse leaves at the EU's (and its Member States') disposal sufficient leeway for either narrowing or, vice versa, widening the inherently political distance between 'Europe' and 'Russia' as two intersubjectively constructed communities. Discursively, the EU plays the role of a source of international legitimation of Russia's modernization agenda, which means that Europe's growing disinterest in supporting modernization under the increasingly authoritarian regime in the Kremlin would with great likelihood trigger the discontinuation of the modernization project—at least, as designed by Berlin and Moscow in the times of the bygone Medvedev's 'thaw.'

3.3 EU–Russia Security (Mis)communication

Security discourses are important terrains where collective identities and subjectivities of political actors emerge. Russia's self-perception in the world – as well its intersubjective relations with other key members of IS—are constituted through a variety of security discourses, deeply rooted in disciplines such as International Relations, political science, sociology, gender studies, and international law. At the same time, security discourses have extended beyond academia to other professional fields such as public policy, journalism, and even commercials. As a result, the discursive landscapes of security have proliferated and comprise a wide variety of meanings.

In the sphere of security the rift between the EU and Russia looks quite substantial. The EU, being short of military power, basically approaches security issues from a *normative unification* perspective that prioritizes normative components of security community building (adherence to common values, accentuation of soft/HS dimensions, etc.). Russia, on its part, often displays its sympathies to talk security business with major EU Member States, which by and large corresponds to *GPM* model, with clear emphasis on *spheres of influence* as a structural precondition for Russian domination in the post-Soviet Eurasia.

In one of his foreign policy pronouncements, Vladimir Putin has claimed that the Western countries "have developed a peculiar interpretation of security that is different from ours."[382] Unfortunately, his pessimistic assessment seems to be fair enough. Russia on the one hand, and the EU and NATO on the other, indeed differently approach international security issues (such as the NATO enlargement, the deployment of American antimissile system in Central Europe, or the Syrian debate in the UN), as well the key security concepts (in particular, in an effort to delegitimize Western policies Putin lambasted 'illegal instruments of soft power'). Russia accused the West in bellicosity, in aggravation of situation in countries subjected to humanitarian interventions, in violations of their sovereignties, in artificially keeping afloat obsolete stereotypes about Russia, etc. In response, the West accused Russia in neo-imperial ambitions and unilateralism, in using energy weaponry against consuming countries, etc.

One may agree that since the collapse of the Soviet Union the West was not interested in strategic security partnership with Russia[383]—perhaps, to the same extent that Russia was not ready—both politically and technically—for such a partnership. It is this complicated state of relations between Russia and Europe that defines the nature of the problems I am going to tackle in this section. I will argue that there are two key issues for Russia in security sphere. First, Russia is very much enmeshed in *defense* thinking (which is reactive and military based), and lacks a more comprehensive *security* thinking to embrace a wider gamut of social threats, risks, and vulnerabilities. The second problem is the lack of fully fledged international acceptance of Russia's security posture, which stems from a normative dissonance between Russia and the EU, and from Europe's vision of Russia as an untrustworthy

382 Vladimir Putin, "Russia and the Changing World" (2009), http://premier.gov.ru/eng/events/news/18252/ (as of March 10, 2014).

383 Dmitry Trenin, "Putin the Peacemaker?" *Foreign Policy* (February 28, 2011), http://www.foreignpolicy.com/articles/2012/02/28/putin_the_peacemaker (as of March 10, 2014).

international actor with corrupt political and economic systems, which certainly has direct security repercussions.[384]

Being a complex combination of academic and political discourses, embedded in various institutional contexts, security agenda in Russia is very sensitive to communication frameworks with the EU. For comprehending EU–Russia security relationship I employ the concept of securitization which, in my view, catches the immanent variety and changeability of discourses on security, and their intersubjective character. In the traditions of the Copenhagen school I understand by securitization "an articulated assemblage of practices whereby heuristic artefacts (metaphors, policy tools, image repertoires, analogies, stereotypes, emotions, etc.) are contextually mobilized by a securitizing actor, who works to prompt an audience to build a coherent network of implications (feelings, sensations, thoughts and intuitions) about the critical vulnerability of a referent object."[385]

A good example of the inherent interrelatedness of all components of securitization process is Russia's proposal on a new European security treaty and the reaction to this initiative in the EU. As a securitizing actor, Russia pointed to the obvious deficiency and vulnerability of the existing mechanisms of security which failed to prevent a series of violent conflicts, basically resulting from states' disintegration and secession of break-away territories. Russia certainly had a point in raising the issue of conflict prevention, but the efficiency of the Russian proposal was hampered by at least two factors. The first is Russia's reluctance to engage in a dialogue on the substance of security with its major security partners in the West. In particular, Moscow remained relatively indifferent to the 'Helsinki Plus' report of the EU–Russia working group chaired by Javier Solana in 2010, as well as to the Euro-Atlantic Security Initiative (EASI).[386] Russia's indifference reveals deep conceptual gaps in security perceptions in Russia, on the one hand, and the EU and NATO, on the other. The Western approach rejects a formal negotiated treaty

---

384 Robert Rotberg, "How Corruption Compromises World Peace and Stability," in Robert Rotberg (ed.), *Corruption, Global Security, and World Order* (Cambridge, MA: World Peace Foundation and American Academy of Arts and Sciences, 2009): 1–26.

385 Thierry Balzacq, "A Theory of Securitization. Origins, Core Assumptions, and Variants," in Thierry Balzacq (ed.), *Securitization Theory. How Security Problems Emerge and Dissolve* (London & New York: Routledge, 2011): 3.

386 EASI, chaired by Igor Ivanov, Wolfgang Ischinger, and Sam Nunn, makes a strong case for a trilateral cooperation between NATO, EU, and Russia in security domain, with potential participation of OCSE and international NGOs.

with Russia and in its stead welcomes a gradual confidence-building process with transparency as its cornerstone. Besides, along with military security, both the EU and NATO strongly advocate the adoption of HS perspective, though it might be understood in different ways—as encompassing historical reconciliation between former enemies,[387] or as the focusing on the needs of population rather than the interests of states. The unwillingness to seriously discuss HS concept obviously weakens the Russian position in communicating with the EU.

Second, what only exacerbates the weakness of the Russian stand is the lack of support from countries which Russia itself considers its allies, first of all the members of the CSTO and the SCO. There are no evidences that Moscow has even tried to coordinate the drawing up of the European Security Treaty with any of them, which turns the whole idea in an individual speech act that resonated neither with Russian neighbors nor with its Western interlocutors. Moscow's attempts to present the lukewarm reception in Europe of this widely propagated security initiative as a proof of disinterest in partnership with Russia only underpins the existence of profound perceptional gaps between Moscow and Brussels.

Yet the application of the concept of securitization not only sheds light on the mechanisms of miscommunication between security actors, but also helps unveil the flexibility of relations of friendship and enmity among nations whose roles and identities are not necessarily well established. Countries constantly securitize and desecuritize each other. Perhaps, the most notorious examples of countries securitized by Russia are Ukraine (2013–2014), Georgia (the military conflict between Moscow and Tbilisi in August 2008), and Estonia (the conflict caused by the removal of the Bronze Soldier monument from the Tallinn downtown to a military cemetery in 2007). Both cases demonstrate that securitization can be driven by both material and ideational factors, and always includes strong symbolic dimension.

In the meantime, several examples of a more or less successful desecuritization can be given, as epitomized by the improved Russia's relations with Poland and Norway. In both cases, the old conflicts—more politically pronounced in the first case due to the Polish dissatisfaction with the Russian unwillingness to unequivocally take responsibility for the Katyn affair,[388] and

387 *Towards a Euro-Atlantic Security Community*. EASI Final report (February 2012), http://carnegieendowment.org/2012/02/03/toward-euro-atlantic-security-community/9d3j# (as of March 10, 2014).

388 Mass murder of Polish officers by Stalinist security forces.

more technical in the relations with Norway—were transformed into a cooperative type of relationship. Both cases of desecuritization have led to the conclusion of bilateral agreements on visa-free border-crossing procedures for residents of adjacent areas, which is a good addition to the visa-free negotiations between Russia and the EU.

Russia's Visions of International Security: The Challenges of Legitimation

The major problem that Russia faces at the international security scene is the much needed legitimation of its security posture, which is unattainable without institutional participation in the dominating security structures. It is exactly the institutional deficit of Russian security policies that is conducive to major policy failures: Even if in certain situations Russia might have a point, Russian arguments are overwhelmingly rejected, which dooms Russia to a politically costly role of a unilateral security actor. To put it differently, Russia's speech acts often fail to reach the goal of persuading the external audience and as policy tools remain ineffective.

The search for legitimacy takes the form of Russia's gradual adaptation to international security vocabulary. Indeed, Russian security discourse is influenced by a number of Western security concepts, such as 'hard' and soft' security, a dichotomy that was positively accepted in Russian academic community and unleashed intensive discussions on information, energy, environmental, and other types/forms of security. In the meantime, most Russian politicians are more skeptical about the adaptability of European security vocabulary in Russia. In their opinion, a wider approach to security, bereft of clear focus on the most deadly threats, is conducive to unfortunate securitization of the entire gamut of social relations, including environment, human rights, energy relations, and so forth. It is the gradual marginalization of military aspects of security in negotiations with Russia that the EU and NATO are interested in, they believe. It is also claimed that a wider understanding of security leads to the lack of "geographic specialization" in security provision,[389] which is a euphemism denoting division of spheres of influence. In particular, the 'soft security' concept may lead to potentially divisive effects, leaving Russia in a role of a source of security threats to the West.

What is missing in the Russian debate is that the EU's and NATO's extended security agendas may widen the areas of possible cooperation with

389 Elena Khot'kova *et al.*, "O perspektivakh zakliuchenia Dogovora o Evropeiskoi bezopasnosti," *Problemy natsional'noi strategii* 2 (2010): 7–24.

Russia, to include a variety of soft security issues, such as migration, drug trafficking, border control management, etc. The same goes for the HS concept that was intentionally misinterpreted in the official discourse of the Kremlin and reduced to technical matters of survival in conditions of disasters, postcrisis management, state regulation of medical and pharmaceutical standards, etc.

Russia's Security Roles in Wider Europe

In what follows, I will dwell upon a variety of roles that Russia can play in international security politics. The roles in this menu are by no means mutually exclusive, and some of them may be performed simultaneously.

Russia as a Security Architect

The key rationale for Russia's insistence on institutionalization of a new 'security architecture' in a wider Europe is a long-standing fear of being excluded from the mechanisms of decision-making in the key issues of international politics.[390] The problem is that the inclusion in a pan-European security community requires the applicants to become 'more like us' and, consequently, is premised on a sense of we-ness and togetherness. In such a community, difference and pluralism are externalized, and Russia is one of those outsiders that is perceived as external to the Western security.[391] Some of the language games reflect this perceptional gap: While Russia prefers to speak about '*Euro-Atlantic* security' (presupposing Russia's participation), most of Europeans think in categories of '*trans-Atlantic* security' (which does not envision Russia's inclusion).

However, the Russian vision of a new security architecture is grounded in a number of approaches that look either contradictory or ill-conceptualized. Some of them are in disharmony with the dominating Western conceptions. *First*, Russia is sympathetic with the idea of 'network diplomacy,' a concept that seems to be quite in tune with the Western political vocabulary. But this similarity in terms is only putative. In the Russian context, the references to 'network diplomacy' connote traditional state-centric policies of multilateralism at the best, while in the West this concept signifies a globalization-friendly

---

390 Sergey Rogov, "Security Relations between Russia and the Western World," in Kurt Spillmann and Andreas Wenger (eds.), *Russia's Place in Europe. A Security Debate* (Bern: Peter Lang Publishers, 1999): 177.

391 Joenniemi, "Difference within Similarity": 30.

type of horizontal interaction between social and professional groups that constitutes an alternative to state hierarchies.[392]

Second, Russia is committed to the principle of equal security, which also raises a number of conceptual issues boiling down to various understandings of the idea of equality in security domain. It can be interpreted, for example, as the right of each country to choose its own security instruments, including the membership in military alliances.[393] This interpretation evidently does not suit Moscow, which makes some pro-Kremlin experts claim that "autonomy of states in security sphere requires certain limitations," and that "the freedom to join alliances should not be taken as a dogma."[394] These remarks only reveal the real intentions behind Moscow's strategy—to constrain the freedom of choice of its neighbors and strengthen its preeminence in the 'near abroad.'

The Kremlin-friendly version of equal security reduces this concept to its purely legal(ist) components. But this logic seems to be only of limited utility, since references to international law often fail to work in situations of contested norms. That is why at certain point the politicization of the demand for equality becomes inevitable, and this is exactly what happens when Russian authors claim that unrecognized territories, including Abkhazia, South Ossetia, and Transnistria, have to be accepted as fully fledged participants of the all-European security "concert."[395] Yet this apparent radicalization of the concept of equality seems to be hardly acceptable for most of Russia's European partners.

What further complicates the practical implementation of the idea of equality is Russia's skepticism about the existence of spheres with different mechanisms of influence, commitments, and regulations within a wider Europe. Yet security concerns of the Nordic Europe are definitely very different

---

392 Jamie Metzl, "Network Diplomacy," *Georgetown Journal of International Affairs* (Winter–Spring 2001), http://www.carnegieendowment.org/2001/04/01/network-diplomacy/dv3 (as of March 10, 2014).

393 Igor' Yurgens, Alexandr Dynkin, and Vladimir Baranovskiy (eds.), *Arkhitektura Evroatlanticheskoi bezopasnosti* (Moscow: INSOR & Econ-Inform Publisher, 2009): 49.

394 Mark Entin, "Predlozhenia po rabote nad zakliucheniem dogovora o evropeiskoi bezopasnosti obrastaiut konkretikoi," *All Europe* e-Journal, http://www.alleuropa.ru/predlozheniya-po-rabote-nad-zakliucheniem-dogovora-o-evropeyskoy-bezopasnosti-obrastaiut-konkretikoy (as of March 10, 2014).

395 Alexander Sytin, "Aktual'nye aspekty novoi arkhitektury bezopasnosti na post-sovetskom prostranstve," *Problemy natsional'noi strategii* 1 (2009): 48–61.

from—and thus unequal to—security troubles faced by the Black Sea countries. Besides, the idea of equal security may require the repudiation of the spheres-of-influence type of policy that Russia pursues in its 'near abroad.'

Third, Russia is keen on supporting the idea of collective security that again comes in a variety of versions. In one of them, "collective security should not be substituted by bloc-based approaches,"[396] which implies that collective security ought to unfold beyond blocs. Yet in Sergey Lavrov's version, collective security is articulated exactly as a combination of regional security 'segments,' or blocs: NATO plus CSTO, Asia Pacific, Persian Gulf, Middle East, and the South Caucasus.[397] Experts assume that even within CSTO there are three regions of 'collective security': East European, Caucasian, and Central Asian. This fragmented vision certainly presupposes different security instruments and institutions for different regions. Thus, the idea of collective security in the CSTO segment may be interpreted as "an ensemble of inter-state governmental bodies, forces and measures that provide the legally framed defense of member states' interests grounded in sovereignty and territorial integrity."[398] Placing sovereignty as the key reference object of securitization raises a number of substantial issues, since the strongest challenges to sovereignty might emanate from within the states and result from mismanagement, corruption, lack of due transparency, etc.

Fourth, Russia's adherence to the principle of indivisibility of security may also be a matter of debate. Thus, a former Russian Foreign Minister Igor Ivanov claims that indivisibility should not be confused with the belief in almost automatic linkages between regional conflicts and global security—such a vision is a relic of the Cold War and only leads to greater tensions between the key powers. Neither has indivisibility to be equated with the search for universal institutions able to solve the entire plethora of security concerns in the world. In Ivanov's view, the most effective frame for the implementation of the idea of indivisibility is a combination of different security regimes, each one representing a flexible coalition of state and nonstate ac-

---

396 Mark Entin, "Chto trebuetsa dlia propyrva k real'noi mezhdunarodnoi bezopasnosti," *Vsia Evropa* 9: 58 (2011), http://www.alleuropa.ru/chto-trebuetsya-dlya-proriva-k-utverzhdeniiu-realjnoy-mezhdunarodnoy-bezopasnosti (as of March 10, 2014).

397 Sergey Lavrov. Speech at the International Security Conference (Munich, February 4, 2012), http://www.mid.ru/brp_4.nsf/0/45D5CC6F7F1EACF04425799A005B12EC (as of March 10, 2014).

398 Igor' Yurgens (ed.), *ODKB: otvetstevennaya bezopasnost* (Moscow: INSOR, 2011): 13.

tors eager to collectively solve issues of common concerns (energy, environment, migration, cyber crime, etc.). In his reading, regimes are more democratic and inclusive than traditional institutions, since they are not grounded in a domination of great powers, and do not envision the veto power.[399]

Fifth, Russian diplomatic vocabulary contains multiple references to the prospects of a bloc-free structure of global security relations ('*vneblokovost*'). Semantically, this concept may be viewed as applicable to a limited number of countries that have chosen neutrality (Ukraine, Switzerland, Sweden, Finland), but, as seen from the Russian perspective, this principle ought to be foundational for the overall 'security architecture' in Europe. What stands behind the Russian interpretation of a 'bloc-free' structure of international security is the desire to delegitimize NATO as the pivotal military bloc in Europe. Yet the declared propensity to a 'bloc-free' security is in a conflict with Moscow's policy of strengthening CSTO and delineating its sphere of security responsibility.

Yet there is another important hurdle for Russia's security proposals implementation: Russia and the EU, despite significant symbolic and discursive investments from both sides in the common communicative terrain, speak different security languages. *First,* the starting positions of Russia and the EU seem to be quite different. The former—in a *realpolitik*-type of reasoning—is keen to pragmatically make accent on joint interests, while the latter grounds its discourse in a 'family-type constellation' with the issues if identity ('who we are' and 'how we relate to others') and the concept of 'ontological security' at its core.[400] The articulation of identity matters leads to two interrelated bordering effects. One has to deal with democracy vs. nondemocracy contradistinction: It is widely believed in Europe that "only among liberal democracies is the security dilemma sufficiently reduced to allow the states to surrender a part of their sovereignty without the fear that today's partner may become tomorrow's enemy [...] . Regional integration is more successful in liberal-democratic Europe than in regions populated by authoritarian regimes."[401] Another effect introduces the opposition between external and internal sources of danger: The Kremlin perceives EU's emphasis on soft security as quite troublesome and even challenging, since most of these threats, being

399 Igor Ivanov, "Nedelimost' bezopasnosti v globalnom mire," *Index Bezopasnosti* 17: 4 (2011): 33–34.

400 Joenniemi, "Difference within Similarity": 29.

401 Benjamin Miller, "When and How Regions Become Peaceful: Potential Theoretical Pathways to Peace," *International Studies Review* 7: 2 (June 2005): 251.

external for Europe, are *domestic* for Russia. Russia is ill-equipped to effectively deal with the set of issues that get a high profile in the EU policy agenda, including corruption, trafficking, migration, environmental protection, and cannot 'export' successful security practices to other—even neighboring – countries. The EU concept of security sector reform, with its accents on accountable and transparent security relations,[402] does not resonate in Russia. By the same token, the security-development nexus, being pivotal for the European discourse, indirectly marginalizes Russia that evidently cannot boast of grounding its security management in effective and inclusive—primarily with regard to civil society institutions—social policies.

Second, the EU and Russia tend to draw different lessons from military operations beyond their borders. After the conflict in Western Balkans the EU has made a strong emphasis on domestic changes in conflict-torn societies pointing to the rule of law and reforms in judiciary and police institutions, as well as on the perspectives of combining civilian (police-type) and military missions on the ground.[403] Russia's lessons after the Georgia war of August 2008 were quite different: The clear deficiency of political, administrative, and economic systems in South Ossetia and Abkhazia has never drawn attention of the Kremlin which instead preferred to anchor its postwar discourse in the ideas of multipolarity and Russia's presumably growing self-confidence.

Third, the issue of scope also matters. The EU openly claims its role as a 'global security provider' with unique organizational capabilities and resources for peace-making operations worldwide,[404] while Russia can only expect of being recognized as a regional power with rather limited toolkit for effectively approaching security issues beyond its borders. Russia shows weak performance in tackling such global issues as climate change, resource depletion, managerial and financial transparency, etc.

Fourth, the issue of expertise is no less important. Unlike the EU, Russia lacks traditions of peace research as a separate field of IR analysis. Peace and conflict studies in Russia are grossly under-conceptualized and thus could not turn into a meaningful policy-changing tool.

---

402 Isabelle Ioannides, "European Union Security Sector Reform Policy," *Eyes on Europe* (Autumn 2009): 37.

403 *Ibid.*, 38.

404 Javier Solana, "Ten Years of European Peace-building Around the World," *Eyes on Europe* (Autumn 2009): 1.

Russia as a Unilateral Peace Enforcer

This role is an alternative to the previous one, since it presupposes Russia's strengthening of its own power resources in its 'near abroad,' rather than co-sponsoring collective security for the entire Euro-Atlantic area. Thus, an expert in the journal published by the state-funded Russian Institute for Strategic Studies claims that Russia has to choose between the liberal principles of security with their emphasis on collective peace-keeping and humanitarian operations grounded in a wider interpretation of security, on the one hand, and a more traditional balance of forces between the key poles with well-fixed spheres of influence for each of them, on the other. According to him, the second option seems to fit better in the Russian security interests. In this interpretation, instead of participating in multilateral coalitions Russia should opt for freedom of hands in the area of its vital interests, as well as for claiming its 'right' to veto unfriendly enlargement of the rivaling military bloc. Instead of looking for cooperative management of security conflicts, Russia should be wary about its competitors' interference in what it considers zones of its exceptional interest. This role recognizes the possible areas of privileged security responsibilities of countries such as Turkey, but intends to reduce the EU's involvement in the post-Soviet countries to bilateral relations bereft of institutional background.[405]

This largely unilateral type of security conduct deserves critical analysis from at least two vantage points. *First*, Russia often imitates US policies without having comparable resources matching the US military might. The August 2008 Russian military action against Georgia and the Kremlin's recognition of the two breakaway territories were marked by multiple references to the Kosovo precedent. Well before 2008 Russian experts admitted that "we are doing in Abkhazia what NATO did in Kosovo, having separated it from Serbia."[406] In fact, Russia imitated the artificial recognitions of sovereignty and the equal rights stemming from it to territories with no resources for independent development, which in result "undermines the legal and political order and creates a fictional order without substantive content."[407]

Second, Russia has to pay dear political price for unilateral military action, finding itself in a diplomatic isolation on the issue of recognition of the

405 Sytin, "Aktual'nye aspekty", 48–61.

406 Alexei Krasnosiolov, "Tak kto poterial Gruziyu?" *International Trends. Journal of Theory of International Relations and World Politics* 1 (January–April 2003): 123.

407 David Chandler, "The Revival of Carl Schmitt in International Relations: The Last Refuge of Critical Theorists?" *Millennium: Journal of International Studies* 37: 1 (2008): 43.

two rebellious republics. Besides, Russia proved unable to mastermind the political situation in its de facto protectorates: The President of Abkhazia was a target of numerous assassination attempts, while in South Ossetia Moscow was incapable of guaranteeing electoral victory to its favorite for presidency, which resulted in the cancellation of the results of presidential election in Fall 2011. Weak political position on the ground is the price that Moscow pays for its unilateralism in the Caucasus, as well as Transnistria.

Russia as a Peace Mediator

A third role for Russia to play is that one of peace maker in the areas of its 'near abroad.' This role, deduced from Russia's declared 'special' interests in this vast area, however, faces serious challenges. *First*, Russia is not a 'honest broker': In conflicts in Nagorno-Karabakh and Transnistria it does take sides, and by doing so, complicates its relations with more important actors, Azerbaijan and Moldova correspondingly. *Second*, Russia's interest in peace mediation and conflict resolution seems to be dubious by many in the West. Thus, a German expert claims that "Russia continues to use the conflicts in order to exert influence on the participating states and does not have a genuine interest in their resolution [...] . Russia does not see post-Soviet conflicts as a threat to its security, but as a means to maintain its influence."[408]

In the meantime, the then President Medvedev signed the Meseberg declaration that opened the prospects for a more intense Russian–German security dialogue on the basis of cooperation over the Transnistria conflict. Moscow indeed tried to exert strong pressure upon the former head of Transnistria Igor Smirnov, but ultimately failed to dissuade him from running again for the President of this breakaway territory. Nevertheless, the Meseberg process is one of few instances of Russia's tacit acceptance of the principle of conditionality that it verbally rejects.

There are two key explanations of the lack of Russia's success in playing the role of peace maker. One is Russia's reluctance to take political stands and thus make choices that would apparently dissatisfy one of the conflicting parties, while another is the deficit of multilateral diplomatic efforts which are one of the weakest links in Russian diplomacy. Of course, Western countries cannot boast of their success stories in conflict resolution either, but the lack of progress is first of all detrimental to the Russian pretentions to hegemonize the political and security landscape of the post-Soviet region.

---

408 Stefan Meister, "A New Start for Russian – EU Security Policy?" *Genshagener Papiere* 7 (June 2011): 17.

Russia as a Key Element of European Energy Security. Russia's role as energy security provider can be viewed in several aspects. *First*, it represents an extension of the idea of Russia as a corporate state, void of strong value-based identity and interested mainly in economic and financial transactions. This role envisions a domination of energy companies' interests (especially those of 'Gazprom') in Russia's relations with transit and consuming countries. The key paradox here is that this positioning, being conceived in Russia as a manifestation of its propensity to technological approaches in its relations with its partners, is reinterpreted in Europe as a political gesture entailing strong security effects, ranging from the appearance of 'energy gendarme' metaphor in the European media to NATO's readiness to include energy disruption into the list of major security threats to the Euro-Atlantic region.

Second, the practical implementation of this role appears to be most effective within the framework of a bilateral and pragmatic co-management of energy issues between Russia and Germany, as exemplified by the Nord Stream project. The Russian and German interests in energy security seem to largely coincide. For Russia as an exporter country the main source of energy insecurity is dependence on transit across the territory of countries where in political circles the mood is hostile. In addition, at the forefront of the Russian understanding of energy security is maximizing capitalization of petroleum resources, and using them for promoting Russian economic interests in the West. For Germany as a user country raising the level of energy security is connected with partial access to Russia's energy resources through working with 'Gazprom' and other large companies. As most European countries, Germany defines energy security as maintaining acceptable (that is stable and reasonable) prices for oil, gas, and their future equivalents, imported from reliable and diversified sources. There are two main threats from this point of view: high prices for energy and instability of supply. As the Russian–German cooperation makes clear, energy security is a means of creating regulatory regimes that would lower the risks of unexpected price changes, and provide at the same time an appropriate level of openness in the markets.

Yet for potential transit countries, energy security is associated with the possibility of controlling the process of transit itself and receiving rent from it. In particular, in the opinion of a Lithuanian specialist, "losing the position of transit state will make Lithuania more vulnerable to Russian politics."[409] Poland, Ukraine, and the Baltic countries accuse Moscow of marginalizing their

409 T. Janeliunas and A. Molis, "The NEGP Ends Lithuania's Hopes of Becoming a Transit Country," *The Baltic Mosaic. Analytical Notes* 1: 5 (Winter–Spring 2006): 30.

roles and constructing politically motivated energy transportation routes, while Russia itself thinks of its energy projects as strictly technological ones, dictated primarily by economic rationale and in this sense depoliticized. In fact, the Russian message, expressed technologically yet based upon a certain political reasoning, stretches far beyond the energy security matters: It reads in fact that Russia does not need 'assistants'/'facilitators' in its energy dialogue with major European powers—a situation which may drastically question the relevance of such self-ascribed roles for Russia's neighbors as 'brokers,' 'bridges,' 'connectors,' 'communicators,' etc. Moreover, Russia treats most of its neighbors as security challengers. Georgia, Poland, Ukraine, the three Baltic states—all may, in one sense or another, be portrayed as security threats to Russia. In their turn, each of these countries builds its energy security perceptions on the unfriendly portrayal of Russia, which becomes a key factor in securitizing the otherwise technical issues in the oil and gas sphere.

Arguably, this peculiar type of securitization is a product of two clashing logics—that ones of politicization and depoliticization. Each time the parties diverge in their qualification of the problem as either political or economic, the securitization perspective arises. In particular, this is the case of Russian–Latvian relations: Russia claims that it never advanced any preconditions in energy negotiations, while, in her opinion, it is Latvia who demands from Russia to make a political move—namely, to apologize for the 1940 occupation.[410]

The key problem for Russia in this respect is that its energy security policies are in a conflict with its role as the locomotive of the post-Soviet integration. Instead of demonstrating its special, in a way, relations with the near abroad countries, Russia not only charges them at world prices (as each corporation would do), but also intends to bypass some of them (first of all Ukraine) as unreliable and troublesome partners.

Russia and Civil Protection Norms

International humanitarian law (IHL) plays a crucial role in Russia's international socialization and normative convergence with IS. For Russia, acceptance of dominating norms and their implementation is the core criteria for integration in the normative order that is being formed across the globe. Yet this process is hindered by at least two obstacles. One is politicization of

410 Andris Spruds. "The NEPG and Russia's Gas Diplomacy: Latvian Perspective," in Philip Kazin (ed.), *The Baltic Mosaic. Analytical Notes* 1: 5 (Winter–Spring 2006): 18.

legal norms that results from their different interpretations based on dissimilar worldviews. Russia reproaches major Western countries for using humanitarian arguments for covering up their geopolitical goals, while the West accuses Russia for inaction or reluctance to investigate mass-scale crimes against civilian population committed in North Caucasus. The second impediment for effective implementation of civil protection norms in Russia is dysfunctional Russian state, ineffective security governance, and low quality of legal expertise.

Despite the existing legal base (criminalization of tortures, etc.), a series of military actions undertaken against Chechen rebels since the beginning of 1990s made Russia an object of incessant criticism by European governments and NGOs for mistreatment of civilian population and disproportionate use of force that inflicted massive losses of human lives. Faced by condemnation from the West, Russian authorities started playing a language game, arguing that the military operation in Chechnya was not an armed conflict but neutralization of banditry and terrorist groupings. This rhetoric was meant to justify the application of force at the military command's discretion (including the deployment of regular Army instead of Internal Ministry forces), but without declaring the state of emergency. Should the latter be introduced, Russia, according to the international law, would have to report to international bodies (the UN or the Council of Europe), and get approval from the upper chamber of the Russian parliament. Besides, it was not until the end of the second Chechen war that Russia adopted the Federal Law 'On Countermeasures to Terrorism' (2006) which presupposed partial suspension of citizens' freedoms during loosely defined 'counter-terrorist operations,' including documentation control, temporary detention for identity checks, unimpeded access to private apartments and houses, interception of telephone conversations, resettlement, and other extraordinary measures.

Legal uncertainty was a purposeful policy of the Kremlin, since it gave more freedom of hands to Moscow. Its reverse side was heavy losses of civil population. The most typical IHL violations reported by Russian and international human rights organizations were mopping-up operations that led to disappearances of civilians, 'filtration' of noncombatants, practices of warrantless search, mass-scale detentions, mistreatment of detainees, out-of-court tortures, and extrajudicial executions of suspects.

The normative institutions of IS from the outset of the war in Chechnya started exerting pressure upon the Russian government, but international legal mechanisms they used turned out very weak and slow. Since 1995 the European Court on Human Rights in Strasbourg admitted several dozens of claims from citizens of Chechnya against Russia. Most applications were submitted with the assistance of 'Memorial' organization and the European Human Rights Center. The Court ruled that Russia bears responsibility for gross violations of citizens' fundamental rights to live, effective protection, and possession of property. The European Court has established that Russia is guilty of failing to provide due protection to civilian population and later investigation on war crimes committed by the military. Russia was obliged to pay financial compensation to numerous claimants, but these measures were deemed insufficient by the Parliamentary Assembly of the Council of Europe that in 2003 has called for an international tribunal on Chechnya. The Society for Russian–Chechen Friendship, a Nizhny Novgorod-based NGO that supported this idea, admitted that its practical implementation is hardly possible in the nearest future for political reasons.

In August 12, 2008, Georgia brought in an action against Russia in the International Criminal Court for igniting genocide of the Georgians in Abkhazia since 1992. The claim was accepted, but no further action was taken so far. Georgia appealed to the European Human Rights Court, which responded by demanding from both Moscow and Tbilisi to keep it informed on the actions they ought to undertake for avoiding further complications with human rights situation in conflict areas. The Russian representative in the European Court of Human Rights, Georgy Matyushkin, called this body to decline the Georgian claim on the grounds of Russia's lack of legal jurisdiction over South Ossetia and Abkhazia—as if it is only this jurisdiction that would make possible to press charges against his country.[411] From its part, the former Russian ombudsman Vladimir Lukin proposed to convene international tribunal on South Ossetia, and the Russian Foreign Ministry supported this proposal. Russian authorities mentioned their intentions to utilize the experience of the Hague Tribunal and mechanisms of the International Court of Human Rights, but no concrete actions followed afterward.

On the one hand, European institutions and NGOs passing judgments on the most controversial cases of military conflicts with the participation of Russia, try by and large to avoid 'big' political questions, such as whether Chechnya had the right for secession, whether Russia had the right to use armed force, or for whom the August 2008 war was a just one. IHL indeed regulates only tools and methods of military actions, and remains silent on

---

411 Moskva v ESPCh otvergla isk Tbilisi o voibe 2008 goda (September 23, 2011), http://www.newsru.com/world/23sep2011/echrarguments.html (as of March 10, 2014).

political issues. It is violations of the norms of conducting war that are punishable irrespective of political aims behind them. On the other hand, being short of legal counterarguments, the Russian state perceives all attempts to raise the issue of IHL implementation as a political threat. Thus, it is political reasoning that prevailed in discussions about ratification of the Rome Statute of International Criminal Court by Russia, which hypothetically might trigger arrest orders for higher Russian officials.

The issue of interpreting civil protection norms was at the core of Russia's strategic disconnections with the West in 2011 (crisis in Libya), as well in civil war in Syria. This type of politicization is due to the inscription of civil protection issues in wider debates on multipolarity, democracy promotion strategy of the West, and its repercussions for Russia. Russia, who abstained in the UN Security Council voting on the Libya resolution, later complained that under the guise of normative principles, including responsibility to protect (R2P), the Western coalition pursued its political purposes of regime change in Tripoli. The Russian Ministry of Foreign Affairs issued a statement in which it criticized the broad definition of the principles of R2P and humanitarian intervention. Russia seems to be caught in a logical trap: On the one hand, it argues that R2P and other civil protection principles lack universal meaning and have to be adjusted to specific situations on the ground.[412] Yet, on the other hand, the Russian diplomacy claims that all peace-keeping operations have to be implemented based on the approval from the majority of the UN Member States—a condition which Russia itself violates.

These debates reveal divergent understandings of legal norms by Russia and Europe. The Russian government overtly refused to share European claims that the coalition's intervention in Libya saved numerous civil lives. On the contrary, the Kremlin accused the West of killing civilians during the intervention. According to Mikhail Bogdanov, Russian President's special representative on Middle East, Russia pledges to prevent the R2P and humanitarian intervention principles from implementation in the regions where it has political influence. In the words of Sergey Lavrov, the Western policy of "reliance on one-sided support for the opposition, particularly for its most belligerent part [...] run counter to the goal of protecting the civilian population. What seems to prevail in that option are attempts to bring about regime

412 O pozitsii Rossii na 66 sessii Generalnoi Assamblei OON. Russian Ministry of Foreign Affairs web site, http://www.mid.ru/bdomp/ns-dmo.nsf/66d11ad1c1bc0a7bc32576790039c04a/b1d0994f63c95f86c32578ce0039986b!OpenDocument (as of March 10, 2014).

change in Damascus as an element of a larger regional geopolitical game"[413] ultimately targeting Iran.

As we see, the whole lexicon of Russia's Foreign Ministry is explicitly political. Lavrov tries to challenge the Western credibility by accusing NATO in 'failing to pass the exam in Libya.' Russian representative in the UN demanded an investigation of anti-Gaddafi military operation. The UN Secretary-General was also sharply criticized by pro-Kremlin experts for his unconditional support for the Libyan operation as the first case of practically implementing the concept of R2P. This criticism undermines the legitimacy of the very organization that the Kremlin always refers to as the most authoritative international body.

This analysis leads to several conclusions. First, Russia's troubles with the implementation of IHL norms reflect a wider set of problems with Russian deficient political system, including the lack of parliamentary control over executive power, weakness of political parties, the Kremlin's control over mass media, electoral fraud, and the state's crusade against independent NGOs. In result, the civil protection issues were unfortunately marginalized in the Russian public discourse.

Second, in spite of a relative stabilization in Chechnya, the matters of IHL in Russia keep their importance, since the federal government keeps loosing legal cases in the European Court on Human Rights, and the current models of security governance in North Caucasus, practiced by both federal troops and local squads, trigger justifiable concerns from human rights organizations worldwide.

Third, politicization of civil protection norms seems unavoidable since—despite the Kremlin's rhetoric of 'the rule of law'—they are largely perceived through the prism of explicitly political signifiers, such as Russia's territorial integrity and great power ambitions allegedly denied by the unfriendly West whose human rights record, in Moscow's eyes, is far from perfect. Yet there is at least one positive repercussion of this politicization: It makes clear that Russia's proclaimed European identity will always remain incomplete—if not false—unless Russia fully adheres to the judgments of the European Court and complies with IHL norms.

---

413 Sergey Lavrov. "On the Right Side of History," *Huggfington Post*, June 15, 2012, http://www.huffingtonpost.co.uk/sergei-lavrov/russia-syria-on-the-right-side-of-history_b_1596400.html?utm_hp_ref=uk (as of March 10, 2014).

Human Security: Divergent Interpretations

HS has only recently been incorporated in Russia's discursive arsenal. In terms of my analysis, the relative novelty of the concept has at least two important effects. *First*, Russia—unlike most European countries—has no history of incorporating the concept of HS in critical thinking about peace and conflicts. This in part explains how Russian leaders have instrumentalized HS discourses or reduced them to rhetorical exercises—at least in European eyes. For example, Russian Foreign Minister Sergey Lavrov justified Russia's offensive in Georgia in August 2008 with reference to HS.[414] Later, he even suggested that Russia was the first country to practically stand for HS in the battlefields of South Ossetia.[415] Lavrov's awkward statements only underscored a gap between his interpretation and the way in which the HS concept was originally intended as a critical tool to shed light on the failures of state-based security policies and aimed against existing hierarchies of power.[416]

Second, Russia's incorporation of the HS concept, despite being instrumentalized in political ways (i.e., based upon the distinction between 'Us' and 'Them' as the constitutive principle of policy making), has largely been expressed in depoliticized forms (i.e., administrative and managerial). Two of them appear to be of utmost importance. One is civic protection-based, with a focus on effective responses to natural disasters and other catastrophes. Another is an increasingly far-reaching medical discourse on people's health, which appears to be a reaction to social problems such as deteriorating demographic conditions, low life expectancy rates, drug addiction, and problems with healthcare infrastructure.

Whereas in Europe HS initially proposed a stronger role for nonstate actors, in Russia it is more frequently used as substantiation for increased state intervention, meaning that Russia's understanding of this concept seriously differs from those countries where it is more deeply rooted.

The concept of HS can be tackled from two perspectives—academic and policy-oriented. From an academic perspective, I aim to uncover the specificity of the HS concept as a floating signifier, again using categories devel-

414 Sergey Lavrov, Speech at the meeting with the Council on Foreign Relations members (New York, September 24. 2008), www.mid.ru (as of 10 March 2014).

415 Sergey Lavrov, "Litsom k litsu s Amerikoi: mezhdu nekonfrontatsiei i konvergentsiei," *Expert* (October 22, 2008).

416 David Chandler, "Human Security: The Dog That Didn't Bark," *Security Dialogue* 39: 4 (2008).

oped by Ernesto Laclau. In this light, one may see that HS is differently positioned in Russia's domestic and foreign policy discourses; besides, as a floating signifier, HS borders on a group of adjacent and semantically compatible concepts, two of which are of utmost importance—R2P and biopower which, as I will venture to demonstrate, can be viewed as two different yet quite coterminous aspects of the HS concept.

The policy-oriented part of this section develops two major arguments. *First*, I argue that the growth in use of the HS concept must be understood in relation both to the expansion of security agenda in Russia (i.e., the inclusion in it of a growing gamut of risks and dangers), and the general depoliticization of Russian discourse (i.e., its focusing on technicalities rather than on politically polarizing choices). *Second,* I will show that the HS concept has an important international dimension for Russia. By adopting and adapting to the HS vocabulary, the Kremlin plays two games simultaneously: It joins the hegemonic European normative discourse and, in the meantime, tries to reinterpret its key concepts to its own liking.

Explaining the 'Floating' Nature of Human Security. The idea of HS is conceptually broad and open, covering a wide array of challenges that human beings (might) face in the 'risk society,' from economic hardship to sexual exploitation. For example, from the perspective of the Organization for Security and Cooperation in Europe (OSCE), HS involves human(itarian) aspects of security including electoral monitoring, bans on torture, tolerance-friendly legislation and fighting against all forms of discrimination, etc.[417] In Russia too, the academic discussion on HS includes a broad variety of issues such as water resources management, sustainable development, economic competitiveness, quality of life, education, law enforcement, manipulative technologies, arms possession, and even architectural constructions to defend against external invasions.[418] It is for this reason that HS should be understood as a floating signifier, or a concept open to multiple interpretations depending on the discursive contexts it is embedded in.[419] The possibility—even necessity—of infusing this concept with different meanings is exactly what makes it an attractive 'figure of speech' and a powerful discursive tool.

417 *OSZE-Jahrbuch 2007* (Hamburg: Institut fur Friedensforschung und Sicherheitspolitik an der Universitat Hamburg, 2009).

418 Ivan Kurilla (ed.), *The Concept of Human Security in Canada and Russia* (Volgograd State University, 2010).

419 Ernesto Laclau, "Constructing Universality," in *Contingency, Hegemony, Universality. Contemporary Dialogues on the Left* (London and New York: Verso, 2000): 305.

The concept of HS seems to be rather dynamic and provokes a number of discursive shifts. First, it shifts the focus from national and international levels (more familiar terrain for IR scholars) to that of individuals and communities. Second, in terms of *key security actors*, HS refocuses attention from the state to social groups, which can be securitized as both sources of and protectors against dangers. Third, in relation to changing *forms of power*, HS presupposes a move from sovereignty to post/beyond sovereignty worldview(s). Fourth, it contributes to an ongoing shift in academic focus from traditional public policy issues to a variety of much more private, if not intimate, matters related to human bodies. Fifth, the use of the concept of HS has moved increasingly from academic circles to those of policy-makers and international organizations. Finally, HS securitizes the domain of human development, on the one hand, and desecuritizes 'hard security' matters on the other. This contributes to the search for a deeper understanding of the nature of security, expands the concept of security from its original (military/strategic) domain to new areas, and rediscovers security dimensions in otherwise nonsecuritized areas. As a result, HS becomes interconnected with a range of policy domains—such as, for example, energy security,[420] transparency, security sector reform,[421] etc.

To better illustrate the differences between the concepts of HS and a more traditional hard security, the following table might be sketched:

Hard Security Concept	***HS Concept***
Heavily dependent on administrative and/or diplomatic levers	Relies upon a societal vision of security
Main organizing principles are sovereignty, control, hierarchy, and standardization	The key markers are variety and multiplicity of both security perpetrators and security providers
Relations between security actors are more formal (framework oriented)	Security relations are less formal, more flexible, and context-dependent (network oriented)
Implies typically modernist visions of security	Reflects late-modern or postmodern articulations of security[422]

420 Commissioners Draw Link between Energy Security and Human Rights (April 22, 2010), www.csce.gov (as of March 10, 2014).

421 "Almaty Conference Looks at Risks in Central Asia," *Security Matters. Newsletter from the Centre for European Security Studies* (February 2010).

422 Pertti Joenniemi, "Regionality: A Sovereign Principle of International Relations?" in *Peaceful Changes in World Politics* (Tampere Peace Research Institute Research Report 71, 2005).

The discursive shifts provoked by the HS concept have certain policy implications. On the one hand, the use of the concept may further *politicize* global security discourses, evoking the question of 'whose security counts' (e.g., "that of the refugee fleeing from violence or repression, or that of the host community concerned over job competition, welfare, cultural cohesiveness and international crime"[423]). In a more radical reading, this approach implies the assessment of security "from the perspective of the victim."[424] In other words, the politicized versions of HS may involve taking sides in conflict situations, for example resignifying trafficked persons as victims rather than law breakers.

As with any universalizable discourse, HS "holds out the difference between universal principles and those who have adopted them, on the one hand, and those who have failed to, on the other hand, thereby constructing spatial as well as temporal identities."[425] One political implication of this for Russia is that if it dismisses HS as a 'Western' concept inimical to its interests, it would be further set apart from the European IS, and its 'othering' amongst Western powers would be strengthened.

On the other hand, HS discourse may result in *depoliticization* of the international security agenda. A number of security scenarios can be identified in the literature, each affecting the likelihood of 'depoliticization' in different ways. The first is a situation of "invisible violence" that can be "structural," "symbolic," or "normalized"/"everyday violence,"[426] when the state faces "forces that can develop unnoticed by state-based threat perceptions."[427] In this context, a common language of HS, technical, and devoid of political polarization, can be devised as the best way to protect human lives.

Another security scenario involves situations in which attackers exist and are real, yet they might be (re)signified as individual criminals rather than collective enemies. Cases of terrorism fall into this category. As Russian experience testifies, each terrorist attack provokes heated public debates that

---

423 Anne Hammerstad, "Whose Security? UNHCR, Refugee Protection and State Security after the Cold War," *Security Dialogue* 31: 4 (2000): 399.

424 Sabina Lautensach, "Preface: The Concept of Human Security in Canada and Russia," in Ivan Kurilla (ed.), *The Concept of Human Security in Canada and Russia* (Volgograd State University, 2010): 9.

425 *Ibid.*, 10.

426 Phillipp Bourgois, "Recognizing Invisible Violence," in Barbara Rylko-Bauer, Linda Whiteford, and Paul Farmer (eds.), *Global Health in Times of Violence* (Santa Fe: School of Advanced Research Press, 2009): 19.

427 Michael Heazle, "Energy and Human Security in the Asia-Pacific: Exploring the Human Security/State Security Interface," in Michael Wesley (ed.), *Energy Security in Asia* (London and New York: Routledge, 2007): 211.

all too easily result in the construction of collective images of strangers, aliens, and, ultimately, enemies. In this context, a HS discourse can deconstruct these (mis)perceptions through emphasizing legal responsibility and prosecution, enhancement of law-enforcement mechanisms, and so forth. Immigration is another example that fits in this scenario, since migrants are often securitized as posing a threat to national identities of host countries. HS may (pr)offer an alternative view of immigration as an economically indispensable (though socially and culturally controversial) process that deactualizes the importance of politically motivated divisions in society.

The third—and the most complicated—scenario involves interethnic and related conflicts, through which identities are split. Such situations demand much deeper transformations, both in the institutional organization of IS and in human nature. In these cases, it seems particularly difficult for people to strive for the protection of 'any life'—as opposed to Giorgio Agamben's 'politically qualified life,' that is, life of 'our' compatriots, allies, coreligionists, or kinsmen. Yet it is exactly the 'protection of any life' that is a truly HS concept, as opposed to multiple policies focused on 'politically qualified life.'

As a potentially "universal discourse," HS "articulates a boundless political subject [...] with no juxtaposing Other."[428] This perspective implies moving beyond collective memories of victimhood, and toward the reification of mechanisms of forgiveness and forgetting that are believed to be "fundamental to the survival of our species."[429] In this discursive framework, security perpetrators and encroachers—otherwise known as 'enemies'—have to be re-signified as 'criminals' (or 'fanatics'); hence, the response to them has to be formulated in policing—as opposed to political—terms. This discursive shift hopes to prevent those who challenge peace and security from elevating their political status, by refusing to recognize them as equals to 'ourselves.' The consistent implementation of a depoliticized HS agenda would disavow all identity-based social distinctions, since these are prone to 'go political' and provoke divisions. For Russia, this aspect of HS is particularly problematic given the disintegrative rise of regional, ethnic, and religious identities, which seems to prevail over nation-building consolidation.

There were some expectations amongst advocates of the HS perspective that interstate wars would eventually become less probable, along with states' gradual loss of former monopolies on security. However, this does not

428 Lena Hansen, *Security as Practice. Discourse Analysis and the Bosnian War* (London and New York: Rotutledge, 2006): 48.

429 Michael Henderson, *No Enemy to Conquer. Forgiveness in an Unforgiving World* (Waco, TX: Baylor University Press, 2009): 14.

logically imply that the discourses of enmity and friendship are no longer valid as forces of mass mobilization. We may question whether enemy-based articulations of group identity and subjectivity would eventually disappear, or become more sophisticated ('invisible,' 'dispersed,' 'shadowy,' etc.) and thus less identifiable, as the post-9/11 discourse suggests. Certainly, they are central to what seriously impedes the implementation of a HS agenda inside Russia. Moreover, HS is often tied to external interventions in the context of persistently conflictual relations between states in the former Soviet Union, such as Armenia and Azerbaijan, South Ossetia and Georgia, etc. Therefore, HS often postulates an external subject of power, or a group of them.[430] Arguably, to be effective, this external subject would have arisen from "a unipolar Western world or no competition with other [...] states that use different principles,"[431] or—most likely—a 'world international society' and cosmopolitan humanitarian space.

From here stems another dilemma with regard to the effects of the HS concept in the Russian context. On the one hand, HS may indeed become a discursive tool that fosters what Barry Buzan terms 'world society' of limited state sovereignty and growing space for nonstate actors' involvement in setting the global agenda. In this respect, the language of HS "re-centers the subject of security away from the state."[432] At the same time, however, HS is predicated upon the "desirability of a universal human community, committed to egalitarian principles"[433]—a 'global We.' Paradoxically, this seemingly universalizing discourse may be divisive since, in the non-Western world, it is often interpreted as 'external,' 'imposed,' and indicative of perceptional gaps between the West and 'the rest.'

Yet, on the other hand, HS may be considered as an element of national security discourses. For example, it is quite possible to discuss immigration as part of traditional, sovereignty-, border-, and interest-based comprehensions of security.[434] There are critics who argue against HS as reinforcing,

---

430 Marlies Glasius and Mary Kaldor, "A Human Security Vision for Europe and Beyond," in Marlies Glasius and Mary Kaldor (eds.), *A Human Security Doctrine for Europe. Project, Principles, Practicalities* (London and New York: Routledge, 2006): 3–17.

431 Antonio Marquina and Mely Caballero-Anthony, "Human Security: European and Asian Perspective," in Antonio Marquina (ed.), *Energy Security. Visions from Asia and Europe* (Basingstoke & New York: Palgrave Macmillan, 2008): 257.

432 Ryerson Christie, "Critical Voices and Human Security: To Endure, To Engage or To Critique?" *Security Dialogue* 41: 2 (April 2010): 169.

433 Ken Booth, *Theory of World Security* (Cambridge: Cambridge University Press, 2010): 8.

434 Marc Rosenblum, "Immigration and U.S. National Interests: Historical Cases and

rather than challenging, the "existing policy frameworks"[435] determined by nation states. Presumably, HS can be interventionist and discretionary, may strengthen hegemonic interests rather than challenge them, and "reinforce the existing hierarchies of power."[436] Thus, one may argue, "the critical utility of human security has been co-opted by the state and used for nefarious purposes."[437] It is important to bear these tensions in mind when seeking to understand the intricacies of Russia's overwhelmingly polemical relations with Europe in the security domain.

Human Security and the Russian State

In Russia, the problematization of HS is particularly complicated by the unsettled nature of the boundaries between the state, civil society, and the private sphere. The limits of the Russian state's regulatory reach are rather murky. The government is able to extend its powers using, among other justifications, growing public concerns about social and human aspects of security.

There were some expectations among Russian liberals that the evolving notion of soft security would leave greater room for the grassroots initiatives of nonstate actors. Some of NGO activists predicted that political leaders would begin to communicate not only with other political elites, but with a broad variety of civil society actors as well, to develop security policies in an increasingly complex social environment. The changing nature of conflicts in the world seemed to demand a greater emphasis on the societal underpinnings of security. The 'softening' of the traditional, state-centric security model was believed to have proceeded in two ways: (1) through the transfer of important security functions from the central state to either subnational units or nonstate actors; and (2) through the decreasing importance of hard security arguments in policy discourses.[438]

Contemporary Debate," in Terri Givens, Garry Freeman, and David Leal (eds.), *Immigration Policy and Security. U.S., European, and Commonwealth Perspectives* (New York and London: Routledge, 2009): 13–38.

435 Chandler, "Human Security," 428.

436 David Chandler, "Human Security II: Waiting for the Tail to Wag the Dog – A Rejoinder to Ambrosetti, Owen and Wibben," *Security Dialogue* 39: 4 (2008): 463.

437 Taylor Owen, "The Critique That Doesn't Bite: A Response to David Chandler's 'Human security: The Dog That Didn't Bark," *Security Dialogue* 39: 4 (2008): 446.

438 These views are extensively exposed in such Internet resources as www.inliberty.ru; www.liberal.ru; http://www.inion.ru/product/eurosec/home_es.htm; and some others. (as of March 10, 2014)

The infusion of new—human body-related—issues into security field initially could have been conceptualized as part of the long-term erosion of state monopoly on setting security agenda. This was one reason why the HS approach appealed to nongovernmental actors in Russia. There were voices in Russia—mostly in academic and nongovernmental circles[439]—advocating for the adoption and enactment of the concept. However, instead of triggering an activity of nongovernmental institutions, the HS discourse was utilized by the state to reassert itself as the key actor in security relations. The state-centric security vision, advocated by the Kremlin, was eventually capable of incorporating a variety of HS ideas without giving operational freedom to the civil society sector. The degree of nonstate actors' involvement in security relations still remains rather limited, which tends to confirm that "NGOs and civil societies may certainly play an important role in ensuring accountability and respect for human rights, but there is very little to suggest that the eventual product of the process will be anything other than a modern State."[440]

Thus, by using the HS discourse, the state has reinforced its role in the security sphere, a tendency that is identifiable in Europe as well where "the distinctions between national and human security"[441] remain uncertain. Russian policy makers are more ready to recognize the proliferation of threats, rather than to decouple security from state power and reserve space for 'sovereignty-free actors.' An increasingly fragmented and extended security agenda has contributed to the growing ambitions of the state. The two-fold process of pluralization and 'softening' of Russian security discourse was conducive to its subsequent 'over-securitization.' Since security challenges are believed to be everywhere and relate to everybody, there is an obvious temptation to securitize issues of everyday routine, which appears to be a good illustration of how HS discourse can be practically utilized to extend state powers over citizens' lives. As a result, Russian official discourse has been steadily saturated with alarmist security concerns. Some threats are elevated (such as the Avian flu), while others (such as, e.g., the environmental risks of building new atomic power stations or energy transportation projects) are deliberately played down. Security becomes part of both negative

439 Examples are "Strategiya" Center from St. Petersburg (www.strategy-spb.ru); Center for International and Regional Policy (www.cirp.ru); "We Citizens" Coalition (www.citizens.ru), "Megaregion – Networked Confederation" Group (www.megaregion.narod.ru) (as of March 10, 2014).

440 Bjorn Moller, "Civil Society Romanticism": A Sceptical View, www.humsamf.auc.dk/~bm/NGOs-SA.doc (as of March 10, 2014).

441 P.H. Liotta, "Boomerang Effect: The Convergence of National and Human Security," *Security Dialogue* 33: 4 (December 2002): 481.

and positive opinion/image making, and used in political technologies to change public attitudes at the state's own discretion.

Russia's National Security Strategy of 2009 is a good example of the inscription of the soft security problematique into a state-centric security vision. This document mentions a number of concepts such as 'sustainable development' (as ostensibly opposed to the current dependency on oil and gas export) and 'personal security.' It recognizes that living standards, life expectancy and the quality of healthcare, and medical insurance system are the most important aspects of societal security. It explicitly refers to social stability, employment rates, retirement benefits, housing infrastructure, and equal opportunities for physically impaired citizens. In this light, the Strategy underlines the importance for Russia to have effective pharmaceutical industry. Food security is introduced as a separate policy concept to tackle the whole gamut of issues comprising effective employment of biotechnologies, soil amelioration, safety of alimentary products, etc. Investments in human capital, including education, are deemed meaningful elements of social security. The document emphasizes environmental protection, 'rational nature management,' and 'balanced consumption' as significant resources for national security and contains a separate section on security-relevant cultural policy issues, including the promotion of family values, ethnic and religious tolerance, the advancement of moral values, the virtues of sports and tourism, etc. Among domestic sources of insecurity the Strategy points to economic and social imbalances in the structure of federal relations, thus recognizing that regions and municipalities are important security actors. Crime, corruption, and shadow economics are referred to as national security threats. In the conclusion, the document contains an index of key security indicators that includes the level of unemployment, the correlation of income between the wealthiest and the poorest groups of population, consumer prices dynamics, the level of state debts, the scale of resources allocated for healthcare and education, as well as the state of technical cadres for defense industry.[442]

Russia's Climatic Doctrine of 2010 provides another example of the inscription of HS-related approaches into state-based policies. The document discusses the negative effects of climate change such as intensified human migration, potential fall of living standards in disadvantaged regions and urban centers, and increased health risks including the possible spread of infectious diseases.

442 Strategiya natsional'noi bezopasnosti Rossiiskoi Federatsii do 2020 goda (2009), http://www.scrf.gov.ru/documents/99.html (as of March 10, 2014).

In the meantime, however, serious doubts can be cast on the efficacy of the Russian state as the key security provider. Russian experience seems to confirm that state bodies, which are meant to defend society, are themselves widely perceived as a source of danger.[443] Provision of security and production of societal risks may thus—unfortunately—be closely related to each other.[444]

The EU: From Geopolitics to Human Security?

The key target for HS adherents in Europe appears to be the concept of hard security and the consequent hard–soft security distinction. The obsolescence of hard security strategy lies in its sovereignty-grounded nature that foments an inevitable search for external foes as transgressors and sources of threats. To contravene this approach, key HS proponents adduce two chief arguments that deserve utmost attention.

First, they claim that the conception of sovereignty undergoes deep transformations. Seen from the vantage point of HS perspective, sovereignty is conditional on the respect for human rights, and presupposes states' self-restraint in using physical force. Indeed, most of traditional sovereign tools, being applied against new security challenges, fail to work, such as, for example, deterrence against terrorists or rogue states. Against this background, the questions of the status of territories (whether Yugoslavia remained one state or became fragmented, or whether South Ossetia and Abkhazia ought to be recognized as independent states) have to be subordinated to a much more important principle of human rights.

Arguably, the approach introduced above seems to be a useful extension of Michel Foucault's theorizing of the evolution of Europe's power instruments from the sovereign right to kill to the obligation of empowering and enabling citizenry, and protecting their lives. What one may again see at this juncture is a distinction between the protection of 'any life,' regardless of nationality, ethnicity, or religious beliefs, and "politically qualified lives", as Giorgio Agamben would say. Yet what for Agamben is a biopolitical function of sovereign power, for HS authors is a global norm-in-the-making that does not need to be grounded in sovereign will.

---

443 Michael Waller and Victor Yasmann, "Russia's Great Criminal Revolution: The Role of the Security Services," *Journal of Contemporary Criminal Justice* 11: 4 (December 1995): 49.

444 Oleg Yanitskii, "Sotsiologia riska: kliuchevye idei", *Mir Rossii. Universe of Russia* 1:7-28 (2003): 7-28.

Second, what if no clear-cut enemies exist in certain security situations? It is the idea of HS to properly describe security situations that are not about defeating a visible and identifiable enemy, but rather about protecting people from a much more complex mix of threats such as health security, malnutrition, or oil spills.

Some authors introduce a sort of temporal continuum of different types of security thinking gradually moving from 'Westphlian' hard security strategies to allegedly postindustrial, postimperial, postsovereign, and post(inter)national forms of security. It seems that such a teleological vision implies what might be dubbed 'temporal othering' of countries such as Russia: Some countries are positioned in the vanguard of promoting a 'new security language', while others lag behind or even may take transient advantage of artificially constructed relations of enmity.

Since hard security thinking is believed to be outdated, the hard–soft security distinction is equally dysfunctional and even misleading due to the fact that there are global threats—such as terrorism—that appear to belong to both security domains. Besides, what may be considered a 'hard' (military and state-centric) security problem contains a great deal of 'soft' (nonmilitary/nonmaterial and more societal) ingredients. In this vein, one may argue, the significance of military power lies not in the inevitability of its physical application, but mainly in its ability to shape the communicative, perceptional, and discursive terrains of world politics. 'Hard security,' therefore, simply does not exist without meaningful soft elements.

However, HS approaches raise a number of questions for further debate. *First*, as I mentioned above, HS concept perfectly fits with situations short of clearly identifiable security perpetrator(s). Yet, in the meantime, HS mechanisms are supposed to work when violence (such as mass-scale protests or revolutionary movements) does have its source. That is why there exists a military interpretation of HS, which boils down to different strategies of counterinsurgency. Thus, hard security thinking is not necessarily in retreat.

Second, since HS focuses on population rather than on territories, it may be regarded as a-territorial type of security to be viewed as part of global normative structures. Yet in the meantime, HS can be still territorially bound, since it has to be reified in the world composed of states, including non-Western ones to which the West is expected to 'export'/project the normative principles of HS. One of the most principal questions stemming from here is whether the HS ideal is achievable in a state system or in a more cosmopolitan milieu? In other words, does HS paradigm offer an agenda for today or mostly for a distant tomorrow? Arguably, the implementation of HS concept is more feasible in what might be dubbed "single human community" in which "all human lives are considered equal."[445] It is exactly at this point that the implications of HS for Russia can be discussed. The difference between the HS approach proposed by European speakers, on the one hand, and Russian foreign policy discourse, on the other, is stark. While European authors stick to 'human community' perspective, Moscow is adherent of a much more state-centric worldview in which there is still a more or less strict line of demarcation between the internal and the external—a line which the HS concept denies.

A couple of examples can illustrate how far away Russia is from the European understanding of HS. The first one concerns Russia's relations with a number of nonrecognized territories whom Russia supports either militarily (South Ossetia and Abkhazia) or politically (Transnistria). What is *not* a top priority for Russia is unfortunately the living standards in these break-away enclaves and their human conditions. Russia pays little attention to the way the secessionist territories are governed, and ethnic minorities are tackled. The implementation of HS agenda in the case of Russia's relations with South Ossetia and Abkhazia would necessitate two basic conditions—all displaced persons should have returned and receive compensation, and an international presence should guarantee their human rights. The first condition is simply not a priority for Moscow, while the second one seems to be unacceptable for political reasons.

Another example of deep perceptional gaps that separate Russia's official policies and the ideas of proponents of the HS may be found in different interpretation of the essence of energy security that may incorporate elements of HS, along with energy diversification, transparency of oil revenues, and the liberalized access to energy resources. But all these dispositions are in a conflict with the logic of the Kremlin who is not interested in diversification of energy supplies, is critical of international standards of transparency in extractive industries, and eager to treat energy products as commercial merchandise and not as 'public goods.'

International Implication of Human Security Debate in Russia

The idea of 'HS' could become an increasingly dominant source of legitimation in global security policies. What initially seemed a mere shift of research focus in security relations—from a state to individual level—has expanded

445 Mary Kaldor and Shannon D. Beebe, *The Ultimate Weapon is No Weapon. Human Security and the New Rules of War and Peace* (New York: Public Affairs, 2010): 169.

into a much wider and more profound re-thinking of the nature of societal dangers and the means of protecting against them.

As I have argued, the Russian state has nominally adopted the discourse of HS but in so doing reinterpreted key terms and adapted them to its own needs. Russia's security strategy, at present, is aimed at presenting itself as a 'normal country,' whose political practices resemble those of Western powers. As a Russian author put it, the Kremlin's policy is best understood as one of " 'normal great power' which seeks to move away from Soviet-style isolationism and turn Russia into a full-fledged member of the international society."[446] This explains why Russia refers to a set of norms which it believes would secure its universally recognized status.

Russia's frequent recourse to normative rhetoric in general, and attempts to integrate the idea of HS in its discursive arsenal in particular, are tools used by the Kremlin to enable acceptance as a legitimate and constitutive member of the 'civilized' IS which, by and large, is grounded in the Western normative tradition.[447] Since Russia portrays itself as allegedly standing for HS implementation, it can label its opponents 'uncivilized outcasts'—a role Russia ascribed, for instance, to the Saakashvili regime in Georgia, despite this depiction not being supported by European countries who mistrust the Kremlin's arguments. Normative concepts, HS included, are a tool for Russia's reformulation of its key messages addressed to the world, and in this context they are embedded in Russia's enhancement of its soft power worldwide. Therefore, HS for Russia is a normative and political concept simultaneously[448] (Brauch 2005: 8), in which power-related components seem to prevail.

Through adopting—at least superficially—Western security discourse, the Kremlin reveals the deep gaps between itself and the West in understanding the nature of security. The paradox is that nowadays it is Russia who buttresses the split between hard and soft security as two supposedly separate spheres, while both NATO and the EU are in favor of a more complex vision of security with no strict divisions between hard and soft aspects. In

446 Andrey Tsygankov, "Vladimir Putin's Vision of Russia as a Normal Great Power," *Post-Soviet Affairs* 21: 2 (2005): 134.

447 Dmitry Trenin, *Integratsiya i identichnost: Rossiya kak noviy Zapad* (Moscow: Evropa Publishers, 2006): 206.

448 Hans Gunter Brauch, *Threats, Challenges, Vulnerabilities and Risks in Environmental and Human Security* (New York: United Nations University, Institute for Environmental and Human Security 1, 2005): 8

the meantime, Russia appears to be skeptical about a value-ridden understanding of security, an attitude that stands against the dominating EU and NATO logic.

A number of recent documents explicitly advocate the inscription of HS into global political discourses to which Russia could have been integrated.[449] NATO too in its new 'Strategic Concept' suggests an expanded version of security that includes disruptions of energy and maritime supply lines, assistance in constructing more stable societies, dealing with environmental decay and climate change, addressing minority protection and gender equality, as well as demographic changes that aggravate problems of hunger, migration, and mass-scale epidemics.[450] These, and many other reports, portray HS as comprising both hard and soft dimensions, and see no use in drawing lines between them. Yet this vision, dominant in the West, remains sharply contrasted to Russia's re-actualization of the hard–soft separation. According to the logic of the Russian Foreign Minister, Sergei Lavrov, soft security is already institutionalized and does not require novelties, which is not the case of hard (military and strategic) security domains.[451] Behind Lavrov's logic is the Kremlin's belief that Russia holds critical material resources and power in the domain of hard security, whereas in the realm of soft security it faces a range of problems. Consequently, a thorough acceptance of a HS agenda, in contrast to hard security, would necessitate deep domestic transformations in Russia, painful, and perhaps unacceptable to the governing elite.

The HS discourse is still new to Russia. This section has explored how the Russian state has employed HS to extend its reach. I have looked at the ways in which the floating nature of the HS concept has enabled the Russian state to expand its room for maneuver, enabling it to interpret itself as the key HS provider. HS has thus been used as a justification for expanding surveillance techniques sponsored and promoted by the state.

One may expect that HS discourse will continue to be a contested concept loaded with normative disagreements. At the same time, the growing number of interpretations of HS within Russia could in the long run undermine

---

449 *Helsinki Plus: Towards a Human Security Architecture for Europe*. The First Report of the EU–Russia Human security Study Group (London and Barcelona, May 2010).

450 *Active Engagement, Modern Defense* (Strategic Concept for the Defence and Security of the Members of the North Atlantic Treaty Organization adopted by Heads of State and Government in Lisbon, 2010), http://www.nato.int/cps/en/SID-59CE38F9-D9F6F824/natolive/official_texts_68580.htm? (as of March 10, 2014).

451 Sergey Lavrov, Interview with "*Defense Nationale*" journal (May 2010). http://www.ln.mid.ru/bdomp/brp_4.nsf/2fee282eb6df40e643256999005e6e8c/11767a9c3045022cc325772d00415746!OpenDocument (as of 10 March, 2014).

the coherence of the concept. Due to the floating nature of the HS concept it could become a conglomerate of segmented interpretations used by different administrative, social, and political actors at their liking and discretion.

***

As I have shown in this subchapter, the Russian case seems to prove that security is not a static concept, but is always in the making. The variety of Russia's security roles reflects the flexibility and mobility of Russian security agenda and the discourses that sustain it. The key problem that looms large at this juncture is the lack of conceptual clarity, which not only sometimes makes Russian discourses on security either disassembled or hollow, but also impedes the search for understanding between Russia and the EU in security domain.

Security itself is a very volatile and fuzzy concept, and its merging with other not more certain concepts, such as sovereignty, identity, or equality, only complicates the comprehension of Russian discourses as related to issues pertinent to the whole Europe. Thus, the pointing to sovereignty as the major reference object of securitization is presumed on a specific political logic of modernity, but becomes vulnerable in situations of dispersion of sovereignty as an effect of globalization and transnationalization. Politically and instrumentally, the rigidity of the security—sovereignty nexus opens possibilities for securitizing domestic protests and opposition forces, which only dissociates Russia from the European normative order. Not less problematic is the grounding of security in the issues of identity, which, being a fuzzy concept by itself, is open to endless interpretations. This makes possible to securitize the broadest variety of issues pertaining to culture, mentality, language, religion, ethnicity, worldviews, and even the uncanny Russian spirituality. The same is true for advancing the concept of equality as the key determinant of Russia's security ideal: This conceptualization makes Russia an anti-status quo actor, a role that Russia most likely loathes to play, and even disavows by its sympathies to the hierarchical structure of IS.

As a reaction to the discursive extension of security terrain, the Kremlin—as the key securitizing actor in Russia—tends to move to explicitly narrow vision of security in its hard, that is, army- and physical force-based version. Yet this artificial reduction of security agenda to the matters of military balance and state financing of defense industry is of little help for building a communicative milieu with Russia's European partners, who are committed to a significantly wider transnational security agenda.

Arguably, neither overall securitization of the whole spectrum of social phenomena and processes, nor the reductionist limitation of security to the issues of military force may constitute a fertile ground for Russia's positive and constructive interaction with its European security counterparts. Concomitantly, Russia needs to keep searching the most effective signifiers of its security discourse which would prevent it from taking retrograde positions (such as, e.g., de facto defending repressive autocrats in countries such as Syria, Belarus, or Ukraine) and, vice versa, allow for full-fledged security cooperation with the strongest and normatively appealing members of IS. As a minimum, Russian security agenda has to embrace two most important issues—multilateralism (as opposed to spheres of influence and unilateral security policies) and HS (as opposed to regime security). To bring results, both ideas, well articulated academically, need much stronger political backing and institutional framing.

3.4 Russia and Germany in a Wider Europe: Dynamics of Rapprochement and Alienation

Russia's relations with Germany, a key EU Member State, give another example of perceptional gaps between the two parties grounded in their orientation to different models of IS. Russia is interested in Germany's role as one of the main actors in the desired *GPM* structures and a political lobbyist for Russia's *spheres-of-influence* policies. Yet Germany develops a Russia policy based on a combination of procedural/*technical approximation* and *normative convergence*, which in the German political parlance is known as 'changes through trade' (Wandel durch Handel).

Many observers view a potential German hegemony in the EU as one of probable effects of the Eurozone crisis. It is not that Germany consciously and purposely strives to occupy a dominant position within the EU. *The Guardian* has appropriately coined Germany "The Accidental Empire."[452] Rather, a complex configuration of economic and political circumstances requires a stronger European role for Berlin. The precise nature of this role, however, remains wide open. Germany can play a role of 'normalized power,' yet deeply embedded in European institutions. Or it can strengthen its leadership through unilateral policies toward undemocratic but economically important countries (such as Russia, China, Kazakhstan, and Azerbaijan), thus

452 "Germany: The Accidental Empire," *The Guardian*, January 25, 2013, http://www.guardian.co.uk/world/series/germany-the-accidental-empire (as of March 10, 2014).

turning into a 'mercantilist state' that reduces its foreign policy strategy to the accrual of economic gains. Germany might also be a sponsor of weaker EU Members or conduct an austerity policy to eventually push the weakest economies out of the EU. Germany could be a loyal member of the transatlantic security community, or a more autonomous and self-minded security partner for the United States and NATO.

Russia and Germany: Two Normalization Projects

I will start this analysis with unpacking the idea of normalization that apparently resonates in both German and Russian foreign policy discourses, but in a very dissimilar way. For Russia normality is connotative with forcing other countries to recognize its belongingness to a club of great powers without undertaking domestic transformations. For Germany to be a 'normal country' means to find a right balance between its national interests and integration with European and transatlantic institutions.

There are at least two readings of normalcy in international relations. First, normal behavior can be connotative with staying in line and/or imitating the conduct of major world powers. In this logic, if application of military force is practiced by key international actors, it can be considered as a norm to be followed. Second, states' normal behavior can be derived from their observance of certain regulatory principles, rules, and standards that ideally ought to find their institutional forms.

The first approach can be dubbed '*normalization,*' whereas the second one can be conceptualized in terms of the idea of '*normativity*' in general and its widely discussed derivative 'normative power' in particular. Despite the common linguistic root, these two approaches significantly differ from each other in many respects. Drawing on constructivist premises, I claim that Germany's and Russia's international identities are molded by divergent interpretations of normalcy that compete with each other and streamline different models of international socialization, that is, inclusion in dominating regional and global institutions.

For Germany and Russia, two countries whose political trajectories overwhelmingly shape the contours of a wider Europe, discourses on normalcy are among the most pivotal triggers of their identities. In at least two aspects the German and Russian discourses seem to be quite close to each other:

- In both cases, debates on normalcy are shaped by posttraumatic experiences and sentiments, although these traumas are strikingly dissimilar—the Nazi crimes and their effects in the case of Germany, and the dissolution of the USSR in the Kremlin's political narrative.

- Both discourses on normalcy are grounded in the events of 1989–1991 that, however, are differently interpreted in the dominating discourses—what triggered the 'geopolitical catastrophe' lambasted by Putin has been the core condition for Germany's reunification.

Despite similarities and the common vocabulary (sovereignty, self-respect, de-ideologization, etc.), the two normalization projects—very much based on realist worldviews—do not easily get along with each other. Thus, both Russia and Germany accept multipolarity, but other realist concepts—GPM, spheres of interest, balance of power, etc.—are much less shared by Berlin and Moscow.

There are two distinctions between the two countries that play major roles for their identities. The first one deals with dissimilar structures of identity discourses in the two countries. *Germany*'s identity is grounded in a combination of commitments to the European normative project and the retrieval of national sovereignty that lies at the core of the normalization debate. On the one hand, Germany overcame nationalism by integration; on the other, it is eager to drop its long-time cultivated antinationalist attitude in order to join the ranks of self-confident nations. *Russia's* identity structure is different—it is split between nationalism and imperial nostalgia, both understood in realist terms, yet with strong addition of civilization-based rhetoric. In its normalization discourse, Russia seems to be rather close to those countries for whom postcommunist transition heralded 'a new normalcy.'

The second gap between the two countries boils down to the different correlations between 'normalization' and 'normativity.' In *Germany*, these two platforms tend to produce an interpretative conflict between the two versions of German identity, while in *Russia* they are drifting closer to each other. The Kremlin discourse is based both on the premises of normalization (portraying Russia as allegedly coming back to its historical roles in Eurasia) and its own version of conservative normativity (arguing that Russia—unlike the West—defends traditional values, including sovereignty, noninterference, equality, and Christian ethics).

Paradoxically, even if Moscow and Berlin speak the language of political realism, the outcome of the two 'normalization' projects is evidently an alienation between them. Berlin was frustrated by the return of Putin to the presidency in 2012, which certainly fostered a further disconnection between the two countries.[453] The Kremlin, in its turn, is unhappy with EU's policy of supporting alternative energy pipelines, EU's accents on human rights issues, etc.

The German advocates of normalization claim that Berlin has to be prepared to clash with Moscow in some issues, including the common neighborhood, since the interests of Berlin and Moscow do not coincide.[454] Here is a good example of a conflict of interpretation: While the Kremlin accuses the EU in interfering in its 'near abroad,' Stefan Meister deems that "with the October 2012 announcement of the establishment of a Eurasian Union by 2015, Vladimir Putin opened a central area of conflict with the EU [...] . This is a direct challenge to the EU's Eastern Partnership and the planned free-trade agreement between the EU and Ukraine."[455] Against this background, the German diplomacy is called for less symbolic gestures and more Realpolitik toward Ukraine.[456] In South Caucasus, Germany's (as well as EU's) central partners have to be Azerbaijan as an oil-producing country and Georgia as a transit country. The strongest of EU Member States are advised to render adequate political support to the Nabucco project.[457] Putin's Russia is viewed as an opponent of Germany due to the lack of interest in Moscow to contribute to the resolution of frozen conflicts, or at least to stop arms sales.[458]

This situation constitutes a serious communicative problem for Russian–German relations, since it demonstrates that the Kremlin lacks an interlocutor in Berlin that would be eager to share Moscow's agenda. For evident reasons, a dialogue between the Putin regime and the value-oriented political groups in Germany is hardly imaginable. Moscow seeks to rely on communicating with the realist segment of the German political community with its valorization of interests and pragmatism, yet it should have to be ready to deal with the intention of the realists to engage more robustly with most of

453 Stefan Meister, *An Alienated Partnership. German-Russian Relations After Putin's Return* (Helsinki: FIIA Briefing Paper 105, May 2012): 3.

454 Stefan Meister, *A New Start for Russian – EU Security Policy? The Weimar Triangle, Russia and the EU's Eastern Neighborhood* (Genshagener Papiere 7, July 2011): 18.

455 Stefan Meister, *The Failure of Managed Modernization* (Berlin: DGAP Standpunkt 14, December 2011): 2–3.

456 Stefan Meister, "Nach der Wahl ist vor der Wahl: Die Ukraine vor der Parlamentswahl," *Deutsche Beratergruppe Newsletter*, Ausgabe 50 (October 2011).

457 Stefan Meister, "EU Policy in the Caucasus Must Be Scrutinized." DGAP web site (October 26, 2012), https://dgap.org/en/article/22544/print (as of March 10, 2014).

458 Stefan Meister, "Sicherheitspolitische Stagnation im Sudkaukasus" (Berlin: DGAP Analyse No. 2, March 2013): 4.

the countries constituting Russia's 'near abroad,' especially Ukraine, Moldova, Georgia, Azerbaijan, and Kazakhstan. Even if symbolic gestures would prevail in German *Realpolitik*, they would anyway prompt conflicts with Moscow rather than cooperation.

Russian–German Disconnections: A Critical Overview

The Kremlin is likely to keep treating the EU as a relatively weak international actor, while in the meantime expecting Germany to remain the most loyal to Russia among the EU Member States. It is expectable that in the light of the current crisis in eurozone the role of Germany in EU's Common and Security Policy will further increase, and Russia has all reasons to stake on the key European country, whose special role among EU Member States is based upon traditions of *Ostpolitik* and encompasses both geopolitical and normative components. Yet how does the seemingly pro-European discourse of the Kremlin resonate in Germany? In this section, I will address the issue of compatibility of Russian and German policies in a wider Europe, and try to identify both conceptual gaps between the two countries and possible areas of common concern.

Today's German foreign policy debate is shaped by three key issues. First, the Germans deem that in the 21st century power has less to do with military force, and much more with a combination of economic strength, technological innovations, and 'soft power' resources of attraction. Second, for the Germans the EU is a democracy project, a sort of a 'republic Europe', open for transnational civil society engagement and sensitive to issues of democracy and human rights in the entire world. Third, Germany looks for a more supranational integration that weakens nation states' monopoly on solving financial and budgetary issues at their liking. The ideas of a supranational federation and 'post-classical' nation state are intrinsic parts of the German public debates.

On all three accounts, Russian political premises are different. Moscow still believes that its strength derives from huge extractive resources and military potential. It keeps favoring nation state-centric structure of IS. And it pays little attention to the variety of normative matters, intentionally marginalizing the issues of democracy both domestically and internationally.

Even when Russian and German international positions seemed to formally coincide, the logics that drive the two countries, as well as the lessons that they learn from international crises, are markedly different. Both Russia and Germany are supportive of the P4M, yet the very meaning of this concept is understood differently. A mix of postpolitical and authoritarian versions of modernization that prevails in Russia creates some discursive disconnections in the relations with Germany, which much more strongly accentuates socio-political connotations of this concept. All debates on Russia's modernization in Germany raise the most acute and troublesome issues for the Kremlin's regime—rampant corruption as inalienable mechanism of power relations, chronic ineffectiveness of state institutions, and a substantive deficit of the state–civil society communication.

Another example of political disconnections is Libya: Many political leaders and opinion makers in both Moscow and Berlin appear to deplore their countries' abstention votes on the UN resolution that gave a start to the military campaign against the Gaddafi government, yet the reasons for criticism are entirely dissimilar. In Russia, the key point for debate is material losses inflicted by its permissive stand, which provoked a much more anti-Western position taken by the Russian diplomacy in blocking outside humanitarian intervention in Syria. In Germany, the debate is focused on the prospects of a much closer association of this country with the Western institutions of security, and on finding a better combination of soft and hard power tools (in particular, as one German author claimed, his country is by now 'a civil power without civil courage'). Both countries deem that they were unprepared for tackling the Libyan conflict, but Russia is mostly concerned about carving out its individual strategy beyond the West, while Germany clearly sees the problem in its unfortunate detachment from the Western coalition. Both countries are eager to be 'normal European powers', but—again—in starkly different ways.

Against this background, Vladimir Putin's third presidential term appears to be a particular challenge to Germany whose political elite until September 2011—informally yet markedly—counted on the continuation of Dmitry Medvedev's tenure. Of course, the German political elites clearly understand the degree of this country's dependence on Russian energy supplies, and Moscow will undoubtedly remain the key economic partner for Berlin. But Moscow may be wrong in hoping to rely upon Germany's ongoing political support. The German political discourse is becoming increasingly critical of the Kremlin and skeptical about strategic partnership with Russia. As the prime minister, Putin has already received a warning signal in summer 2011 when the Board of the Quadriga Foundation withdrew the prize awarded to him earlier, under the pressure of angry public opinion. It is quite indicative that the German Foreign Minister issued an unusually harsh statement after the March 4, 2012 presidential election: "I hope that Russia now, after the elections and with a clear view, will see that it stands on the wrong side of history." Then German Foreign Minister Guido Westerwelle had obviously in mind Russia's intransigent position on Syria, but his words may be certainly projected onto other fields of Russian foreign policy which are of interest to Germany, including the regions of EU–Russia common neighborhood. In particular, the appointment of Dmitry Rogozin, with his highly controversial reputation in Europe, as presidential representative on Transnistria is indicative of Moscow's adherence to old approaches in the regional conflict which both Moscow and Berlin a couple of years ago agreed to tackle as the cornerstone of a wider dialogue on security in Europe within the framework of the 'Meseberg process.' Yet the anticipated Russian–German cooperation on Transnistria is currently stalled because of the insufficient Russian unwillingness and inability to streamline political changes in this break-away territory.

The German expert community—in particular, the German Society for Foreign Politics, DGAP—increasingly raises the issue of reactivating the German engagement with the EaP countries, even if this might ignite new tensions with Russia. Arguably, Germany does not accept the legitimacy of Russian ambitions in the so-called 'near abroad,' and looks for new openings for regional multilateral diplomacy. For Russia this means that the alleged separation of actors in the common neighborhood into the categories of 'local' ('authentic') and 'external' (extra-regional, alien) is increasingly problematic and even troublesome. In practical terms, Russian foreign policy is expected to prioritize not a de facto division of spheres of influence (a geopolitical scheme which appears to be unworkable due to the drastic complication of the fabric of IS, as compared with the heydays of the domination *of a Realpolitik* type of thinking), but a search for more flexible forms of positive interaction with major European actors in neighboring areas.

Germany–Russia: Islands of Communication

Germany's roles in developing EU's policies toward Russia are two-fold. *On the one hand*, Germany was always eager to include Russia in pan-European security structures and avoid offensive notes in EU's Eastern policy. Many German experts and diplomats call Germany 'Russia's key to the West.' For example, it was Germany who facilitated Russia's inclusion in the search for diplomatic solution of the Kosovo crisis. It was Germany who offered to Russia a continuation of security dialogue on the condition of joint management of Transnistrian conflict. It was Germany who viewed the Black Sea Synergy initiative as a test case for EU–Russia cooperation.

On the other hand, it was Germany who in 2007 came up with an 'ENP Plus' project, aimed at a more dynamic engagement with East European countries constituting Russia's 'near abroad.' It was Germany who stood behind the idea of South-Eastern European Energy Community to include Ukraine and Moldova, and promoted an idea of 'new partnership' with Central Asia.

There are serious political tensions tainting German–Russian relations. The Meseberg process and the P4M are ineffective, and the public policy dialogue is almost nonexistent. Guido Westerwelle has critically reacted to the Pussy Riot verdict, while Andreas Schockenhoff, one of Merkel's aides on Russia, has called to close down the St. Petersburg Dialogue thus provoking extremely harsh reaction from Moscow. Sometimes contradictions between Berlin and Moscow are allusive: Thus, the title of Russian Foreign Minister Sergey Lavrov's article '*Russia is on the right side of history*' contains hidden polemics with his German colleague Guido Westerwelle who in the aftermath of the March 2012 presidential election in Russia made a diametrically contrary statement.

Against this complicated background, there are two communicative strategies that constitute the core elements of Germany's policy toward Russia: to engage pro-Kremlin speakers in a dialogue, and to communicate with the opposition.

Engaging the Kremlin Elite

In communicating with politicians and experts close to the Kremlin, the German foreign policy community is eager to promote Germany as a country with rich experience of pragmatic dialogue with Moscow, open to keep engaging Russia in European affairs. In the meantime, the German political class wants to find out whether the Kremlin might articulate new messages addressed to Europe, how they differ from opposition's discourses and from discourses emanated in Eastern European countries.

On their part, the Kremlin speakers use these communicative opportunities to address the German political audience. They do their best to legitimize the Putin regime in the eyes of Europeans, explain the rationale for the Eurasian Union, and claim that Germany is Russia's closest partner in Europe. They argue that Europe ought to accept Russia as it is, without expecting significant changes in its behavior, since Russia's European identity is derived from history and geography, and Europe is not in a position to teach Russia. The Kremlin desperately wants to prove Russia's 'normalcy,' yet without undertaking any serious domestic reforms.

Direct communication with German audience is a challenge for the Kremlin speakers who try to vindicate Russia's belongingness to Europe, but without subscribing to the European criteria of human rights, democracy, civil society, etc. There are at least two weak points in their argumentation which the German hosts tried to underpin. First, even if Russia and Germany care only about trading with each other, they must think of how trustful they are as partners, and whether they are committed to common rules. Second, in international debates Europe is discussed not as a territory, but as a socially constructed concept. The whole logic of international socialization is about studying and learning, and Russia's refusal to be part of this process raises doubts about her ability to be part of the European normative milieu.

Debates on these issues uncovered an interesting paradox in Germany's perception of Russia. On the one hand, the Germans often implicitly treat Russia as a 'normal country,' thus applying European standards for dealing with Moscow. In particular, many German politicians expected that the P4M will bring Russia closer to Europe. Yet, on the other hand, Russia is viewed as Europe's external Other which has to be tackled more critically.

Unfortunately, it is hard to find evidences supporting the expectations of gradual convergence of German and Russian international positions as a result of direct dialogues with Putin's supporters. The pro-Kremlin speakers usually see their mission neither in unveiling the sources of Europe's discords with the Kremlin, nor in moving toward integration with the European normative order, but rather in reiterating political arguments of the officialdom.

Communicating with the Opposition

Since Fall 2011 Russian society made huge steps in voicing public demands for greater freedom and transparency, trying to bring Russia closer to the European norms of democracy and human rights. That is why it is important to give floor in Germany to those public figures who participate in protest movement and for whom the EU is a source of inspiration.

In the opinion of speakers representing liberal opposition, to become a 'normal European country,' Russia has a lot to do. First, it has to attract more foreigners for coming to Russia, especially the most mobile social group—students. Second, the quality and intensity of Russian cultural presence in Europe have to be drastically upgraded in order to introducing a fresh, dynamic, and open-minded Russia to Europe. These two steps toward Russia's Europeanization seem to bring greater effects than loud political declarations.

The most radical opponents of Putin insist that modernization in Russia under the current regime is impossible, which sheds doubts on the utility of the EU–Russia modernization partnership. They suggest that the key political question from the EU side is whether major European countries would help to legitimize Putin's rule, and call the German government to unveil information on bank accounts held by the top Kremlin's officials in German banks. Apparently, these appeals may question the basic premises of the 'Russia first' policy practiced for many years by Germany. But in the meantime they strengthen argumentative positions of those groups within German foreign policy community who insist in abandoning the 'business-as-usual' type of policy toward Putin's regime and in exerting more normative pressure on it.

How Effective is German Communication with Russia?

German communicative strategies offer some chances to strengthen Russia's European identity. Yet Moscow prefers to develop its own narratives rather than plug into the Europeanization framework. Intensive discourse on Russia's European vocation did not bring so far fruits, as many in Berlin have anticipated. In spite of developing a rather 'thick' infrastructure of communication with Russia, the German government is losing confidence in Russian leaders, which turned 'strategic partnership' in a term without specific content.

Against this backdrop it is understandable that the session of St. Petersburg Dialogue in Fall 2012 turned into an exchange of mutual complaints, especially in such contentious areas as the Pussy Riot affair and visa facilitation talks. Putin's characterization of EU's policy toward Russia as a 'cartel collusion' reveals the degree of Moscow's misperception of the nature of the European supranational project. Yet the Kremlin's nervous reaction to the raising feelings of futility of St. Petersburg Dialogue among German politicians testifies to Moscow's interest in maintaining the whole infrastructure of communication with Berlin as the most indispensable element of (what remains of) political partnership between the two countries.

Forging the German–Polish–Russian Trialogue

What has a clear repercussion for German–Russian relations is Germany's willingness to implement its leadership functions within coalitions of EU Member States, such as the 'Weimar triangle' (Berlin–Paris–Warsaw) or the reinvigorated German–Polish nexus. This is what Berlin means by the idea of 'more Europe for Germany' that dominates the German foreign policy debate. With the softer approach toward Russia from the part of Donald Tusk´s government, the cooperation with Poland plays an increasingly important role for Germany's 'Eastern policy.' Yet Russia's role in this policy is far from certain:

it can be either incorporated in it by means of such relatively new formats as the German–Polish–Russian 'trialogue,' or can be left aside.

The Russian–Polish rapprochement, mediated and even lobbied by Germany, is one of few concrete testimonies of effectiveness of the German communicative power. It was the pacification of relations between Moscow and Warsaw that made possible the concept of German–Polish–Russian trialogue, politically supported by the German government and sustained by German expert community.

The Trialogue project started with a trilateral summit held in Kaliningrad in 2010 that legitimized an important visa facilitation agreement between Russia and Poland, mediated by Germany. In parallel, a joint letter of German and Polish Foreign Ministers with an appeal to develop joint policy approaches toward Russia was published, and a series of networked project supported by German Foreign Ministry and German foundations were launched. The Trialogue was instrumental in implementing the Russian–Polish visa-free regime for the Kaliningrad *oblast* and two neighboring Polish *voivodship*. Yet Germany seems to expect more from this political geometry. Within the triangular format, Berlin is ready to talk to Moscow on matters of mutual concern before Brussels takes position, and wants to engage Warsaw. From the German perspective, the rising role of Poland in Europe can alleviate Poland's fears of marginalization and the German domination, and be beneficial for the EaP. Besides, the trialogue is a good example of Germany's institutional leadership through multilateral commitments.

In fact, the idea of the Trialogue is a continuation of a stronger emphasis on the German–Polish co-management of the Eastern policy.[459] In the meantime, the Trialogue also opens one more track to Russia's integration into a wider Europe, including the issues of energy security and transportation projects. The German government tries to bracket out the politically flammable issues and focus on technicalities. Russia too is obviously eager to pursue a nonnormative foreign policy based on purely economic considerations.

There are many reasons for Germany to support the trialteral project. First, the EU generally lacks policy initiatives toward Russia (as toward some other countries in the post-Soviet region). While the EU hesitates, Germany is ready to talk to Russia on matters of mutual concern but prefers to have Poland on its side. The Germans deem that this Trialogue provides greater stability both within the EU and on its borders, and, to some extent, blurs the

459 Stefan Meister, "German Eastern Policy. Is a Partnership with Poland Possible?" (Berlin: DGAP Analyse Kompakt 7, September 2011).

lines between insiders and outsiders, opening up another track for Russia's inclusion into wider Europe.

Second, Poland used to complain that Russia and Germany tend to speak 'about us, but without us.' Now, the Germans are encouraging the Poles to play the role of an interlocutor with Russia.

Third, the Trialogue is a potential model for other 'win-win-win' scenarios that could gradually eliminate the obsolete mentality of zero-sum games in the region. It is not only Poland that can secure gains from Germany's growing role in Europe, but Russia can too.

However, the Trialogue faces a number of serious problems. First, hiding behind this 'triple win' project is the tacit acceptance of a value-free foreign policy based mainly on material gains. Second, the anticipated spillover effect of triangular cooperation is not guaranteed. It is hard to foresee how the positive outcomes of the Berlin–Warsaw–Moscow rapprochement can be projected eastwards and produce results in South Caucasus or Central Asia.

Third, Ukraine remains a huge problem for both Russia and the EU. Ukrainians fear that Germany and Russia will continue to strike deals at their expense (the Nord Stream pipeline being a case in point). Ukraine sharply criticizes the EU for failing to accept Ukraine as a candidate country, and often accuse the EU of adhering to a 'Russia first' policy. European experts and politicians respond that Ukraine has only itself to blame for failing to meet Europe's expectations. They hold that the Ukrainian government missed an opportunity to build a European polity and has seriously spoiled its image, starting with the politically motivated prosecution of former Prime Minister Yulia Tymoshenko. In particular, German Chancellor Angela Merkel equated Ukraine under Yanukovich's presidency with Belarus—lumping them together as two EU neighbors with undemocratic and repressive regimes.

The improvement in Russian–Polish relations made clear that it is possible for Moscow to get Central European countries to be its partners. But to obtain true partnerships across the region, Russia will need to do away with a simplistic approach to its Western neighbors and base policy on a more complicated and multidimensional picture of a wider Europe that defies artificial divisions between 'old' and 'new,' or 'false' and 'true,' Europeans. It will have to view Eastern and Central Europe as a conglomerate of transnational identities and spaces that defy top-down policies and are sympathetic to a long-discussed model of a 'Europe of regions,' in which Russia's place and role are far from certain.

Germany's Ostpolitik and Russia's Near Abroad Policy: Values, Interests, and Beyond

In this section, I compare Russia's near abroad policy and Germany's *Ostpolitik*. This comparison is justifiable given Berlin's crucial role for shaping the policies of the entire EU toward its Eurasian neighbors. I will argue, *first*, that German Eastern policy is split between two major platforms—one is normative (value ridden), another is interest based. The first platform is much more homogenous due to the very structure of the value discourse that relies on a set of norms more or less uniformly accepted by its proponents (democracy, human rights, freedom of speech, free election, independent judiciary, etc.) This is not the case of interest-based discourse that, as it always happens with the realist interpretations of specific policy prescriptions, is split apart between two fractions. One deems that it is in Germany's best interest to prioritize its relations with Russia (even at the expense of attention to its neighbors' problems), while their opponents from the same interest camp claim that priority has to be given to the opposite strategy of ceasing to build Germany's *Ostpolitik* on the basis of 'Russia first' approach.

Second, a similar split between 'pragmatics' and 'ideologues' is to some extent part of Russia's discourse on the near abroad. Yet Russia's version of a value-based policy—mostly exemplified by different versions of civilizational discourse—only alienates this country from both Europe and most of Russia's neighbors. As far as proponents of an interest-based vision of Russia's policy are concerned, their alleged realism is vulnerable in two senses: It seems unable to properly conceptualize and operationalize Russian interests in the neighboring areas, and underestimates the conflictual potential of interest-based policies pursued by competing actors.

Germany, Russia, and the EU–Russia Common Neighborhood

Germany and Russia are the key countries whose policies shape developments within the EU–Russia common neighborhood. A certain number of German initiatives acted as a spur to projects aimed at engaging Russia in pan-European affairs. As a response to Dmitry Medvedev's plea for European Security Treaty Berlin came up with an idea of the Meseberg initiative, which tried to link a possible Russian–EU security dialogue to the joint resolution of the conflict in Transnistria. It was Berlin's idea to launch a program known as the EU–Russia P4M. Berlin also is the driving force for developing the concept of 'trialogue'—a (still potential) policy forum for governments and public policy groups from Germany, Poland, and Russia. Undeniably, should these concepts and ideas be implemented, they would drastically improve political climate in the EU–Russia common neighborhood.

Yet unfortunately this is not the case due to the increased alienation in bilateral relations that prompted disillusionment and decrease of interest in fostering cooperation from the German side.[460] What Russia and Germany share is unfulfilled (or perhaps simply wrong) expectations. Indeed, intensive discourse on Russia's European vocation did not bring so far fruits, as many in Berlin (or Brussels) have expected. Trade and economic interdependence, especially in energy sector, does not automatically translate into political cooperation, as the Kremlin anticipated. Berlin's understanding of Russia's possible contribution to stabilizing some regions of Eurasia does not go as far as accepting Russia's spheres of interests. Lack of positive news from Moscow frustrate the German political class. Russia is not a personal priority for Chancellor Angela Merkel and President Joachim Gauk who are reluctant to engage in talks with the Kremlin. For many German companies Gazprom as a partner is viewed as inflexible as the Kremlin is for diplomats. Despite wishful thinking, many issue areas declared as parts of bilateral relations are in fact simulacra—this is the case of a 'legal dialogue' between Russia and Germany, as well as a 'dialogue between civil societies,' which do not make sense unless Russia wishes to comply with European standards of democracy.

Yet still there are some opportunities for the emergence of overlapping institutional tools and commitments in Russian–EU relations in their shared neighborhood. These overlaps of activity and interests definitely contain the elements of both competition and mutual readjustment/accommodation. The possibilities for intensification of exchanges and communicative regimes in the common neighborhood area are still open, as an effect of hypothetical visa liberalization, Russia's WTO accession, and the proliferation of networking trans-/cross-border practices. On a more theoretical level, this scenario by and large corresponds to the idea of open regionalism, which instead of the search for unilateral domination of key actors (for instance, in the form of 'exclusive' energy projects such as South Stream or Nabucco) looks for wider regional frames of inclusive interactions on the basis of debordering and desecuritization strategies. One of the most positive effects of such a model would be 'selective integration': the common neighborhood countries can integrate with the EU in some fields, and with Russia—in other domains. This variant is even more feasible against the background of the growing appeal of the concept of 'Europe of different speeds,' which opens more possibilities

460 Meister, *An Alienated Partnership*, 2.

for selective integration. This scenario will require more flexibility from the Russian diplomacy that is indispensable for acting in highly institutionalized and/yet competitive milieu. Both symbolic-discursive and institutional changes in Russian conduct will be mandatory, but this process of learning and readjusting is the only antidote against the prospects of the gradual shrinking of the area of 'common neighborhood.'

Despite the sharp intra-European problems, Germany keeps its interest to—and presence in—most of the post-Soviet states, above all Ukraine, Moldova, Belarus, Georgia, Kazakhstan, and Azerbaijan. Along with inevitable competition with Russia and attempts to balance the Moscow's influence in these countries, Germany's *Ostpolitik* can also open new possibilities for a closer interaction with Russia. Even if these possibilities are unintended results of Moscow's and Berlin's individual policies, they should be anticipated, identified, and properly used by the two countries.

As I have mentioned earlier, within *Germany* there is a split between a value-based and interest-based communities, which the federal governments tries to balance. The *value-based* camp posits that Germany's priorities lie in political domain, and Berlin must more robustly raise the issues of democracy and human rights while talking to the Kremlin. Resilience of such an approach is explained by the eagerness of the German diplomacy after the reunification "to break from a *Realpolitik* conception of foreign policy as a pursuit of national interest based on power, and to embrace instead ideals built on multilateral cooperation and institution-building" that gave Germany a "post-sovereign identity."[461] Adherence to a set of European values was for decades the key priority for Germany's foreign policy, while the concept of national interest was marginalized as having unwelcome connotations with Germany's *Sonderweg*.

Proponents of *interest-driven Ostpolitik,* on the contrary, claim that this is an interest-based framework that is the most instrumental for understanding both developments within the post-Soviet area and the policies of other major powers (China, Russia, Turkey, Iran, the United States) in the whole Eurasia. Director of the Berlin-based DGAP think tank has summarized their position as follows:

> There is no alternative to dealing with dictators. We do not have to love them, but we do have to cooperate with them. The peaceful collapse of East Germany would hardly have been possible during Brezhnev's regime. While he was in power, West

461 Scott Erb, *German Foreign Policy. Navigating a New Era* (Boulder and London: Lynne Rienner Publishers, 2003): 3.

> Germans worked with him and his system without any of the misgivings that today leave a bad taste in some mouths. Was it because our policies at the time were motivated by the noble cause of world peace rather than by economic interests—the driving force that some see lurking behind Germany's current foreign policy? [462]

However, the *Realpolitik* camp does not speak with a single voice. The interest-based group is split between supporters of 'Russia first' policy, and their opponents who deem that it is in Germany's national interest to foster cooperation with other post-Soviet countries. These are two different versions of German national interest.

Advocates of the *'Russia first'* policy are sure that Germany benefits a lot from Russia's energy supplies, and the only problem in bilateral relations is unfortunate but corrigible miscommunication. This group—exemplified, for example, by Alexander Rahr or Peter Schultze—is reluctant to publicly discuss the most problematic issues of governance in Russia (corruption, lack of state–civil society dialogue, etc.), and prefer to focus on pragmatic issues (trade, investments, and security).

Those preferring to *focus on Russia's neighbors* challenge these assumptions. As Stefan Meister put it, the German goal in Eurasia is to transport energy resources from the Caspian Sea to Europe, skipping Russia's brinkmanship. South Caucasus plays the key role in implementing this project. Yet Germany, in his view, keeps a low profile in South Caucasus, and German actions here are too much fixed on Russia, which prevents Berlin from developing a policy of its own aimed, among other priorities, at emancipating the common neighborhood states from the Russian domination. In Meister's view, Germany is capable of playing a much-needed role of a speaker and a lobbyist for the Caucasian countries at the EU level—perhaps the same way as France plays the role of an advocate of Mediterranean states in Brussels.[463]

The realist logic makes inevitable differentiation between the countries within South Caucasus. Armenia is viewed as isolated and too much dependent upon Russia both economically and militarily, and lacks a strong and viable economic appeal. Georgia has discredited itself under Saakashvili's rule and cannot be considered as an effective security partner. In Meister's view,

---

462 Eberhard Sandschneider, "Leaving the Moral High Ground" (Berlin: DGAP, March 11, 2013), https://dgap.org/en/think-tank/publications/further-publications/leaving-moral-high-ground (as of March 10, 2014).

463 Stefan Meister, "EU Policy in the Caucasus Must Be Scrutinized" (Berlin: DGAP web site, October 26, 2012), https://dgap.org/en/article/22544/print (as of March 10, 2014).

the most important Caucasian country is Azerbaijan, possessing vast resources in the Caspian Sea and open to constructively engage with Europe.[464] Azerbaijan deserves a special partnership with the EU, since it is key to Europe's access to Central Asian energy resources and to the success of South Energy Corridor.[465]

For realists the issues of humanitarian or ethical nature are important only unless they do not impede cooperation in the most lucrative economic spheres. In their view, the EU has "to export security, stability and economic prosperity rather than democracy to its Southern and Eastern neighbors."[466] Thus, it was too strong a fixation of the EU on the Yulia Timoshenko affair that led EU policies toward Ukraine to a dead end. In fact, German realists reduce the normative and political issues to economic calculations—pretty much the same way as their Russian colleagues do, looking at the EU mostly through the prism of financial lenses.

Yet a Russia committed to corporate logic of profit-making does not become closer to Germany—quite the contrary. The key complaint many German experts address to Moscow is that it "does not see the post-Soviet conflicts as a threat to its security, but as a means to maintain its influence."[467] Indeed, it was Moscow who supports the two break-away Georgian territories, Abkhazia and South Ossetia, hinders negotiations on Transnistria by insisting to keep there its troops until a final solution to the conflict will be found, and supplies weaponry Armenia and Azerbaijan, which undermines the international mediation efforts in the conflict on Nagorno-Karabakh.

These hot points reveal the degree of politicization and securitization inherent in the German realist discourse. Its proponents openly state that there are political motives behind energy transportation projects skipping Russia and Iran. Opponents of the 'Russia first' approach seem to offer a rather cohesive version of alternative to the current German diplomacy in Eurasia. Yet one of the key problems for this type of discourse is its eagerness to combine

---

464 Stefan Meister, "Mehr Verantwortung, bitte. Warum die EU eine kohaerente Sudkaukasus-Strategie braucht," *Internationale Politik* (November–Dezember 2010): 97–101.

465 Stefan Meister, "Recalibrating Germany's and EU's Policy in the South Caucasus" (Berlin: DGAP Analyse No. 2, July 2010): 7.

466 Tanja Borzel and Vera Hullen, "Good Governance and Bad Neighbors? The Limits of the Transformative Power of Europe" (Berlin: Free University, KFG Working Paper 35, December 2011): 17.

467 Stefan Meister, *A New Start for Russian – EU Security Policy?* (Berlin: Stiftung Genshagen, *Genshagener Papiere* 7, July 2011): 17.

the model of Germany as a trade state with substantial normative orientation as exemplified, for instance, by appeals to foster Ukrainian reforms.[468] German realists call the EU to commit itself more strongly in South Caucasus "beyond the development of energy relations," and thus get engaged in transferring good governance practices and fostering communication with NGOs. Yet this normativity is of a very limited, selective, and utilitarian sort: It applies on a country-specific basis and averts excessive generalizations.

Another problem is that the realist logic seems to indirectly justify the very policies of Russia that it lambastes: In Meister's opinion, the hypothetical resolution of post-Soviet conflicts would lead to a loss of Russia's power in the entire region.[469] This is exactly what Russian adherents of Realpolitik think, and this is exactly what hinders the win-win solutions in the common neighborhood area.

Russia: Self-ascribed Values, Uncertain Interests

Though Russian discourse is also split along the values vs. interest lines, the content of key arguments looks drastically different.

Value-based Approaches

The Western normativity is often portrayed as inimical to Russia.[470]. Moscow's engagement with European normative order is believed to lead to Russia's marginalization, expose its unalienable otherness and consequent loss of its subjectivity in a world dominated by 'the wealthy West.'

Yet Russia not only displays its irritation as to the European liberal discourse, but is also eager to articulate its own value-based approaches that are more ideological than normative. Thus, Eurasianism is dubbed an 'ideology' which presupposes Russia's turn to its Asian neighbors on the basis of alleged common worldviews. This is a good example of such a narrative: "China won't prefer Russian railways to sea transportation routes only because it is faster and cheaper; Chechens won't stop jihad only because it is more lucrative to do business in Russia; Islamic investments won't go to Russia only because of the chance to make profit. Russia has to make its own—

468 Stefan Meister, "Nach der Wahl ist vor der Wahl: Die Ukraine vor der Parlamentswahl," *Deutsche Beratergruppe Newsletter*, Ausgabe 50, Oktober 2012.

469 Meister, *A New Start*, 17.

470 Vadim Tsymbursky, "Eto tvoi posledniy geokulturniy vybor, Rossiya?" ("Polis" journal portal), http://www.politstudies.ru/universum/esse/7zmb.htm#14 (as of 10 March 2014).

independent from Europe and the United States - civilizational choice to shape its policies for decades to come."[471]

Unlike European normativity, the Russian mix of civilizational and ideological discourses does not entail institutional effects and thus basically remains in the sphere of rhetorical exercises. Russian value discourse is a set of self-perceptions rather than an agenda to be shared by—or within – a certain community of states. This discourse is not only Russia-focused, but also overtly exclusive (as opposed to European normative inclusiveness). Thus, the head of the Russian Institute for Strategic Studies—funded by the government—claims that the Russians are only those who share Orthodox ideals of clemency and integrity. Russia's tsarist regime was, in his interpretation, an authentic form of democracy worth of restoration. He obviously favors "Russian nationalism's mission to keep the light of Jesus in the soul and bring it to others," and dubs "an absurd" Russia's "loss" of Kiev, Sebastopol and Chernigov.[472] It is obvious what kind of repercussions in Russia's 'near abroad' countries these revisionist and simply retrograde statement can entail. One cannot but agree with Sergey Karaganov's regret about Russia's inability and unwillingness to live as all others and, therefore, to become a normal country.[473]

Interest-based Approaches

It is typical to assume that Russia's foreign policy approach is of realist background. While the EU stresses that the development of common values is essential as a basis for successful cooperation, Russia emphasizes the importance of interests and spheres of influence. The concept of multipolarity, the core element of Russian foreign policy philosophy, is of realist pedigree. Other realist concepts, such as balance of power or 'concert of great powers' are not acknowledged publicly, but do play their roles in the Russian diplomatic and expert circles.

Arguably, Russia relies on a defensive version of realism, with survival—rather than power maximization—at its core. In the Kremlin's world outlook, there is always a place for Self–Other distinctions, including the artificially

---

471 Yaroslava Zabello *et al.*, "Tsivilizatsionniy vybor Rossii," *Otechestvennie Zapiski* 5 (2003), http://www.strana-oz.ru/2003/5/civilizacionnyy-vybor-rossii (as of March 10, 2014).

472 Piotr Mutatuli and Leonid Reshetnikov, "Rossiya, vstan' i vozvyshaisia!" *Problemy natsionalnoi strategii* 2: 11 (2012): 12–26.

473 Sergey Karaganov, "Sila ot bessilia." *"Russia in Global Politics"* portal (October 14, 2012), http://www.globalaffairs.ru/pubcol/Sila-ot-bessiliya-15666 (As of March 10, 2014).

constructed enemies as incarnations of radical alterity. The Kremlin views unipolarity not as a purely structural phenomenon, but as a direct effect of the US force-based policies.

Yet the key problem with the Russian alleged realism is that the concept of national interests remains vague and fuzzy. National interest is one of the most politicized concepts in international relations vocabulary, which is due to two reasons. First, the conceptualization of national interests is a discursive process that involves many 'floating signifiers' open to dissimilar interpretations, and thus necessarily involves debates between different political platforms. Second, the content of national interest cannot be derived from 'objective' factors lying beyond political debate (such as geography, e.g.) and thus is directly linked to—if not defined by—the deeply political (though changeable) distinctions between friends and enemies. Thinking in terms of national interests thus usually implies political choices between different alternatives.

On each of the two accounts Russia's understanding of national interest looks deficient. The hegemonic discourse of the Kremlin tries to depoliticize the concept of national interests by deriving them from geographical, cultural, historical, or civilizational matters, which in the Kremlin-sponsored discourse feature as 'evident' and requiring no debate. In the meantime, the Kremlin's technocratic mentality prevents it from developing normative relations of friendship—especially, with neighboring countries. Russia, in fact, had never displayed a sense of deep respect to its neighbors, despite political rhetoric. Pro-Kremlin experts see Russia's neighborhood as consisting of states overloaded by historical and even psychological complexes,[474] lacking political subjectivity and sovereign qualities, economically unviable, and prone to anti-Russian nationalism.[475] This makes them, as the head of the CIS Study Section of the Russian Diplomatic Academy deems, objects of malign influence and pressure from Europe, which Russia has to block off.[476]

Such thinking reveals one more trouble with the Kremlin's realist discourse. National interest can be justifiably viewed as "a set of objectives designed to enhance the material utility and ideational values of the polity."[477] It is the lack of a value-based ingredient in Russian interest discourse that

474 Sergey Bukharin and Nikolai Rakitianskiy, "Psykhologo-politologicheskiy analiz fenomena limitrofizatsii Polshi," *Problemy natsionalnoi strategii* 1 (2010).

475 Sytin, "Aktual'nye aspekty."

476 Sergey Zhiltsov, "Politicheskie protsessy na Ukraine: itogi i vyzovy dlia Rossii," *Problemy natsional'noi strategii* 4: 9 (2011): 8.

477 Stephen Krasner, *Power, the State, and Sovereignty. Essays on International Relations* (London & New York: Routledge, 2009): 6.

makes it incomplete, superficial, and underconceptualized. Many experts deem that Russia's adherence to *Realpolitik* includes the underestimation of nonmaterial ('soft') instruments of power. This incapacitates Russian diplomacy as soon as it faces situations shaped by the issues of values and identities—thus, Moscow interprets normative sympathies to Europe in many post-Soviet states as effects of hegemonic imposition of Western geo-cultural instruments of domination.

What is interesting for my analysis is not the predominance of realist thinking in Russia's foreign policy making, but the discontinuity, interruptions, and ruptures within the realist logic. The chief problem therefore is not that the Kremlin adheres to the *Realpolitik* type of thinking, but that it does it inconclusively and ineffectively. Moscow pursues realist agenda without comprehensive debate and deep conceptualization of national interests that are always politically constructed and involve hard political choices. This is something that does not fit into a largely technocratic and depoliticized world outlook of the ruling regime. Should Russia be genuinely concerned about building its foreign policy upon solid foundation of national interests, it would most likely come to the conclusion that cooperative relations with Chişinău—and, concomitantly, with Bucharest and Berlin—will open much better prospects for Russia in Europe than politically and economically sponsoring Transnistria, a break-away and unrecognized Moldovan territory with energy debts. Perhaps, deeper debate would make clear that Russia's national interests would be better served by friendly relations with Georgia than by supporting its separatist regions with uncertain future. Equally, it would be completely in lines with the realist logic to rethink Russian policies in South Caucasus and make stronger accents on economically beneficial cooperation with oil-rich Azerbaijan, as opposed to investing Russian resources in providing security for an economically weaker Armenia.

The Russian version of interest-based international politics illuminates one more problem: The Kremlin seems to idealize interest-based foreign policy as a means for avoiding conflicts between states. Yet the pursuance of interests ('possession goals')—as opposed to norms ('milieu goals', to refer to the distinction made by Arnold Wolfers)—contains deep conflictual potential. The case of Ukraine appears to be very illustrative in this respect: The EU adherence to an explicitly normative policy toward President Viktor Yanukovich was beneficial for Moscow's policy of pressurizing Ukraine and pushing it to the Eurasian Union. And, on the contrary, the possible strengthening of realistic—that is, business interest-based—attitudes to Ukraine in Germany and the EU in general would pave the way for intensifying competition between the EU and Russia for this country's future orientation.

By the same token, even void of a normative content, the EU–Russia interest-based relations can be extremely troublesome. "Russia is irritated by Europe's backing for 'selective projects' (above all, the Nabucco and Trans-Caspian pipelines); the European Commission's unclear position on long-term contracts; the marked opposition in some political circles to export pipelines under construction by Gazprom [...] an, most important, by EU's efforts to diversify its gas supplies."[478] What the Kremlin misses in this debate is that normative consensus—either negated or underestimated by Moscow—can serve as an effective means to reduce transactional costs by enhancing mutual trust and avoiding detrimental competition between partners.

Yet does Russia have its own interest-based 'grand project' at all? As Konstantin Kosachev, the head of 'Rossotrudnichestvo' (a Foreign Ministry-subordinated agency for humanitarian cooperation) admits, for Russia's reintegrationist policy the key stimulus was not domestic (with the exception of a 'moral obligation' toward its 'compatriots' living abroad) but external, namely the "escalating activity of other major players in the post-Soviet region aimed to integrate it in military and political alliances."[479] What this high-ranking Russian foreign policy maker frankly admitted is the lack of authenticity in Moscow's interests in the CIS, and an ostensibly reactive character of Russia's policies in neighboring countries.

Another pro-Kremlin speaker Fiodor Lukianov echoed this logic, characterizing Putin's foreign policy motivation as "fending off external pressure." Putin, in this assessment, does not believe in strategies and prefers a reactionary type of action, which leads to avoiding or procrastinating with hard political decisions. Thus, Putin's successes are only possible as failures of his opponents.[480] This policy style hardly corresponds to the principles of foreign policy realism.

478 Tatiana Mitrova, "New Approaches in Russian Foreign Energy Policy – East and West," in Kristin Linke and Marcel Vietor (eds.), *Prospects of a Triangular Relationship? Energy Relations between the EU, Russia and Turkey* (Berlin: Friedrich Ebert Stiftung and DGAP, April 2010): 20.

479 Konstantin Kosachiov, "Ne rybu, a udochku." "*Russia in Global Politics*" portal (October 4, 2012), http://www.globalaffairs.ru/number/Ne-rybu-a-udochku-15642 (as of March 10, 2014).

480 Fiodor Lukianov, "Otets dostroiki." "*Russia in Global Politics*" portal (October 1, 2012), http://www.globalaffairs.ru/redcol/Otetc-dostroiki-15672 (as of March 10, 2014).

Thus, in this section, I have shown not only normative and interest-based gaps between Russia and Germany in their approaches to the common EU–Russia neighborhood, but also demonstrated the deficiency of Russian versions of both realist and ideological narratives. Challenged by mass-scale protest movements from inside and the growing criticism from outside, the Kremlin discourse drastically simplified its key arguments and messages to the world, having reduced them to a 'black-and-white' worldview. Russian officialdom much more openly than before declared its unwillingness to take into due account European normative arguments and to use normative justifications for explaining its policies to European audiences. The Kremlin and its speakers, in fact, are gradually detaching themselves from the European discursive contexts. Arguably, the rise of German voices challenging the Russia-biased foreign policy of Berlin is a reaction to Russia's self-isolation from the European normative order and concomitant communicative ruptures in bilateral relations.

Some Russian foreign policy experts, having borrowed constructivist ideas of discursive identity-making, made a false conclusion that it is feasible to change perceptions without altering the substance of its policy. Such a simplistic attitude was heavily influenced by the wide spread of domestic PR technologies. This is exactly what characterizes Russia's policies in its 'near abroad.' But the key problems of Russian foreign policy are grounded not in its poor image and misperceptions in the West or elsewhere, but with the content of the policy itself. Russian foreign policy so far has failed to find its niche in world politics. Unlike European versions of realism, its Russian counterparts ignore the impact of domestic constituency on foreign policy—the key factor that became a matter of sharp concern all across Europe in the aftermath of mass-scale protest movements in Russia against Putin's presidency. The Kremlin's version of *Realpolitik* seems not only impractical, but also inconsistent: Russia is reluctant to accept a junior position vis-à-vis its principal counterparts from Europe, but is fully conscious of their economic and financial superiority.

As far as Germany's policy in the common neighborhood is concerned, it is gradually becoming more interest-oriented, and the focus of these interests shifts away from Russia, which opens new opportunities for common neighborhood countries. In spite of the debt crisis within the EU, Germany keeps high its engagement with *Ostpolitik* partners. German foreign policy machinery—unlike the Russian one—contains a number of semi-official institutions that are widely used for formulating policy changes and delivering new messages to other countries (think tanks, political foundations, policy fora, etc.). Germany took rather serious the challenge posed by the Russia-led projects of reintegrating post-Soviet states, and appears to be willing to act more proactively and take maximum advantage of the key Russian weakness—complete lack of a normative appeal in its policies toward its neighbors.

Conclusions

In this book, I have analyzed Russian–EU relations as seen from the viewpoint of a number of conceptual models developed by major international relations schools, and in particular the English school with its concept of IS. I have explained, *first*, that bilateral relations between Moscow and Brussels are deeply inscribed in structural frameworks of multilateral institutions and practices. Therefore, the explanation of deteriorating relations between Moscow and Brussels requires structural analysis by unpacking a number of models of IS presented in this book. All of them in one way or another fit in the concept of multipolarity that constitutes a structural frame for Russia's foreign policy. Yet in the European reading multipolarity does not go as far as challenging the US security roles—it is more about finding more operational space for European strategies, including those of multilateralism that do not seem to be among Russia's strongest assets.

Second, in communicating and interacting with each other, Russia and the EU often stem from different models of IS, and it is these conceptual cleavages that hinder their bilateral relationship and render them ineffective. Consequently, the most substantial problems arise when Russia and the EU stick to dissimilar visions of IS and, therefore, rely on different mechanisms of international socialization.

The empirical cases I have touched upon attest the stark differences in attitudes to the structural underpinnings of IS of which the EU and Russia are unalienable parts. Russia presumes that in a wider Europe there is an ample space for dividing spheres of interests and drawing 'red lines' that should not be crossed for the sake of security. Russia deems that most of the security problems have to be decided by a 'concert' of major powers—if needed, at the expense of smaller states. This policy philosophy constitutes the gist of Russia's understanding of multipolarity as a pluralist structure of different norms, sometimes referred to as multiplicity of civilizations. The ideal of multipolarity advocated by the Kremlin is based on an overt indifference to each other's domestic affairs and equal acceptance of each type of regime under the guise of valorization of difference as such.

Against this background, the EU stems from a more clearly articulated philosophy of international socialization that does display its sensitivity to the principles constitutive for political identities of its partners and particularly neighbors. By the same token, the EU wishes to pluralize the area of common neighborhood by stimulating practices different from the dominating post-Soviet authoritarianism. Paradoxically, these attempts can be perceived as being close to reproducing Russia's spheres-of-influence rhetoric, but this only confirms that even pursuing different strategic goals, the EU and Russia remain in an intersubjective mode of relationship.

Therefore, this study unveiled that Russia's conception of *spheres of influence* is contested by the EU who, however, has to recourse to *balancing* and containment mechanisms to prevent Russia from monopolizing its 'near abroad.' This tactics confirms that balance-of-power politics better explains dynamics in the periphery than on a global level, though, of course, the practical implementation of this model may be questioned by the multiplicity of forms of power that cannot mechanically balance each other. As for *multiregionalism*—an opposite to both balance of power and spheres of influence models—it is constrained by the competitive relations between Russia and the EU in their common neighborhood, as well as by conceptual uncertainty of the Moscow-led integrative project that may be interpreted either as an alternative to the European integration, or as an imitation of the EU success.

Another realist concept—that of *balance of power*—has some roots in European expertise, but it may include Russia only on a case-by-case basis—for example, as it was the case of counterbalancing American interventionist policies in Iraq. China seems to be a much stronger matter of concern for Western followers of balance-of-power approach than Russia. As I suggested in this book, Russia's great power ambitions are questioned in Europe, along with Moscow's claims to have an upper hand in the post-Soviet Eurasia as a precondition for effective relations with the EU and NATO.

The normatively loaded idea of a multiplicity of civilizations, grounded on Russia's civilizational autonomy and self-sufficiency, contains even scarcer communicative potential. In its radical version it denies the need for Russia to institutionally integrate with the West and discursively construct Russian identity through constitutive references to Europe. It seems that the third presidency of Vladimir Putin gave a green light to such an understanding of Russian grandeur. Yet if Putin's isolationist scenario comes true, it will only sharpen debates on alternative, less confrontational and richer in content models of Russia's integration with IS.

The model of *GPM* is enmeshed in its own controversies. First, Russia's great power style of behavior is problematic for Europe due to a couple of reasons. From a geopolitical viewpoint, Russia's attempts to intervene in the European 'concert of great powers'—in particular, by way of participation in the Berlin–Paris–Moscow axis–can split up the transatlantic alliance and weaken a common EU foreign and security policy. On a more conceptual level, Russia's understanding of the great power qualities (strategic independence from cooperative commitments, indisputable sovereignty, free pursuit of interests abroad, etc.) and attempts to portray all of them as 'genuine values in international relations' are not completely shared by its European interlocutors who pay much greater respect to the ability of great powers to use multilateral tools and soft power resources as vindications of their ambitions in the world.

As for the normative unification model, it is subject to two competing and highly divisive interpretations. Russia sympathizes with norms as procedural commitments that basically touch upon the sphere of foreign relations, while the EU favors norms as value-based concepts that require adaptation and adjustment of domestic rules to the internationally dominating ones. A good illustration of the width of such a perceptional gap between Moscow and Brussels is my analysis of security domain, where I have identified a meaningful difference between the Common Space on external security (which was agreed upon by both parties) and the European Security Treaty project (proposed unilaterally by Moscow). The Common Space—at least, in words—is a typical element of a solidarist type of IS, grounded in a combination of GPM and procedural unification. Moscow's proposals on new security architecture in Europe were grounded in the same solidarist logic which, however, was regarded as insufficient by the EU who requested Russia's adjustment to much more explicit value-based commitments. EU's insistence on Russia's acceptance of European values was a perfect pretext for Russian speakers to dub the European approach to Russia as 'ideologized.' Yet the Russian stand, self-defined as 'pragmatic,' is largely perceived by its Western neighbors as 'an ideological enterprise' as well.

Even when Germany—the key EU Member State—abandoned the expectations of a common normative background and offered to Russia a continuation of security dialogue in exchange for Russia's closer cooperation in the resolution of Transnistrian conflict, this deal also failed to work—first, because of Russia's insufficient leverages to foster the political changes in Tiraspol, and second, because of Russia's rollback to old approaches in Transnistria and Ukraine.

The utmost the EU can do in the normative terrain is to maintain the issues of democracy and human rights in its political agenda with Russia. The EU has to insist that Russia must observe the documents it signed in previous years, where it took quite explicitly normative obligations—this legal argument can be more understandable for the Kremlin than purely humanitarian talks. The EU has to insist on expanding the agenda of bilateral relations through including and incorporating the NGOs with their concerns and interests, thus contributing to the practical implementation of the idea of public diplomacy. And the EU Member States have to abstain from the practice of symbolically supporting the ruling regime, which only enhances its authoritarian inclinations. Realistically speaking, the utmost the current regime can do is to foster Russia's openness to Europe, mostly in nonpolitical domains (cultural exchanges, educational and academic projects, supporting civil society initiatives, etc.). Yet even this agenda seems to be questionable due to the dominating in the Kremlin attitudes to Russian NGOs working with foreign funds as 'foreign agents.'

The concept of Russia's *procedural integration* with the West, being the core of the Kremlin-supported depoliticized discourse, might have better perspectives and finds many supporters beyond Russia. Their voices seem to be particularly strong in Germany with its focus on pragmatism and the belief in positive involvement of Russia in the practices of modernization. From the practical perspective, much will depend on the sustainability of positions of European proponents of gradual technical rapprochement with Russia, as opposed to the adherents of more normative—and thus less Russia-friendly—approaches. The key problem at this juncture is that even technical cooperation ultimately implies such normative issues as the rule of law, transparency, accountability, good governance, etc., where Russian positions are vulnerable and weak.

Both in Russia and in the West there were many enthusiastic assessments of Putin's foreign policy as "pro-Western, and especially pro-European."[481] Usually the utterances of this sort—which intensified in the Kremlin discourse after Putin's comeback to the Kremlin for his third presidential term—are not more than exercises in wishful thinking. Foreign policy analysts should have taken a more sober and less politically motivated outlook at the prospects of the EU–Russian relations which boil down to the pace and tempo of Russia's Europeanization. In this book, I have shown that the disagreements between Russia and the EU on seemingly technical and procedural issues are deeply political, since both parties adhere to different inter-

481 James Goldgeier and Michael McFaul, "Russians as Joiners: Realist and Liberal Conceptions of Postcommunist Europe," in Michael McFaul and Kathryn Stoner-Weiss (eds.), *After the Collapse of Communism: Comparative Lessons of Transition* (Cambridge: Cambridge University Press, 2004): 253.

pretations of power—perhaps, the key concept that frames the relations between the subjects in communication. As Stefano Guzzini rightfully observed, "deciding what power really means has obvious political implications," since the very acceptance of nonmilitary (and nonmaterial, in a wider sense) forms of power may advocate "a more varied foreign policy strategy sensitive to claims of legitimacy and cultural attraction."[482]

Political gaps are usually the most difficult to bridge; that is why I do not expect intense positive dynamics in relations between Moscow and Brussels. Politically, the EU and Russia keep drifting away from each other, and it is hard to foresee so far whether they can come up with more or less coordinated solutions in either Eastern Europe or South Caucasus. Multilateral diplomacy is still a wish for these regions, which seems to be more a challenge to the EU than to Russia who traditionally has a much stronger preference for unilateral policies. Conflicts between Russia and the EU abound, and even technical disagreements may go political, as a legal trial against Gazprom in the EU illuminates. Sometimes even without any political issues at stake, there might be strong disconnections – take, for example, the divergent attitudes in Berlin and Moscow to shale gas exploration, environmental protection, or energy-saving technologies.

Anti-European rhetoric in Russia is on the rise. Russian Foreign Ministry keeps publishing its reports on human rights violations all across Europe; 'Russia Today' keeps continuing the unfinished Soviet job of revealing all imperfections of Western democracies, yet beyond Russia this discourse remains deeply reactive and repetitive. The Russian version of Euro-skepticism is an interesting phenomenon since it develops in a country with neither intentions nor chances to join the EU. Thus, unlike similar platforms within the EU, the Russian anti-European discourse is much more political than economically based. Previously the Kremlin was trying to play a more sophisticated language game of formally accepting the key European normative signifiers (democracy, human rights, etc.) yet simultaneously infusing their own (sometimes implicitly non-European) meanings in them. Nowadays, the strategy is simplified, and a less nuanced and more clearly articulated anti-European narrative appeared.

For Putin's Russia the values of the Europeanization paradigm are decreasing. Moscow's offensive in Crimea in 2014 is a clear signal of Moscow's resolve to challenge the entire system of borders in post-Cold War Europe

---

482 Stefano Guzzini, "The Concept of Power. A Constructivist Analysis," in Felix Berenskoetter and Michael Williams (eds.), *Power in World Politics* (London and New York: Routledge, 2007): 36.

(as well as Eurasia) and, by so doing, to question the way the Soviet Union was dissolved, along with such legal arrangements as the 1994 Budapest memorandum on international guarantees for Ukraine's independence and territorial integrity. Putin's characterization of the fall of the USSR as the greatest geopolitical catastrophe of the 20th century has to be understood exactly in this context, as well as his most recent remarks on Ukraine 'not perfectly legal' separation from the Soviet Union. The annexation of Crimea and the threat of waging a military campaign in the rest of Ukraine mark a profound shift in Russian foreign policy philosophy—from a status quo power to a revisionist one; from mainly nonideological diplomacy to hyper-politicization and ideologization of the whole array of Russia's international relations; and from nation state building to the imperial momentum. It seems obvious that these changes seriously challenge the previous efforts of internationally legitimizing Russia's policies by complicating both Russia's strategy of reintegrating former Soviet republics in Eurasian Union and Russia's communication with the West in general and the EU in particular. Since mid-1990s it was Russia who has been gradually but steadily contesting the de facto established structures of EU-centric order in a wider Europe. Yet Russia's support for irredentist groups in Crimea, along with a possible projection of this policy to Eastern Ukraine, the roles of the two parties have inverted: Nowadays, it is Russia who de facto establishes its own rules of the games with potentially profound repercussions for the whole Europe, leaving the EU with no other choice than resist and contest Russia's growing ambitions.

Global governance, GPM, and normative convergence seem to be the most apparent victims of Russia's de-Europeanization and voluntary detachment from the European normative order. Chances for the EU and Russia to pool their resources for coordinating their policies in regions of common neighborhood are scarce as well. The capital problem for the years—if not decades—to come is how to prevent the ideas of multiplicity of civilizations and spheres of interests from evolving into a dangerously conflicting balance-of-power structure of the IS. With the accelerating imperial momentum in Russian foreign policy and the growing intention of Moscow to identify its global roles beyond European context the EU faces not only the strongest challenge to its own identity, but also a need to reconsider the whole array of its Eastern policies.

SOVIET AND POST-SOVIET POLITICS AND SOCIETY

Edited by Dr. Andreas Umland

ISSN 1614-3515

1 *Андреас Умланд (ред.)*
Воплощение Европейской конвенции по правам человека в России
Философские, юридические и эмпирические исследования
ISBN 3-89821-387-0

2 *Christian Wipperfürth*
Russland – ein vertrauenswürdiger Partner?
Grundlagen, Hintergründe und Praxis gegenwärtiger russischer Außenpolitik
Mit einem Vorwort von Heinz Timmermann
ISBN 3-89821-401-X

3 *Manja Hussner*
Die Übernahme internationalen Rechts in die russische und deutsche Rechtsordnung
Eine vergleichende Analyse zur Völkerrechtsfreundlichkeit der Verfassungen der Russländischen Föderation und der Bundesrepublik Deutschland
Mit einem Vorwort von Rainer Arnold
ISBN 3-89821-438-9

4 *Matthew Tejada*
Bulgaria's Democratic Consolidation and the Kozloduy Nuclear Power Plant (KNPP)
The Unattainability of Closure
With a foreword by Richard J. Crampton
ISBN 3-89821-439-7

5 *Марк Григорьевич Меерович*
Квадратные метры, определяющие сознание
Государственная жилищная политика в СССР. 1921 – 1941 гг
ISBN 3-89821-474-5

6 *Andrei P. Tsygankov, Pavel A.Tsygankov (Eds.)*
New Directions in Russian International Studies
ISBN 3-89821-422-2

7 *Марк Григорьевич Меерович*
Как власть народ к труду приучала
Жилище в СССР – средство управления людьми. 1917 – 1941 гг.
С предисловием Елены Осокиной
ISBN 3-89821-495-8

8 *David J. Galbreath*
Nation-Building and Minority Politics in Post-Socialist States
Interests, Influence and Identities in Estonia and Latvia
With a foreword by David J. Smith
ISBN 3-89821-467-2

9 *Алексей Юрьевич Безугольный*
Народы Кавказа в Вооруженных силах СССР в годы Великой Отечественной войны 1941-1945 гг.
С предисловием Николая Бугая
ISBN 3-89821-475-3

10 *Вячеслав Лихачев и Владимир Прибыловский (ред.)*
Русское Национальное Единство, 1990-2000. В 2-х томах
ISBN 3-89821-523-7

11 *Николай Бугай (ред.)*
Народы стран Балтии в условиях сталинизма (1940-е – 1950-е годы)
Документированная история
ISBN 3-89821-525-3

12 *Ingmar Bredies (Hrsg.)*
Zur Anatomie der Orange Revolution in der Ukraine
Wechsel des Elitenregimes oder Triumph des Parlamentarismus?
ISBN 3-89821-524-5

13 *Anastasia V. Mitrofanova*
The Politicization of Russian Orthodoxy
Actors and Ideas
With a foreword by William C. Gay
ISBN 3-89821-481-8

14 *Nathan D. Larson*
Alexander Solzhenitsyn and the Russo-Jewish Question
ISBN 3-89821-483-4

15 *Guido Houben*
Kulturpolitik und Ethnizität
Staatliche Kunstförderung im Russland der neunziger Jahre
Mit einem Vorwort von Gert Weisskirchen
ISBN 3-89821-542-3

16 *Leonid Luks*
Der russische „Sonderweg"?
Aufsätze zur neuesten Geschichte Russlands im europäischen Kontext
ISBN 3-89821-496-6

17 *Евгений Мороз*
История «Мёртвой воды» – от страшной сказки к большой политике
Политическое неоязычество в постсоветской России
ISBN 3-89821-551-2

18 *Александр Верховский и Галина Кожевникова (ред.)*
Этническая и религиозная интолерантность в российских СМИ
Результаты мониторинга 2001-2004 гг.
ISBN 3-89821-569-5

19 *Christian Ganzer*
Sowjetisches Erbe und ukrainische Nation
Das Museum der Geschichte des Zaporoger Kosakentums auf der Insel Chortycja
Mit einem Vorwort von Frank Golczewski
ISBN 3-89821-504-0

20 *Эльза-Баир Гучинова*
Помнить нельзя забыть
Антропология депортационной травмы калмыков
С предисловием Кэролайн Хамфри
ISBN 3-89821-506-7

21 *Юлия Лидерман*
Мотивы «проверки» и «испытания» в постсоветской культуре
Советское прошлое в российском кинематографе 1990-х годов
С предисловием Евгения Марголита
ISBN 3-89821-511-3

22 *Tanya Lokshina, Ray Thomas, Mary Mayer (Eds.)*
The Imposition of a Fake Political Settlement in the Northern Caucasus
The 2003 Chechen Presidential Election
ISBN 3-89821-436-2

23 *Timothy McCajor Hall, Rosie Read (Eds.)*
Changes in the Heart of Europe
Recent Ethnographies of Czechs, Slovaks, Roma, and Sorbs
With an afterword by Zdeněk Salzmann
ISBN 3-89821-606-3

24 *Christian Autengruber*
Die politischen Parteien in Bulgarien und Rumänien
Eine vergleichende Analyse seit Beginn der 90er Jahre
Mit einem Vorwort von Dorothée de Nève
ISBN 3-89821-476-1

25 *Annette Freyberg-Inan with Radu Cristescu*
The Ghosts in Our Classrooms, or: John Dewey Meets Ceauşescu
The Promise and the Failures of Civic Education in Romania
ISBN 3-89821-416-8

26 *John B. Dunlop*
The 2002 Dubrovka and 2004 Beslan Hostage Crises
A Critique of Russian Counter-Terrorism
With a foreword by Donald N. Jensen
ISBN 3-89821-608-X

27 *Peter Koller*
Das touristische Potenzial von Kam''janec'–Podil's'kyj
Eine fremdenverkehrsgeographische Untersuchung der Zukunftsperspektiven und Maßnahmenplanung zur Destinationsentwicklung des „ukrainischen Rothenburg"
Mit einem Vorwort von Kristiane Klemm
ISBN 3-89821-640-3

28 *Françoise Daucé, Elisabeth Sieca-Kozlowski (Eds.)*
Dedovshchina in the Post-Soviet Military
Hazing of Russian Army Conscripts in a Comparative Perspective
With a foreword by Dale Herspring
ISBN 3-89821-616-0

29 *Florian Strasser*
Zivilgesellschaftliche Einflüsse auf die Orange Revolution
Die gewaltlose Massenbewegung und die ukrainische Wahlkrise 2004
Mit einem Vorwort von Egbert Jahn
ISBN 3-89821-648-9

30 *Rebecca S. Katz*
The Georgian Regime Crisis of 2003-2004
A Case Study in Post-Soviet Media Representation of Politics, Crime and Corruption
ISBN 3-89821-413-3

31 *Vladimir Kantor*
Willkür oder Freiheit
Beiträge zur russischen Geschichtsphilosophie
Ediert von Dagmar Herrmann sowie mit einem Vorwort versehen von Leonid Luks
ISBN 3-89821-589-X

32 *Laura A. Victoir*
The Russian Land Estate Today
A Case Study of Cultural Politics in Post-Soviet Russia
With a foreword by Priscilla Roosevelt
ISBN 3-89821-426-5

33 *Ivan Katchanovski*
Cleft Countries
Regional Political Divisions and Cultures in Post-Soviet Ukraine and Moldova
With a foreword by Francis Fukuyama
ISBN 3-89821-558-X

34 *Florian Mühlfried*
Postsowjetische Feiern
Das Georgische Bankett im Wandel
Mit einem Vorwort von Kevin Tuite
ISBN 3-89821-601-2

35 *Roger Griffin, Werner Loh, Andreas Umland (Eds.)*
Fascism Past and Present, West and East
An International Debate on Concepts and Cases in the Comparative Study of the Extreme Right
With an afterword by Walter Laqueur
ISBN 3-89821-674-8

36 *Sebastian Schlegel*
Der „Weiße Archipel“
Sowjetische Atomstädte 1945-1991
Mit einem Geleitwort von Thomas Bohn
ISBN 3-89821-679-9

37 *Vyacheslav Likhachev*
Political Anti-Semitism in Post-Soviet Russia
Actors and Ideas in 1991-2003
Edited and translated from Russian by Eugene Veklerov
ISBN 3-89821-529-6

38 *Josette Baer (Ed.)*
Preparing Liberty in Central Europe
Political Texts from the Spring of Nations 1848 to the Spring of Prague 1968
With a foreword by Zdeněk V. David
ISBN 3-89821-546-6

39 *Михаил Лукьянов*
Российский консерватизм и реформа, 1907-1914
С предисловием Марка Д. Стейнберга
ISBN 3-89821-503-2

40 *Nicola Melloni*
Market Without Economy
The 1998 Russian Financial Crisis
With a foreword by Eiji Furukawa
ISBN 3-89821-407-9

41 *Dmitrij Chmelnizki*
Die Architektur Stalins
Bd. 1: Studien zu Ideologie und Stil
Bd. 2: Bilddokumentation
Mit einem Vorwort von Bruno Flierl
ISBN 3-89821-515-6

42 *Katja Yafimava*
Post-Soviet Russian-Belarussian Relationships
The Role of Gas Transit Pipelines
With a foreword by Jonathan P. Stern
ISBN 3-89821-655-1

43 *Boris Chavkin*
Verflechtungen der deutschen und russischen Zeitgeschichte
Aufsätze und Archivfunde zu den Beziehungen Deutschlands und der Sowjetunion von 1917 bis 1991
Ediert von Markus Edlinger sowie mit einem Vorwort versehen von Leonid Luks
ISBN 3-89821-756-6

44 *Anastasija Grynenko in Zusammenarbeit mit Claudia Dathe*
Die Terminologie des Gerichtswesens der Ukraine und Deutschlands im Vergleich
Eine übersetzungswissenschaftliche Analyse juristischer Fachbegriffe im Deutschen, Ukrainischen und Russischen
Mit einem Vorwort von Ulrich Hartmann
ISBN 3-89821-691-8

45 *Anton Burkov*
The Impact of the European Convention on Human Rights on Russian Law
Legislation and Application in 1996-2006
With a foreword by Françoise Hampson
ISBN 978-3-89821-639-5

46 *Stina Torjesen, Indra Overland (Eds.)*
International Election Observers in Post-Soviet Azerbaijan
Geopolitical Pawns or Agents of Change?
ISBN 978-3-89821-743-9

47 *Taras Kuzio*
Ukraine – Crimea – Russia
Triangle of Conflict
ISBN 978-3-89821-761-3

48 *Claudia Šabić*
"Ich erinnere mich nicht, aber L'viv!"
Zur Funktion kultureller Faktoren für die Institutionalisierung und Entwicklung einer ukrainischen Region
Mit einem Vorwort von Melanie Tatur
ISBN 978-3-89821-752-1

49 *Marlies Bilz*
Tatarstan in der Transformation
Nationaler Diskurs und Politische Praxis 1988-1994
Mit einem Vorwort von Frank Golczewski
ISBN 978-3-89821-722-4

50 *Марлен Ларюэль (ред.)*
Современные интерпретации русского национализма
ISBN 978-3-89821-795-8

51 *Sonja Schüler*
Die ethnische Dimension der Armut
Roma im postsozialistischen Rumänien
Mit einem Vorwort von Anton Sterbling
ISBN 978-3-89821-776-7

52 *Галина Кожевникова*
Радикальный национализм в России и противодействие ему
Сборник докладов Центра «Сова» за 2004-2007 гг.
С предисловием Александра Верховского
ISBN 978-3-89821-721-7

53 *Галина Кожевникова и Владимир Прибыловский*
Российская власть в биографиях I
Высшие должностные лица РФ в 2004 г.
ISBN 978-3-89821-796-5

54 *Галина Кожевникова и Владимир Прибыловский*
Российская власть в биографиях II
Члены Правительства РФ в 2004 г.
ISBN 978-3-89821-797-2

55 *Галина Кожевникова и Владимир Прибыловский*
Российская власть в биографиях III
Руководители федеральных служб и агентств РФ в 2004 г.
ISBN 978-3-89821-798-9

56 *Ileana Petroniu*
Privatisierung in Transformationsökonomien
Determinanten der Restrukturierungs-Bereitschaft am Beispiel Polens, Rumäniens und der Ukraine
Mit einem Vorwort von Rainer W. Schäfer
ISBN 978-3-89821-790-3

57 *Christian Wipperfürth*
Russland und seine GUS-Nachbarn
Hintergründe, aktuelle Entwicklungen und Konflikte in einer ressourcenreichen Region
ISBN 978-3-89821-801-6

58 *Togzhan Kassenova*
From Antagonism to Partnership
The Uneasy Path of the U.S.-Russian Cooperative Threat Reduction
With a foreword by Christoph Bluth
ISBN 978-3-89821-707-1

59 *Alexander Höllwerth*
Das sakrale eurasische Imperium des Aleksandr Dugin
Eine Diskursanalyse zum postsowjetischen russischen Rechtsextremismus
Mit einem Vorwort von Dirk Uffelmann
ISBN 978-3-89821-813-9

60 *Олег Рябов*
«Россия-Матушка»
Национализм, гендер и война в России XX века
С предисловием Елены Гощило
ISBN 978-3-89821-487-2

61 *Ivan Maistrenko*
Borot'bism
A Chapter in the History of the Ukrainian Revolution
With a new introduction by Chris Ford
Translated by George S. N. Luckyj with the assistance of Ivan L. Rudnytsky
ISBN 978-3-89821-697-5

62 *Maryna Romanets*
Anamorphosic Texts and Reconfigured Visions
Improvised Traditions in Contemporary Ukrainian and Irish Literature
ISBN 978-3-89821-576-3

63 *Paul D'Anieri and Taras Kuzio (Eds.)*
Aspects of the Orange Revolution I
Democratization and Elections in Post-Communist Ukraine
ISBN 978-3-89821-698-2

64 *Bohdan Harasymiw in collaboration with Oleh S. Ilnytzkyj (Eds.)*
Aspects of the Orange Revolution II
Information and Manipulation Strategies in the 2004 Ukrainian Presidential Elections
ISBN 978-3-89821-699-9

65 *Ingmar Bredies, Andreas Umland and Valentin Yakushik (Eds.)*
Aspects of the Orange Revolution III
The Context and Dynamics of the 2004 Ukrainian Presidential Elections
ISBN 978-3-89821-803-0

66 *Ingmar Bredies, Andreas Umland and Valentin Yakushik (Eds.)*
Aspects of the Orange Revolution IV
Foreign Assistance and Civic Action in the 2004 Ukrainian Presidential Elections
ISBN 978-3-89821-808-5

67 *Ingmar Bredies, Andreas Umland and Valentin Yakushik (Eds.)*
Aspects of the Orange Revolution V
Institutional Observation Reports on the 2004 Ukrainian Presidential Elections
ISBN 978-3-89821-809-2

68 *Taras Kuzio (Ed.)*
Aspects of the Orange Revolution VI
Post-Communist Democratic Revolutions in Comparative Perspective
ISBN 978-3-89821-820-7

69 *Tim Bohse*
Autoritarismus statt Selbstverwaltung
Die Transformation der kommunalen Politik in der Stadt Kaliningrad 1990-2005
Mit einem Geleitwort von Stefan Troebst
ISBN 978-3-89821-782-8

70 *David Rupp*
Die Rußländische Föderation und die russischsprachige Minderheit in Lettland
Eine Fallstudie zur Anwaltspolitik Moskaus gegenüber den russophonen Minderheiten im „Nahen Ausland“ von 1991 bis 2002
Mit einem Vorwort von Helmut Wagner
ISBN 978-3-89821-778-1

71 *Taras Kuzio*
Theoretical and Comparative Perspectives on Nationalism
New Directions in Cross-Cultural and Post-Communist Studies
With a foreword by Paul Robert Magocsi
ISBN 978-3-89821-815-3

72 *Christine Teichmann*
Die Hochschultransformation im heutigen Osteuropa
Kontinuität und Wandel bei der Entwicklung des postkommunistischen Universitätswesens
Mit einem Vorwort von Oskar Anweiler
ISBN 978-3-89821-842-9

73 *Julia Kusznir*
Der politische Einfluss von Wirtschaftseliten in russischen Regionen
Eine Analyse am Beispiel der Erdöl- und Erdgasindustrie, 1992-2005
Mit einem Vorwort von Wolfgang Eichwede
ISBN 978-3-89821-821-4

74 *Alena Vysotskaya*
Russland, Belarus und die EU-Osterweiterung
Zur Minderheitenfrage und zum Problem der Freizügigkeit des Personenverkehrs
Mit einem Vorwort von Katlijn Malfliet
ISBN 978-3-89821-822-1

75 *Heiko Pleines (Hrsg.)*
Corporate Governance in post-sozialistischen Volkswirtschaften
ISBN 978-3-89821-766-8

76 *Stefan Ihrig*
Wer sind die Moldawier?
Rumänismus versus Moldowanismus in Historiographie und Schulbüchern der Republik Moldova, 1991-2006
Mit einem Vorwort von Holm Sundhaussen
ISBN 978-3-89821-466-7

77 *Galina Kozhevnikova in collaboration with Alexander Verkhovsky and Eugene Veklerov*
Ultra-Nationalism and Hate Crimes in Contemporary Russia
The 2004-2006 Annual Reports of Moscow's SOVA Center
With a foreword by Stephen D. Shenfield
ISBN 978-3-89821-868-9

78 *Florian Küchler*
The Role of the European Union in Moldova's Transnistria Conflict
With a foreword by Christopher Hill
ISBN 978-3-89821-850-4

79 *Bernd Rechel*
The Long Way Back to Europe
Minority Protection in Bulgaria
With a foreword by Richard Crampton
ISBN 978-3-89821-863-4

80 *Peter W. Rodgers*
Nation, Region and History in Post-Communist Transitions
Identity Politics in Ukraine, 1991-2006
With a foreword by Vera Tolz
ISBN 978-3-89821-903-7

81 *Stephanie Solywoda*
The Life and Work of Semen L. Frank
A Study of Russian Religious Philosophy
With a foreword by Philip Walters
ISBN 978-3-89821-457-5

82 *Vera Sokolova*
Cultural Politics of Ethnicity
Discourses on Roma in Communist Czechoslovakia
ISBN 978-3-89821-864-1

83 *Natalya Shevchik Ketenci*
Kazakhstani Enterprises in Transition
The Role of Historical Regional Development in Kazakhstan's Post-Soviet Economic Transformation
ISBN 978-3-89821-831-3

84 *Martin Malek, Anna Schor-Tschudnowskaja (Hrsg.)*
Europa im Tschetschenienkrieg
Zwischen politischer Ohnmacht und Gleichgültigkeit
Mit einem Vorwort von Lipchan Basajewa
ISBN 978-3-89821-676-0

85 *Stefan Meister*
Das postsowjetische Universitätswesen zwischen nationalem und internationalem Wandel
Die Entwicklung der regionalen Hochschule in Russland als Gradmesser der Systemtransformation
Mit einem Vorwort von Joan DeBardeleben
ISBN 978-3-89821-891-7

86 *Konstantin Sheiko in collaboration with Stephen Brown*
Nationalist Imaginings of the Russian Past
Anatolii Fomenko and the Rise of Alternative History in Post-Communist Russia
With a foreword by Donald Ostrowski
ISBN 978-3-89821-915-0

87 *Sabine Jenni*
Wie stark ist das „Einige Russland"?
Zur Parteibindung der Eliten und zum Wahlerfolg der Machtpartei im Dezember 2007
Mit einem Vorwort von Klaus Armingeon
ISBN 978-3-89821-961-7

88 *Thomas Borén*
Meeting-Places of Transformation
Urban Identity, Spatial Representations and Local Politics in Post-Soviet St Petersburg
ISBN 978-3-89821-739-2

89 *Aygul Ashirova*
Stalinismus und Stalin-Kult in Zentralasien
Turkmenistan 1924-1953
Mit einem Vorwort von Leonid Luks
ISBN 978-3-89821-987-7

90 *Leonid Luks*
Freiheit oder imperiale Größe?
Essays zu einem russischen Dilemma
ISBN 978-3-8382-0011-8

91 *Christopher Gilley*
The 'Change of Signposts' in the Ukrainian Emigration
A Contribution to the History of Sovietophilism in the 1920s
With a foreword by Frank Golczewski
ISBN 978-3-89821-965-5

92 *Philipp Casula, Jeronim Perovic (Eds.)*
Identities and Politics During the Putin Presidency
The Discursive Foundations of Russia's Stability
With a foreword by Heiko Haumann
ISBN 978-3-8382-0015-6

93 *Marcel Viëtor*
Europa und die Frage nach seinen Grenzen im Osten
Zur Konstruktion ‚europäischer Identität' in Geschichte und Gegenwart
Mit einem Vorwort von Albrecht Lehmann
ISBN 978-3-8382-0045-3

94 *Ben Hellman, Andrei Rogachevskii*
Filming the Unfilmable
Casper Wrede's 'One Day in the Life of Ivan Denisovich'
Second, Revised and Expanded Edition
ISBN 978-3-8382-0594-6

95 *Eva Fuchslocher*
Vaterland, Sprache, Glaube
Orthodoxie und Nationenbildung am Beispiel Georgiens
Mit einem Vorwort von Christina von Braun
ISBN 978-3-89821-884-9

96 *Vladimir Kantor*
Das Westlertum und der Weg Russlands
Zur Entwicklung der russischen Literatur und Philosophie
Ediert von Dagmar Herrmann
Mit einem Beitrag von Nikolaus Lobkowicz
ISBN 978-3-8382-0102-3

97 *Kamran Musayev*
Die postsowjetische Transformation im Baltikum und Südkaukasus
Eine vergleichende Untersuchung der politischen Entwicklung Lettlands und Aserbaidschans 1985-2009
Mit einem Vorwort von Leonid Luks
Ediert von Sandro Henschel
ISBN 978-3-8382-0103-0

98 *Tatiana Zhurzhenko*
Borderlands into Bordered Lands
Geopolitics of Identity in Post-Soviet Ukraine
With a foreword by Dieter Segert
ISBN 978-3-8382-0042-2

99 *Кирилл Галушко, Лидия Смола (ред.)*
Пределы падения – варианты украинского будущего
Аналитико-прогностические исследования
ISBN 978-3-8382-0148-1

100 *Michael Minkenberg (ed.)*
Historical Legacies and the Radical Right in Post-Cold War Central and Eastern Europe
With an afterword by Sabrina P. Ramet
ISBN 978-3-8382-0124-5

101 *David-Emil Wickström*
Rocking St. Petersburg
Transcultural Flows and Identity Politics in Post-Soviet Popular Music
With a foreword by Yngvar B. Steinholt
Second, Revised and Expanded Edition
ISBN 978-3-8382-0600-4

102 *Eva Zabka*
Eine neue „Zeit der Wirren"?
Der spät- und postsowjetische Systemwandel 1985-2000 im Spiegel russischer gesellschaftspolitischer Diskurse
Mit einem Vorwort von Margareta Mommsen
ISBN 978-3-8382-0161-0

103 *Ulrike Ziemer*
Ethnic Belonging, Gender and Cultural Practices
Youth Identitites in Contemporary Russia
With a foreword by Anoop Nayak
ISBN 978-3-8382-0152-8

104 *Ksenia Chepikova*
'Einiges Russland' - eine zweite KPdSU?
Aspekte der Identitätskonstruktion einer postsowjetischen „Partei der Macht"
Mit einem Vorwort von Torsten Oppelland
ISBN 978-3-8382-0311-9

105 *Леонид Люкс*
Западничество или евразийство? Демократия или идеократия?
Сборник статей об исторических дилеммах России
С предисловием Владимира Кантора
ISBN 978-3-8382-0211-2

106 *Anna Dost*
Das russische Verfassungsrecht auf dem Weg zum Föderalismus und zurück
Zum Konflikt von Rechtsnormen und -wirklichkeit in der Russländischen Föderation von 1991 bis 2009
Mit einem Vorwort von Alexander Blankenagel
ISBN 978-3-8382-0292-1

107 *Philipp Herzog*
Sozialistische Völkerfreundschaft, nationaler Widerstand oder harmloser Zeitvertreib?
Zur politischen Funktion der Volkskunst im sowjetischen Estland
Mit einem Vorwort von Andreas Kappeler
ISBN 978-3-8382-0216-7

108 *Marlène Laruelle (ed.)*
Russian Nationalism, Foreign Policy, and Identity Debates in Putin's Russia
New Ideological Patterns after the Orange Revolution
ISBN 978-3-8382-0325-6

109 *Michail Logvinov*
Russlands Kampf gegen den internationalen Terrorismus
Eine kritische Bestandsaufnahme des Bekämpfungsansatzes
Mit einem Geleitwort von Hans-Henning Schröder und einem Vorwort von Eckhard Jesse
ISBN 978-3-8382-0329-4

110 *John B. Dunlop*
The Moscow Bombings of September 1999
Examinations of Russian Terrorist Attacks at the Onset of Vladimir Putin's Rule
Second, Revised and Expanded Edition
ISBN 978-3-8382-0608-0

111 *Андрей А. Ковалёв*
Свидетельство из-за кулис российской политики I
Можно ли делать добро из зла? (Воспоминания и размышления о последних советских и первых послесоветских годах)
With a foreword by Peter Reddaway
ISBN 978-3-8382-0302-7

112 *Андрей А. Ковалёв*
Свидетельство из-за кулис российской политики II
Угроза для себя и окружающих (Наблюдения и предостережения относительно происходящего после 2000 г.)
ISBN 978-3-8382-0303-4

113 *Bernd Kappenberg*
Zeichen setzen für Europa
Der Gebrauch europäischer lateinischer Sonderzeichen in der deutschen Öffentlichkeit
Mit einem Vorwort von Peter Schlobinski
ISBN 978-3-89821-749-1

114 *Ivo Mijnssen*
The Quest for an Ideal Youth in Putin's Russia I
Back to Our Future! History, Modernity, and Patriotism according to *Nashi,* 2005-2013
With a foreword by Jeronim Perović
Second, Revised and Expanded Edition
ISBN 978-3-8382-0578-6

115 *Jussi Lassila*
The Quest for an Ideal Youth in Putin's Russia II
The Search for Distinctive Conformism in the Political Communication of *Nashi,* 2005-2009
With a foreword by Kirill Postoutenko
Second, Revised and Expanded Edition
ISBN 978-3-8382-0585-4

116 *Valerio Trabandt*
Neue Nachbarn, gute Nachbarschaft?
Die EU als internationaler Akteur am Beispiel ihrer Demokratieförderung in Belarus und der Ukraine 2004-2009
Mit einem Vorwort von Jutta Joachim
ISBN 978-3-8382-0437-6

117 *Fabian Pfeiffer*
Estlands Außen- und Sicherheitspolitik I
Der estnische Atlantizismus nach der wiedererlangten Unabhängigkeit 1991-2004
Mit einem Vorwort von Helmut Hubel
ISBN 978-3-8382-0127-6

118 *Jana Podßuweit*
Estlands Außen- und Sicherheitspolitik II
Handlungsoptionen eines Kleinstaates im Rahmen seiner EU-Mitgliedschaft (2004-2008)
Mit einem Vorwort von Helmut Hubel
ISBN 978-3-8382-0440-6

119 *Karin Pointner*
Estlands Außen- und Sicherheitspolitik III
Eine gedächtnispolitische Analyse estnischer Entwicklungskooperation 2006-2010
Mit einem Vorwort von Karin Liebhart
ISBN 978-3-8382-0435-2

120 *Ruslana Vovk*
Die Offenheit der ukrainischen Verfassung für das Völkerrecht und die europäische Integration
Mit einem Vorwort von Alexander Blankenagel
ISBN 978-3-8382-0481-9

121 *Mykhaylo Banakh*
Die Relevanz der Zivilgesellschaft bei den postkommunistischen Transformationsprozessen in mittel- und osteuropäischen Ländern
Das Beispiel der spät- und postsowjetischen Ukraine 1986-2009
Mit einem Vorwort von Gerhard Simon
ISBN 978-3-8382-0499-4

122 *Michael Moser*
Language Policy and the Discourse on Languages in Ukraine under President Viktor Yanukovych (25 February 2010–28 October 2012)
ISBN 978-3-8382-0497-0 (Paperback edition)
ISBN 978-3-8382-0507-6 (Hardcover edition)

123 *Nicole Krome*
Russischer Netzwerkkapitalismus
Restrukturierungsprozesse in der Russischen Föderation am Beispiel des Luftfahrtunternehmens "Aviastar"
Mit einem Vorwort von Petra Stykow
ISBN 978-3-8382-0534-2

124 *David R. Marples*
'Our Glorious Past'
Lukashenka's Belarus and the Great Patriotic War
ISBN 978-3-8382-0574-8 (Paperback edition)
ISBN 978-3-8382-0675-2 (Hardcover edition)

125 *Ulf Walther*
Russlands "neuer Adel"
Die Macht des Geheimdienstes von Gorbatschow bis Putin
Mit einem Vorwort von Hans-Georg Wieck
ISBN 978-3-8382-0584-7

126 *Simon Geissbühler (Hrsg.)*
Kiew – Revolution 3.0
Der Euromaidan 2013/14 und die Zukunftsperspektiven der Ukraine
ISBN 978-3-8382-0581-6 (Paperback edition)
ISBN 978-3-8382-0681-3 (Hardcover edition)

127 *Andrey Makarychev*
Russia and the EU in a Multipolar World
Discourses, Identities, Norms
ISBN 978-3-8382-0529-8

128 *Roland Scharff*
Kasachstan als postsowjetischer Wohlfahrtsstaat
Die Transformation des sozialen Schutzsystems
Mit einem Vorwort von Joachim Ahrens
ISBN 978-3-8382-0622-6

129 *Katja Grupp*
Bild Lücke Deutschland
Kaliningrader Studierende sprechen über Deutschland
Mit einem Vorwort von Martin Schulz
ISBN 978-3-8382-0552-6

ibidem-Verlag / *ibidem* Press
Melchiorstr. 15
70439 Stuttgart
Germany

ibidem@ibidem.eu
www.ibidem-verlag.com
www.ibidem.eu